PRAISE FOR Raisin

"Catherine Ann Clemett gives the Christ-Magdalene energies a voice for this time of inner and outer chaotic change. In telling her life's story, she fearlessly reveals herself with humor and compassion. Resolute courageous wisdom rises forth from her lived experiences providing you with a down-to-earth reflection of what it means to embody your divine impulse to awaken. Reading these pages may catalyze you to discover your own intrinsic, liberating wisdom. This may help you trust the familiar inner knowing that intuitively knows how to fearlessly embrace every opposing, resistive obstacle to being the love you already are. This is the way of the Christ-Magdalene."

Claire Heartsong, author of *Anna, Grandmother of Jesus* (Mt Shasta Area, CA)

"Catherine Ann, I have to say you have connected to the heart of humanity in your adventurous, yet gentle, amazing book. It is like you are reading the minds of people who are awakening to spirit and letting them know they are NOT alone. Thank you so much. You can certainly RAISE the frequency with a little nudge of the heart."

Marilyn Harper, channel for Adironnda & Company (*Branson, MO*)

"Intrigue, Comedy, Danger, and most of all Insightful. Catherine has chronicled her life in a way that grips the reader. The stories and experiences that molded the awakening of this remarkable woman is nothing short of amazing. In her succinct way, Catherine Ann shows us how Awakening begins by realizing that synchronicity of thought and action are the building blocks to awareness. Each moment builds on the next. The awakening comes when we get to the moment, we understand that synchronicity will continue on and there is nothing we need to do but trust and have faith that all is a part of the bigger picture. Each piece is part of the whole. I recommend this book to anyone that has any doubt that the pieces are perfectly orchestrated by a power outside of ourselves."

Diane A Light, DCP, MOL (*Sun City, AZ*)

"This mesmerizing look at a Soul's golden, absolutely genius, path to the Higher Dimensions unlocks for the reader new and detailed awareness of their own Sacred Journey Home. Catherine Ann allows us to see the intricate details designed by her Soul to take her to an ever-expanding higher vibration in preparation for the completion of her Earthly Mission and Ascension into the Higher Realms. She and her Soul dance with magical, mystical, delicate steps to the music of wisdom, love, laughter, sorrow, fun, adventure, overwhelm and tears. And we are invited to partake. Thank you, Catherine Ann, for this life changing experience!!!"

Jan Deeter (*Litchfield Park, AZ*)

"I love a book that takes me on a journey. This latest book by Catherine Ann Clemett does exactly that. Her journey through all the twists and turns, multiple seemingly mishaps or perhaps divine intervention, had me following the writing while watching a movie in my mind. I could literally see the scenes as she was describing them. This experience was so vivid, I suggest she write the screenplay. It seems the right time to start telling our life's adventures through a spiritual lens. Catherine Ann does just that."

Salvatore Candeloro, Medium by Design (Phoenix, AZ)

"I will always be grateful to Catherine for coming into my life in 1980. This was the beginning of my spiritual awakening! I have been quite an admirer of her adventurous nature, inquiring mind, and creative talent. In this book, Catherine shares a wondrous journey of her life's experiences. She inspires us with her vivid and colorful recounting of events, tireless pursuit to find truth, and refreshing candor in uneasy times!"

Barry Neal Levin (*Rainier, WA*)

"Catherine Ann Clemett is a gifted empath who provides hope and essence to thrive in today's disrupted world. She channels you into new spaces. Move over Marianne Williamson."

Greg Hutchins, author of *Working It (Portland, OR)*

"Catherine, as the older sister in the family.... seemed not a part of the family. She felt invisible. This wonderful memoir is an inside look at being an outsider! It's about 'learning to love myself.' The wonderful song from "King and I"..."Getting to Know You" ... would be retitled for this book, "Getting to Know Me." It's a book about 'opening up' to the larger aspects of ourselves–of living life to the fullest even when things look bleak. Digging down....to dig out. What a wonderful trip through her incredible life!

Lee Kalcheim, Playwright, author of *Father Knows Less (West Stockbridge, MA)*

Catherine Ann Clemett embraces a multitude of energies as she journeys within to discover the dance between the physical and the non-physical... As she delves deeper within to reveal her inner true Self, she does so with great compassion and love. She embraces life to the fullest as she experiences her spiritual awakening and the understanding that she is a spiritual being.

Finbarr Ross, Author of *Sacred Mystical Journey (Montrose, CO)*

I had known part of Catherine Ann's life story before I read her book. By the time I finished reading it (and it is hard to put it down!), I was in awe of how she has even survived up till now. It is an amazing story of continuous miracles, synchronicities and plot twists. You'll love it!

Heather M. Clarke, Author of *You Already Know This, Volumes 1 & 2 (Litchfield Park, AZ)*

Raising My Frequency

A Spiritual Journey
Awakening to More of Life

Also, by Catherine Ann Clemett

Anna, the Voice of the Magdalenes, co-authored with Claire Heartsong

Twin Flame Union, the Ascension of St. Germain and Portia, co-authored with Claire Heartsong

Finding the One True Love, Why Breaking the Rules Will Change Your Life, co-authored with Angelina Heart

Soulweaving, Return to the Heart of the Mother

Are You a Magdalene?

Is This All There Is? The Call to Awaken
Book 1: The Awakening Series

Finding Your Inner Jewel, How to Access Your Authentic Self
Book 2: The Awakening Series

Partnering with Divinity

Raising My Frequency

A Spiritual Journey
Awakening to More of Life

Catherine Ann Clemett

Copyright © 2022 Catherine Ann Clemett

Published by LightRiver Media
Surprise, AZ

All rights reserved. All rights reserved. All rights reserved. No part of this book may be reproduced without written permission from the publisher, except by a reviewer who may quote brief passages or reproduce illustrations in a review; nor may any part of this book be reproduced, stored in a retrieval system, or transmitted in any form or by any means electronic, mechanical, photocopying, recording or other, without written permission from the publisher.

ISBN # 978-0-9847209-6-5

Library of Congress Control Number: 2022913370

"When there is trauma in your drama,
change the tragic into magic."

~ St. Germain

Table of Contents

Acknowledgments..
Foreword...xiii
Preface..
Chapter 1: How Did I End Up Here?...
Chapter 2: It's All Energy!...
Chapter 3: The Breadcrumb Trail Begins......................................13
Chapter 4: Imprint for the Soul's Growth....................................19
Chapter 5: Dance to the Rescue..33
Chapter 6: Thwarted Again...37
Chapter 7: My Major Stumbling Blocks..45
Chapter 8: The Other Side Beckons...51
Chapter 9: Opting for a Career Path...61
Chapter 10: Elevating My Career Prospects...................................71
Chapter 11: Becoming More Conscious...79
Chapter 12: Meeting the Masters...89
Chapter 13: Mystery Solved, Yet Deepens....................................103
Chapter 14: Men, Money, and Miracles.......................................113
Chapter 15: The Cult Years...127
Chapter 16: Seeds of Discontent..139
Chapter 17: Freedom..147
    Kay's Message to Me in August 2003.................................152
Chapter 18: It's All Inward from Here......................................157
Chapter 19: Opening to New Directions......................................169
    Grid Work Excerpt..171

St. Germain and the Hosts of Heaven Message..........176

Chapter 20: The Larger Plan Unfolds..........181

Chapter 21: Finding My Soul's Purpose..........203

Chapter 22: Coming Full Circle..........213

Chapter 23: Back on Track Again..........223

Chapter 24: On the Move Again..........227

Chapter 25: International Travel Begins..........233

11/11/11 Lourdes, France Message..........244

11/15/11 St Marie la Mer Message..........246

Chapter 26: Amazing Occurrences..........251

Ephesus Turkey, November 11, 2014..........265

Magdalene Grid Activation Message..........265

Chapter 27: Integration..........269

Conclusion..........285

Hosts of Heaven Message..........288

Afterword: Know Thyself..........293

Images..........301

Events Calendar..........341

Books and Products..........347

The Awakening Series..........349

Meditations..........352

Programs and Sessions..........353

About the Author..........355

Acknowledgments

Foremost is my gratitude to my I AM presence and my soul for instigating and initiating this journey of self-discovery, helping me to understand who I am and how I fit into the bigger picture. Many people have played either inspiring roles or challenging roles in my journey of awakening or have assisted me including family members, mentors, teachers, friends, roommates, event hosts, lodging hosts, boyfriends, clients, tour and workshop participants, dancers, and collaborators most notably: Claire Heartsong, Virginia Essene, C.W., Vickie Moyle, Arthur Clemett, Evelyn Clemett, my siblings, Gila Cadry, JZ Knight, Penny Torres Rubin, Ramtha, Mafu, Zanzoona, St. Germain, Jean Trebek, Alex Trebek, Barry Levin, Judith Rose Moore, Pam Barker, Karen Holden, Lee Kalcheim, Suzanne Rollow, Cynthia Slon, Philip Burley, Mark Degange, Mark Litvin, Rich Dunkle, Dan Shaw, Dean Thompson, Thomas Sharkey, Linda Barnes, Kathy Christiansen, Bob Dredge, Guru P., Jan Deeter, Salvatore Candeloro, Stephanie Skura, Evelyn Ochoa, Geoffrey Lennon, Jill Adams, Bill Nakagawa, Finbarr Ross, Mariangela Landau, Kay Geist, Patricia Giles, Margaret Ruby, Sheila Murphy, Martha Myers, Jan Whalen, David Walker, Ani Williams, Joanie Proctor, Flo Magdalena, Sheryl Mercer, Heather Clark, Amy Fleetman, She-Lah, Uria, Jim Shawvan, Sharon Ludlow, Diane Light, and many other people whom I have not specifically named, or have changed their names to protect their privacy.

Foreword

by Finbarr Ross

Catherine Ann Clemett takes us on a beautiful journey embracing the Divine Feminine and the energies of unified consciousness as she moves through a chaotic world from Connecticut to Hawaii and beyond.

She embraces a multitude of energies as she journeys within to discover the dance between the physical and the non-physical. On this journey she reveals her true Self. As she delves deeper within to reveal her inner true Self, she does so with great compassion and love. She embraces life to the fullest as she experiences her spiritual awakening and the understanding that she is a spiritual being.

Guided by spirit, she embodies and anchors her inner knowing as she quests the many spiritual disciplines ranging from the metaphysical to Zen contemplation, understanding energy, Kundalini rising, and more. As you read this book you may also come to an understanding of inner knowing and self-awareness leading you to understand the power of love that resides within the heart.

Preface

A pearl would never become an object of exquisite beauty without irritation.
Bless the process.

Magic abounds. Yet it often hid from my perception like a forgotten, cherished toy. I am referring to the magic of Source, that which uplifts, inspires and allows for synchronicity and miracles to occur. Even as a young child, I kept searching, searching, and searching for the magic that I instinctively knew was there somewhere, yet it continued to elude me. Exhilarating moments of insight like standing atop a high mountain in clarity and joy would inevitably give way to valleys and volumes of disappointment and disillusionment, feelings that I never fit in or could get what I really wanted, which only furthered my self-doubt. Nothing I did seemed to matter.

The peaks and valleys of terror and exhilaration became my companions, gripping me equally throughout my journey of awakening. Eventually, I came to realize I couldn't control who or what was outside of myself. I could only affect that which was within me.

Terror arose in me when facing the unknown, when taking risks, and through the willingness to expose my deepest, darkest fears, insecurities, and human failings-the most vulnerable parts of myself. As I brought these vulnerable shadow parts up into the light for examination, my terror yielded to understanding, wisdom, and exhilaration. In my willingness to go into the murky depths of this shadow examination, profound strength, conviction,

Frequency Raising

courage and compassion for myself emerged that I never knew I had. Bit-by-bit the magic started softly, revealing itself to me once again enabling me to climb out of the murky depths and raise my frequency. It came about when I allowed myself to just be present with whatever was happening without trying to make it wrong, override it, or dismiss it.

Raising one's frequency is a relatively simple task, yet it takes lifetimes and perseverance to accomplish. When one will face themselves and do their inner work to address and shift the lower frequency states of fear, anger, rage, hostility, doubt, inadequacy, exclusion, and manipulation to higher frequency states based on love, unity, cooperation, support, inclusion, and creativity; a raising of one's frequency naturally occurs. This is because space is created for more wisdom, insight, and expanded awareness to occur.

All states of our consciousness, whether they originate out of the lower or higher registers of frequencies profoundly affect and program our world around us. When we emanate from the higher frequency states of consciousness, life around us becomes harmonious, uplifting, and inspiring. When we emanate most often unconsciously from the lower frequency ranges, then life is often painful, challenging, and can become a constant struggle. This was a lot of what I experienced particularly in my early life.

All I wanted was the 'more' of life. To my teenage conscious mindset, this meant more of what I felt I didn't have; friends, boyfriends, outings, dates, thrilling experiences; a feeling of belonging and excitement in my life. However, to my subconscious mind, this plea had a different meaning. This plea put me on the path of awakening to who I really am as a multidimensional spiritual being way beyond my human understanding or experience at age fourteen. When I first put forth this passionate plea, I had no clue what I was really asking to unfold in my life. Ultimately, I was asking to awaken and raise my frequency.

Awakening happens when we can face and embrace the truth, clear the obstructions and allow light to flood into those spaces and places where there was previously negativity, obfuscation, and pain. Awakening is the most profound personal journey one ever takes. The journey tears away any false illusions, coveted belief systems, or opinions and thoughts we have about

Preface

ourselves or others so that we can find the magic of the inner jewel we are within.

Only when we will face ourselves honestly, find the truth, and continually move forward without getting mired in the mud or stuck in the weeds do the obstructions clear, allowing our frequency to rise. Besides sharing the magical and really bizarre occurrences which have happened in my life, I find it is also imperative to share my challenges and struggles, which sometimes were negative and depressing. In this roller coaster ride of being human, often I couldn't seem to change it no matter how hard I tried. While many shy away in fear from going within and confronting their shadow aspects, I found it was only through confronting my issues head-on, seeking their truth rather than sweeping them under the rug that awakening occurs through the insight, comprehension and freedom that is gained.

When our soul signals to us it's time to awaken, we may often have some challenge or disaster befall us or we may be shocked in certain ways, leading us to question our foundational reality. This shock to our system or challenge in our life serves to crack open the hard nut of our ego. This is the catalyst for our awakening, moving us towards greater insight, wisdom, and a more fulfilled existence both on a spiritual and physical level.

In this book I share my journey of awakening advancing beyond the limitations of an emotionally-charged childhood in which I tried to make myself small and invisible for self-preservation, to later in life becoming a published author, workshop leader, international speaker and spiritual mentor, none of which I consciously planned nor ever could have imagined earlier in my life. Eventually, I came to understand this unexpected journey was my soul's blueprint for my awakening, not my personality's intended goal plan for my life.

Awakening doesn't just happen in one instance, but through a never-ending series of initiations which furthers the evolution of our soul. Even though it may be a long and arduous process, perhaps taking many lifetimes for our soul to crack the ego-personality's hard exterior, it is only through surrendering the tight grip of the personality self to that of our soul and the God within that brings about the *great awakening* and the return of magic.

Frequency Raising

When we recognize our Divinity through a clear lens, we then transcend to the power and joy of forever-ness!

So, it is within this framework of understanding that I share my human challenges, the conquering of my fear, and the ensuing triumphs that uncovered the "more," the *magic, manifestations, and miracles* which are forever present if we only know where to look. I invite you to come along as I share my journey, hoping it will help you navigate your own journey of awakening as well. The next-to-the-last chapter of the book starting on page 301 provides images that illustrate many of the stories that are shared.

Catherine Ann Clemett
June 2022

Chapter 1: How Did I End Up Here?

I never felt I belonged, not in my family, not in my school, and not in my social circles, except with a few select friends. I was never part of the in-crowd and probably would have found them boring had I been accepted into that group. At home, I remained mostly invisible as I withdrew from sharing my feelings, longings, upsets and dreams with my family for self-protection and self-preservation, as a means to escape ridicule. So how could I belong?

Not belonging even went so far as non-existence in my perception. When I was away at college, my brothers had become friends with an older boy whom they knew through sailing. For over a year, Doug had become a fixture in our house, spending nearly all of his time there and eating most of his meals with my siblings. It was almost like he was another brother. Although I hadn't yet met Doug, I'd heard stories about him.

Returning to my family's home in Westport, Connecticut for the weekend from college I came up the basement stairs. As I entered the house through the garage door which led into the basement, my brothers' friend Doug confronted me at the top of the stairs, questioning why a stranger would just walk into the house.

"Who are you?" he barked.

"I'm Beegee (the nickname I had growing up). I live here."

"You live here?" He asked in a bewildered tone.

"Why have I never seen you before?"

"I've been away at school," I replied. "Yeah, I'm the older sister."

"Older sister? I never knew there were five children in the family," he stammered.

"I always thought there were only four Clemett children."

"Are you kidding me?" I squeaked, my voice cracking on the edge of tears.

Confronting my brothers, "You mean to say for an entire year none of you ever mentioned my name or ever said anything about me?"

Stunned that I was so overlooked, this took my perception of being invisible and not mattering to a whole new level. I felt excluded, even by my siblings. They obviously did not see me as part of their world.

Whatever belonging meant, I knew it didn't apply to me. Growing up with a brilliant, but narcissistic bi-polar father, the drama and trauma of mental and emotional abuse stalked me throughout much of my childhood. As a hyper-sensitive kid, I didn't have the strength, self-worth, or clarity to repel these assaults. My father's cruel attempts to help me develop a thick skin only resulted in shredding what thin skin protection I had left.

I hadn't yet developed my own inner authority and conviction to know I had a right to be listened to, and a right to express my own personal views and opinions. Being constantly steamrolled by the father's authority and know-it-all attitude, I'd just shut down and internalize these assaults into my personal battleground, determined to not let them define me nor let my father win. These assaults, however, were the catalyst that cracked open my ego and started my process of awakening.

What is awakening? Awakening means different things to different people. It can be a moment of clarity, insight, discovering truth or an ah-ha moment where answers to a problem or dilemma bubble up from within. However, awakening rarely happens without some type of catalyst. Most often the catalyst comes from an experience of drama, trauma, or upheaval in our lives, which devotees on spiritual paths for eons have always referred to as initiations.

Much later, I came to understand the assaults I experienced growing up, along with other unexplained experiences were the essential building blocks, the alchemical ingredients which propelled me into my journey of awakening. These experiences were my first initiations. Initiatory experiences can also come about when our perception of reality suddenly shows up differently than how we expect in ways we can't fathom. Initiations prompt us to ask questions about our situation or challenges. In trying to make sense of these challenges or strange occurrences, our soul often leads us to go within to seek answers through assessing our attitudes, belief systems, assumptions, and behavioral patterns which shape our perception of the world and what occurs in our lives.

As if feeling alienated from most people around me wasn't enough to convince me I didn't belong, I also had several out-of-the-ordinary experiences which seemed magical or impossible to me which further stretched my boundaries of perception which I instinctively knew was unsafe to share with others.

In the mid-nineteen nineties, I'd been visiting my family in Rhode Island for a week. I offered to help my mother out by going grocery shopping for her. Returning to her house with three sacks of groceries and a heavy two gallon plastic jug of spring water, lugging these up the narrow wooden staircase of her 1750 Historical Register house was the most challenging part of the task. My ingrained habit was to struggle to get everything upstairs in one fell swoop. This time, however, even though my habitual desire to get everything upstairs in one trip was overwhelmingly strong, I made a deliberate, conscious decision to stop this pattern of behavior. Instead of racing to get everything up the stairs all at once, I sat in the car for a few minutes, took a few deep breaths, calmed myself into a meditative state and mentally asked, "How can I be kinder and more loving to myself with this task?"

The obvious answer which came to me was to make two trips. So, I took the three sacks of groceries and headed up the stairs, resigned to the fact I would need to go back to the car for the water. Upon reaching my mother's apartment on the second floor, I placed the grocery sacks on the kitchen table and made a quick pit-stop in the bathroom.

Coming out of the bathroom after less than a minute, I was astonished to see the two-gallon jug of water sitting on the corner of the kitchen table.

How on earth did that get there?

Perplexed, *were my eyes playing tricks on me?*

Did someone put it there, but who?

Someone else must be here, I thought.
I'd heard no one. It made no logical sense.
"Hello mom? David? Is anyone home?"
Dead silence—no response.

I was there alone. I couldn't fathom how the heavy jug of water could have ended up on my mother's kitchen table all by itself when I hadn't put it there. Later, when my mother and brother returned home, I asked if they knew anything about how the jug of water got upstairs. They were just as bewildered as I was.

Even though I didn't understand it, I knew with absolute certainty something mysterious, and beyond logical explanation, had happened. I hadn't made it up, nor had I somehow forgotten that I'd gone back down to the car for the water. It was a mystery which I knew no one would believe anyhow. I didn't, however, immediately dismiss this experience as impossible. I just put it on the back burner for the time being, allowing it to remain a mystery.

Now, decades later, as I've come into awareness that we live in a multidimensional reality in which the vibratory frequency of the planet is being raised, I've come up with a new theory about this seemingly magical occurrence. Maybe my strong intention, coupled with a deliberate choice to love myself by changing my habitual pattern, possibly catapulted me out of the third-dimensional reality up into the fifth dimension in that instance. The conscious choice to be loving to myself may have raised my frequency up in that moment to where the laws of physics behaved differently, or perhaps I crossed a timeline into an alternate reality. Even though I had no way of tangibly explaining it, my assumption of what makes up reality would never be quite the same, ever again. This event would prove to be another catalyst for my journey of awakening. It served only to deepen my commitment and quest to know myself at this causation level beyond usual human understanding.

Growing up, I had my life path all planned out in my mind. I had two dreams. First, was to become a dancer in a professional ballet or modern dance company, and second, to find and marry my soulmate. This was everything I was working towards. As a kid, I alternated between exhibiting two different aspects of my personality. My dancer self was outgoing, creative, engaged with, and passionate about, my craft. Dance was my refuge, sanity, and reason for living. To be a successful dancer required me to show up larger than life, to become known, recognized and sought after. My personality at home in the family unit, however, was much more reserved, introverted, and self-protective as my father believed his role was to help his children develop a thick skin. Almost all of my interaction with him occurred through a constant barrage of criticism, usually in the guise of sadistic humor aimed at me.

Relentlessly, I'd hear, "*suck it in,*" as he struck me in the stomach with the back of his hand.

Almost every time he passed by me, he added comments like, "I'd hate to be the guy that has to lift you in ballet class!"

Even though I was a normal weight, he had this warped idea that women should look like anorexic models. This all started when, as a prepubescent preteen, I chunked up a bit, getting ready for a growth spurt. He wouldn't let it alone. The ensuing barrage of this hurtful commentary became so rampant that I would circumvent any room he was in to avoid interacting with him. My brothers had heard this type of interaction between my father and me so much that they even began repeating stories at the dinner table about how I was the best baseball player on the team. This was because my stomach was so big that it encompassed the whole outfield so the ball would just bounce off my stomach! Mortified, I didn't know how to defend myself against this kind of slander and cruel behavior, so I just retreated into my shell and took it.

A brilliant, well-known doctor who was a pioneer in medicine, my father could be very charming to everyone around him. However, if he thought you should know better, or that you've asked a stupid question, without a word he'd cut you down, putting you in your place just by glaring at you over the rim of his glasses. And he not only reserved this behavior for his children but also applied it to the doctors who were fellows in radiology whom he was mentoring.

After my father passed away, at his memorial service, I overheard a group of five or six prominent radiologists from New York City talking about my father. They were all sharing how disregarded they felt and how unjustly my father treated them while they were doing their radiology fellowships under him. It was oddly reassuring to know it wasn't just me or my siblings whom he singled out and treated this way! This was a further sign that the fault lay with my father rather than me, as he always led me to believe.

There were no boundaries. I didn't feel my father even saw me as a separate person. To him, I was just an extension of his views, his interests, and what he thought and believed. Now as an adult, I recognize this as narcissistic behavior. I had to fight hard to preserve my sense of identity, my preferences, opinions, and feelings. I found it hard to believe that other kids actually had back-and-forth communication with their fathers and that their fathers respected them and listened to them. Communication with my father always felt one-sided. If there were any issues or shortcomings, he always found fault with everyone else, not with himself.

Chapter 2: It's All Energy!

Football, sports, or whatever my father and brothers were interested in wasn't of any interest to me. Being cajoled into competing against my siblings to see who could do the most push-ups or whatever contests my father dreamed up just made me mad. One-upmanship was the name of the game. Although he admired this trait, I didn't. Feeling bullied, I'd cave and retreat as fast as I could.

My father almost never asked me about my interests, what I wanted, or how I felt. Most of the comments he made about my interest in dance were only ridicule. Nothing I did or was interested in seemed to matter. I came to believe I just wasn't good enough. I longed for the *more* of life, for the love, support, communication, nurturing and adventure which I knew was 'out there' somewhere for me. Yet I didn't have a clue what that was, nor how to go about finding it.

It sucks here!

I want to be in touch with the excitement, the promise and exploring the curiosity and magic of life!

This was the passionate plea of my fourteen-year-old self to the universe to either get me out of here or to help me understand why my existence felt so limited, confined, confused, and unhappy. I knew there must be more to life than what I'd been experiencing. The year was 1965. The underpinning of this plea was that again, I felt I didn't belong anywhere, particularly with my family, as I felt so different from them. After school, when I'd retreat into my bedroom, my mother always thought I was upstairs, studiously doing my homework, as I was a dutiful student who received good grades. But I didn't work hard at it. Most of the time, I'd do most of my homework on the school bus on the way to school. This left plenty of time in the privacy of my bedroom for me to lie sideways across my bed and space out for hours on end in thought. I was curious about everything and had a deep desire to understand the universe - what comprised it, how it worked, and how I fit into that picture. One day, I was surprised that I seemed to have received an answer to my plea that helped me understand the *more* of life that I'd been seeking. It caught me totally off-guard! This was the first time I remember having what later I understood to be a *download*.

The answer I received which just dropped into my mind seemingly out of nowhere was, *it's all about energy*.

Energy?

What?

What energy?

Energy was never a thought that entered my mind until it mysteriously 'dropped in' from somewhere else which I couldn't identify. It was certainly not something I was consciously entertaining in my mind. At age fourteen, I didn't even know what those words meant, but I knew somewhere within the core of my being it was true. Everything was energy! I didn't know how to articulate it or research what it meant. Who the heck was talking about energy in 1965, anyway? I vowed that someday, I'd find out. Setting out to find and understand the *more* of life beyond what I was experiencing, along with my staunch resolve to not let my father win by surrendering to his dictates, views and demands, prompted my initial inner search which wasn't safe to share with anybody, so I had to search in secret.

Growing up in a middle-class family with a certain amount of privilege, my experience of abuse or victimization wasn't nearly as bad as what many other people have had to endure growing up. However, I didn't understand the extent of the emotional and psychological abuse we suffered as children until after I grew up. My upbringing left me with enough of a negative imprint of low self-esteem, immobilizing my ability to succeed that I knew to move forward I would eventually need to make peace with it and release it.

As a kid, you just think the environment you grow up in is normal because you know nothing different. Over time, I realized I was developing an acute *psychic* ability, a psychic antenna, to help me circumvent this emotional and psychological abuse. Instinctively, I was unconsciously training myself to read the energy of a room, a person, or a situation so I could determine if it was safe to engage in it or if it was better to make myself scarce. I made myself scarce a lot.

My vow someday to understand this *energy* created a burning desire to explore all the different manifestations of it and pathways it takes so I could to gain some comprehension of it. What occurred was a great unfolding of experiences, which gradually led me to greater understanding. I couldn't have fathomed any of this back when I first had the download that everything is *energy*. It became even clearer that my deep yearning to learn more, along with the alienation I felt from my family, and my hypersensitivity were, without doubt, the *initiations* that propelled me into the journey of self-discovery and spiritual awakening. My motivation to not only understand this *energy* but also how to use it to create greater happiness and fulfillment now became my mission. Eventually I came to understand it wasn't just *energy*, but the frequency of that *energy* that was important.

The quest to understand *energy* became my connection to both the physical and non-physical realms. It also helped me to understand the greater role dance played in my life. Besides giving me a reason to get out of the house, dance offered me the opportunity to develop some control in my life through fine-tuned mastery of my physical body, even if I didn't have a clue how to control my home environment or the world around me. Although unconscious, this mastery also taught me a lot about how *energy* works and flows in the body.

My goal as a dancer was to become so in control of my body that I could dance effortlessly from balance point to balance point, which took extreme dedication and focus as I didn't have a natural, lithe, highly flexible dancer's body like other dancers I knew. My physique was compact and strong, better suited to jumps and large movements. Moving across the floor-soaring through the air high off the ground felt like flying to me.

Later, as a more seasoned performer, I realized I'd not only learned how to harness and maximize my *energy*, but to extend it out to the audience to increase their attention and engagement. Eventually I would come to understand that my long-term love affair with dance, unbeknownst to me, would later give me the foundation and mechanism to anchor higher dimensional experiences and wisdom through my physical body.

Years down the road, when doing a lot of inner shadow work, I realized that an even more basic driving force about my love of dance was that dance was something which was totally my choice, not something dictated to me by someone else. It was also a means of getting attention, admiration, and love. Excelling as a dancer was a way for me to receive approval and support because of my performing abilities. Never feeling I was good enough growing up, instead of shying away, I now had something in which I could prove my worth and mastery. I challenged myself through competing with other dancers in class, while also competing with myself, as I was continually striving to improve my skills and ability. I came to realize this foundation of dance wasn't only about the physical mastery but was also to serve as a foundation for my spiritual mastery.

Looking back, I've noticed three things. The first was I didn't deliberately or consciously set out to be on a *spiritual* journey. Instead, the journey *found* me like when a stray cat or dog shows up at your door and decides, rather unexpectedly, you're their owner. In a similar way, I felt this path of awakening somehow *claimed* me as its owner. That first *download* of *it's all about energy* started me on this spiritual trail of *breadcrumbs*. I didn't understand where it was leading me, but I sensed there was some plan or purpose for which I wasn't yet privy.

The *breadcrumbs*, which have appeared and developed over many decades, are the clues in what I call the *treasure map of your soul*. This translates to the exact path of facing and overcoming your most significant challenges along with receiving the most beautiful blessings in life in which you gain wisdom and insights through your own experience. This develops you as a soul.

Chapter 2: It's All Energy!

The second was a willingness to be open to unknown possibilities, going beyond the conventional ways of thinking and versions of what I knew as my reality. This also entailed being willing to address and mend the patterns of abuse and victimization within me. With time, I realized that when one is willing and able to face themselves within, no matter what is there or what shows up, transformation inevitably occurs. As we make changes within, it mirrors them in one's external reality. This concept also became an integral part of my awakening, which required courage and tenacity to step into these strange and foreign lands of the conscious and subconscious mind. It forced me to find conviction and belief in abilities which were previously crushed out of me.

The third was coming to recognize there was always a deep divine inner presence within me, guiding me, sustaining me and frequently *saving my bacon*. No matter what situation I was in, or how terrified I may have been, in astonishing ways I've always landed on my feet like a cat, which reminds me of an incident that I witnessed in my early twenties.

My family's house in Westport, Connecticut, built on a hill, had two-stories in the front and three stories at the back because of the sloping backyard. The kitchen, on the middle floor, had windows that faced the backyard. My mother and I were sitting at the kitchen table looking out the second-story window only to see our family cat, Cindy, all four paws with her claws extended and her fur wafting in the breeze as she sailed past the window. I guess she had somehow climbed up onto the roof and had gotten knocked off. After flying three stories down to the backyard below, she landed in the grass, looked dazed for a few moments, shook herself off, and walked away without a scratch.

I realize my pattern of always landing like a cat on all fours, no matter what is happening in my life, has helped me to relax and develop more confidence in my inner being's guidance and direction. So, just as Cindy's fall from the roof meant she survived one of her nine lives, I also realize I've encountered at least nine situations in which I've faced my mortality in some fashion. Not only were these often-terrifying events, but I know something more significant was operating beyond my conscious awareness, coupled with *Divine Intervention* occurring as some kind of overseeing guidance. I've pulled off extraordinary things in the face of what seemed to be insurmountable challenges. Yet in everything I've done, as I've said, I ended up flying by the seat of my pants.

Even though I came to recognize there was this divine presence within me, I still couldn't understand why my daily human life hadn't automatically straightened out, becoming easygoing, fulfilling, and abundant. Instead, it felt like I faced a continuing series of difficulties and challenges for which I was still searching for answers. I also realized I needed to untangle myself from the ancestral and current Clemett family karmic web of issues for the sake of gaining my self-worth, identity, and spiritual growth. I realized the seed of mastery may have lain dormant for lifetimes, only to be ignited when the right timing and configuration of family dynamics, DNA, and yes, *dysfunction*, comes into play! Soon, the first enormous piece to this puzzle of why I've endured suffering so much in my life unexpectedly showed up, igniting this seed of mastery.

Chapter 3: The Breadcrumb Trail Begins

In 2003, I had my first reading with psychic and channel Cynthia Slon. My guides came in thanking, honoring, and acknowledging me for the fantastic work I'd done. Bewildered, I asked, *"what work?"* In my recollection, I'd done nothing. My guides informed me I did grid work on the inner planes and in my sleep state, which assisted humanity. It was news to me. I wondered if this was why I sometimes woke up tired in the morning! If I was so honored and respected on the inner planes, I wondered, *why was my human life such a mess?*

Everyone faces difficulties in their life, along with disappointment, but I had a pattern of everything I most wanted in life repeatedly being thwarted. It wasn't only my big dreams and desires, but also what happened as a daily occurrence. My friends would comment on how inconsequential matters tripped me up, or how things in my life turned into issues which didn't work out.

Similar to a wounded salmon getting smashed on the rocks as it struggles to return to its spawning ground, I kept fighting for what I wanted as I tried to get to the root but was not getting anywhere. I didn't know why this was happening, but I was sick of it!

Despite hearing about the cosmic level of things I was purportedly performing, I still wondered what I needed to do or change to live a successful human life like others around me were doing. The answer came in another reading in 2006, when Cynthia and I started discussing why my life had been so challenging.

My guides, through Cynthia, said I was living a blueprint which wasn't really mine.

How could this be? I wondered.

She said when my mother told my father she was pregnant with me; he was very upset. Apparently, her emotional response to his behavior was so intense that it released a flood of hormones and toxic chemicals in her body, creating a toxic in-utero environment in my early gestation. The guides said the only way I could live and survive this poisonous environment was to be born as soon as possible, which was why I was born prematurely when my mother was a little over six and a half months pregnant.

To counteract this, my guides gave me a visualization exercise to do to decrease the effects of this pre-birth toxicity within me. They suggested I go back through all the relationships in my life, expressly through all the romantic relationships with male partners, giving back any dysfunctional energy projected onto me which resulted in low self-esteem, low self-worth, abuse and victimization that I'd experienced at the hands of others. They further instructed me to call back in and unite with all the pieces of myself (soul retrieval) which others hadn't acknowledged, loved, or validated.

As an Empath, naturally I'd take on dysfunctional energy (low frequency), not even knowing I was doing it. Now, I was to give this dysfunctional energy back to each partner from whom it had originated, as it was not my energy or frequency to begin with. Cynthia also suggested I go back to the early gestational in-utero environment of my mother where I could reverse the toxic energy of my parent's confusion, arguing, pain, and anger, which had become embedded not only into my DNA but also in my cellular and molecular early gestational development. Through this reversal exercise, it would then be possible to return to my originating state offering to myself all the energy, love, warmth, and nurturing which I did not have when I first entered the world. When receiving a reading, it's often hard to know if the information is accurate or not. However, my mother's account of the early days of her relationship with my father provided confirmation of Cynthia's reading.

Chapter 3: The Breadcrumb Trail Begins

When I was in my thirties while visiting my mother, she began letting out tidbits about her story with my father to me after she had a few drinks. She'd been a nurse at Yale New Haven Hospital where she met my father, who was a new intern. My mother had been interested in becoming a doctor herself, but feared she didn't have enough skill, intelligence or the ability to pull it off financially. Instead, she became a nurse and set out to find the smartest guy she could find to make up for what she felt were her intellectual inadequacies. So, she set her sights on my father, who had the highest IQ ever recorded up to that point at Wesleyan University in Middletown, Connecticut.

Although my father was brilliant, there was serious dysfunction in their relationship. My mother told me when they were dating, he put her on an assessment system, a scale starting at minus twenty in which every time she did something he approved of, he'd add a point which moved her closer towards zero. Every time she did something he didn't approve of, he'd remove a point. When the scale reached zero, he would then ask her to marry him.

Upon hearing this, I thought to myself, *are you kidding?*

What a jerk!

To me, hearing about my father's behavior should have been a red flag for my mother. After a few more drinks, my mother admitted they weren't using any birth control when, as a doctor and a nurse, they should have known better. I assume that the negative assessment deal was off once my mother announced she was pregnant. They devised a way to hide her pregnancy with a wedding date that made sense. Expecting I'd be a full-term baby, they'd claim I'd come early, making it plausible she got pregnant on their wedding night.

In 1951, people still did whatever they had to do to keep their family skeletons in the closet. In response to this situation, my father was pushing for the Justice of the Peace to marry them. However, my mother wanted to have a traditional Catholic wedding for her very devout Irish Catholic mother. For her, being married by the Justice of the Peace wasn't an option. So, they set a date for a Catholic Church wedding for late July, which fit in with their plan to keep the skeleton in the closet as my mother was apparently only a few months pregnant.

As the months went by, people weren't even aware my mother was pregnant. She was slender and only bought maternity clothes for the first time six days before I was born, when her regular clothes were getting too tight. The morning before I was born, my mother said she awoke with a strange rash all over her body, which nobody could diagnose.

Not feeling right, she told my father she needed to go to the hospital. They admitted her and gave her a bed. Alone in her room with no signs of labor, my tiny head suddenly emerged. Instinctively, she locked her legs together to prevent me from slipping out before help arrived. Yelling for help, she kept pressing the buzzer for the nurse, who eventually came and I was officially born.

Growing up, I thought it was odd my parents never discussed their wedding or celebrated their anniversary. There were no wedding photos, either. My Grandparents lived a few hours away. Sometimes I'd stay overnight with them. As a treat, my grandmother would allow me to sleep in her double bed in her bedroom while my grandfather slept in a separate bedroom. One night, I woke up in the middle of the night, freezing. I went to the closet, looking for an extra blanket. On the top shelf, I found an enormous gift box which piqued my curiosity. Opening it up, I discovered it was full of wedding photos and newspaper clippings of my parent's wedding. The wedding date in late July 1951 was only about four and a half months before my birth, as I was born in early December 1951.

Even at age thirteen, I could do the math!

The next morning, I took the newspaper clipping downstairs to my grandmother and asked her about the date of my parent's wedding. She tried to diffuse the issue by telling me the paper printed the wrong year.

Now how often does that happen?

Even as a thirteen-year-old, I knew it was a blatant lie. Again, this confirmed it was a skeleton they wanted to keep in the closet, all right!

It didn't bother me that much. At that point, I figured my parents must have loved each other if they stayed together for several more decades, through two miscarriages and four more children after I was born. I had no judgment or blame on my parents for how my life began. They were young professionals, in their early twenties, under parental and societal pressures from the culture and times in which they lived. In those days, if you got pregnant, you got married—end of story! They did their best under the circumstances. And even though I didn't consciously blame my parents, I still wanted to get beyond the recurring patterns of struggle in my life.

Years later, I came to realize that struggling was a coping mechanism I had as a newborn. If I was struggling, that meant I was still alive. Understanding how to overcome this pattern of struggle has become a lifelong quest. And it's through this constant struggle I came to realize what a strong and determined little being I was.

Chapter 4: Imprint for the Soul's Growth

We are all born as innocent babes. But soon after, for some of us, the indoctrination of the harshness of this world begins. We receive consistent conscious and subconscious training which informs us what to do, what to think, and how to behave. Most of us never question these social conventions. But those of us who often question our perceived reality, the belief systems, and the rules others impose on us, find that this provides the fuel for our soul's growth. I questioned everything. I was always the one seeking to understand the *why* of everything.

As I've mentioned before, "Beegee," was the name I went by throughout my childhood into my late 20s when I started using my given name, Catherine Ann. Because I was born so prematurely, only weighing two-and-a-half pounds at birth, my parents hadn't even decided on a name for me yet. The doctor held me in the palm of his hand as he handed me over to my mother. I was that tiny. My grandmother said I looked like one of the ham bones she used for soup, which is not exactly the most flattering of images. I was long, skinny and very red. The doctors didn't expect I would live.

My first three months of life I spent in an incubator in a naval hospital in Queens, New York being cared for by male Navy Corps nurses in the NICU (Neo-natal Intensive Care Unit). Since I had no name, the staff put a hospital band on my wrist which just said "BG Clemett"—Baby Girl Clemett. So "BG" quickly became my nickname. My grandmother came up with the creative spelling of "BeeGee" long before the rock group the Bee Gees came into existence.

During those first few days after my birth, the parish priest came, baptized me, and gave me last rites. My birth certificate still to this day says Clemett (female) with no first name on the certificate. When it became clear I might survive, my parents eventually came up with the name Catherine Ann. Some months later, I had a baptismal certificate listing my name as (Mary) Catherine Ann Clemett. "Mary" was the emergency baptism name routinely given to all female Catholic babies who weren't expected to live. My first brush with mortality in this life was surviving my premature birth. Different from the other eight of my "nine lives," this first challenge was actually not about dying but about surviving and staying in the body while still in-utero and after birth.

Apparently, I had an intense desire to escape this mortal physical life. I learned of this also during my 2006 reading with Cynthia. She said during the first three months of my life I kept trying to escape to return *home*, but my guides kept shoving me back into my tiny infant body. My mother told me that each day, for months after I was born, they didn't know if I'd survive another day or not. So, even though I tried to leave repeatedly, my soul had a definite plan. My guides were making sure I would stick around for it to come to fruition.

At three months old, I finally came home from the hospital. Soon after, my father, who was then a doctor on active duty, left for Korea to serve in the Medical Corps at the start of the Korean War. I was just six months old when he vanished from my life for two years. When he left for Korea, my mother and I moved in with my grandparents in Connecticut. They took care of me while my mother worked nights as a nurse and slept during the day. I was so used to life without my father that when he returned from Korea, I'd have nothing to do with him, as he was a stranger to me. I was told I'd scream every time he came near me for the next several months.

As a kid, I was smart, innovative, and hyperactive. My mother said if I were born today, instead of in the early 50s, doctors would have put me on Ritalin as I never sat still. As a toddler, my mother put me in a harness on a leash. People stared in horror that she'd do that to her child, but it was the most humane thing she could do as it freed me to wander and explore within a safe radius.

As a young child, I was adventurous and inventive; a real handful. I'd busy myself playing house by taking all of my clothes and my baby brother's clothes, putting them into my plastic swimming pool to *wash* them. Or I'd make pancakes by dumping every ingredient or substance I could find in the kitchen into a bowl: flour, sugar, dish soap, cleanser, juice, milk, and detergent. I was so proud of myself, but my mother was at her wit's end. I wasn't concerned with my mother's approval, however, because I had a friend who helped with these projects. At four years old, I had an imaginary playmate named Herman. Every evening, I'd insist that my mother set a place for Herman underneath the kitchen table before I would eat dinner.

Until I turned eight, life was exuberant and innocent. My happiest years were when we lived in South Portland, Maine. Perched on the cliff above the neighborhood beach, our house had panoramic views of the ship channel leading into Portland Harbor. For the two years we lived there, I had an ideal life, spending most of my time at the beach along with the neighborhood kids. We created a thriving barter system selling all kinds of treasures we found: pieces of ocean glass, crab carcasses, feathers, pretty shells, or whatever washed up on the beach. The white periwinkle shells we used as our currency.

Every morning I'd wake up blanketed by the sweet fragrance of lilacs outside my bedroom window, excited about whatever adventures the day would bring. Just being outside inhaling the salty smell of the ocean, luxuriating in the gentle sea breeze caressing my skin, and being lulled by the gentle lapping of the waves made me feel excited to be alive. But it didn't last. My world would soon come crashing down.

We moved a lot during my childhood. By the time I was eight, we'd moved house eight times. Moving was to become a familiar repeating pattern throughout my life. I've moved more times than I can now count. My father, who had completed two different medical residencies and a fellowship, practiced as a radiologist in Portland, Maine, for a few years and then accepted an academic medicine position at Yale University Medical School in New

Frequency Raising

Haven. It was this move from our wonderful home in Maine to an isolated house out in the country in Connecticut in which my carefree life shattered.

In Connecticut, I had no friends and no opportunity outside of school to make new ones. My only companions were the cows next door in the field on the other side of the barbed wire fence. I'd talk to them, but they just ignored me. Depressed, resentful, and alone, I spent my whole third-grade school year grieving that move from Maine. The following year, my parents finished building a brand-new house in a neighboring town. With this move, life gradually became a little better since most of my time I now spent outside with the other neighborhood children. In an era when parents didn't need to worry about the safety or whereabouts of their children, we were free to roam as we pleased. We would play outside for the entire day until my mother rang a large bell to signal it was time to come home for dinner. Even then, the only one who'd mind the bell and run back on cue was the dog!

Life went on, and I'd still spend the occasional weekend at my grandparents' house. Again, sleeping in my grandmother's bed during one of these visits, one night I needed to go to the bathroom in the middle of the night. I went into the bathroom, but the next thing I knew was I was sitting on a raised platform on the most magnificent, luxurious toilet seat I'd ever sat upon. It was like a throne.

Was I awake or asleep?

Every detail felt so real. Even the color of the bathroom fixtures was crystal clear in my recollection: the sink, the toilet, and the bathtub were all pale aqua blue. Reveling in the exquisite texture of this velvety feeling toilet seat, I debated whether I was actually in the bathroom or still in bed. Eventually, I decided I must be awake and in the bathroom.

The next morning waking up cold and clammy with soaking wet pajamas sticking to my skin, to my horror it quickly dawned on me I hadn't gotten up in the middle of the night and gone to the bathroom as I'd believed. That soft luxurious toilet seat I thought I was sitting upon was really the texture of the bed sheets. I'd wet the bed! I never remembered wetting the bed before.

So how could it happen now?

Chapter 4: Imprint for the Soul's Growth

Maybe if I was three years old, I could understand it, but I was thirteen! Embarrassed, I went to tell my grandmother what happened. Although my cheeks flamed with shame, my grandmother comforted me and showed understanding as she stripped the bed and changed the sheets. I shared the dream I had and that I really thought I was awake. I even described to her the details of the aqua blue fixtures and the platform on which the toilet sat.

My grandmother's eyes widened into saucers. Her face took on a confused look of disbelief as I shared the account of this dream with her. She responded, "That's the exact bathroom we used to have when your mother was pregnant with you. We remodeled it before you were born, taking out the platform toilet and replacing the aqua-colored fixtures with new white fixtures."

How could I have dreamed this?

I never remember hearing any discussions of what their former bathroom looked like. And why would I? The remodeling happened before I was born! This just proved to be one of many yet-to-come ripples in my experience where I questioned the construct and continuity of reality. I knew that some mystery or magic was afoot, which I didn't understand.

Whilst I could talk with my grandmother about uncomfortable things, my mother was a different story. I soon developed a sense of what was acceptable and what my mother considered *taboo*. In the 50s and 60s, it was essential to keep an image of the perfect family. Television shows like "Father Knows Best" and "Leave It to Beaver" portrayed model families with trivial issues and concerns used solely to drive the weekly plot. Otherwise, life depicted on these shows was perfect. And on the "Dick Van Dyke Show", Dick's character, Rob Petrie, and his wife Laurie Petrie (played by Mary Tyler Moore), always slept in twin beds. Never did they share the same bed. Sexuality and actual issues like family problems, mental illness and even expressing your feelings were *taboo* subjects better swept under the rug. That was all well and fine until I realized I had issues I needed help with in this forbidden arena, yet I couldn't bring myself to ask for help.

Growing up, I had learned that to raise any concern or complaint; I had to either be very ill or seriously hurt. Anything less, my parents ignored or dismissed as trivial. As a child, I often had chronic strep throat infections. But as time went by, it was clear if I had a sore throat, it was not worth saying anything unless it was severe. Instead, I would climb up and sit on top of the bathroom counter in front of the medicine cabinet mirror with a flashlight peering down my throat to see how red or inflamed it was. Once I could see the white areas of pus on my tonsils, I knew I could finally tell my parents about my ailment without being made to feel foolish for bringing it up. Whether I should say anything was always a guessing game.

As I grew, and my body changed, it was both exciting and terrifying as I had to internalize anything to do with puberty, which was automatically in the *taboo* zone. I kept my *bodily* questions and concerns to myself. Talking about a problem or mentioning a complaint, ache, pain, or concern happened only under great duress. One February, my parents were having a big dinner party for my father's colleagues. They sent me down the hill to a neighbor's house with our kid's wagon to borrow wine glasses for the party. It was icy outside. As I strained to pull the cart up the hill on our street, I slipped and fell on my arm. When I returned to the house, I complained to my mother about my arm hurting, but my words fell on deaf ears. Trying to appease my endless whimpering, she fashioned a sling of sorts, but still had me vacuuming with my other hand moments later.

The next morning, as I was still complaining, she threatened to take me to the hospital.

"Good. I want to go," was my defiant response.

X-rays revealed I had broken my arm.

I didn't blame my parents for any neglect or abuse—it was just how things were back then. Part of me understood their behavior came out of their own insecurities, being overwhelmed with raising five children, and the pervasive uptight culture of that era in trying to maintain a public image of a perfect family. Trying to adhere to this perfect public image meant that any messy family issues needed to be ignored, or at least kept behind closed doors and not talked about. I took this as a further sign that my needs were inconsequential, and my feelings irrelevant.

Getting my first menstrual period at age fourteen and a half further reinforced these feelings. All of my friends got their first periods at age eleven or twelve. For years, as I expected to get my period, I was afraid something was wrong with me, yet I couldn't bring myself to voice it to my mother. When, to my relief, my period finally arrived, anxiety quickly set in. Desperately trying to summon the courage to tell my mother, I tried approaching her five or six times throughout the day. However, each time I chickened out at the last moment, changing the subject because I knew it was in *taboo* territory.

Finally, I went to the only adult I felt I could talk to—my best friend's mother. She and I had a very open relationship. My friend's parents were both social workers at Yale University. They were very open and talked to us about everything. sex, boys, puberty and answered questions we had. I felt loved, safe and welcomed talking with her mom. Regarding the situation about me getting my period, the only thing she could do was to call my mother and let her know.

The ensuing interaction with my mother was the only time in my life I've ever had a yelling and screaming fight with her. It upset her that I'd gone to my friend's mother instead of to her. Sharing how I tried to bring it up earlier, but just couldn't, I let my mother know how difficult it was for me, as we'd never talked about anything.

"I thought you knew," my mother said, explaining to me how she found a book on puberty in my room one day.

I'd taken that book out of the elementary school library almost three years earlier when I was in 6th grade. I didn't know at the time it was all about physical changes in puberty. When I realized the content was in the *taboo* zone, I hid the book at the bottom of my bed under my covers, thinking no one would find it there. I never knew my mother had seen it.

But the *taboo* zone didn't end with this fight. My mother brought me a sanitary napkin and a belt to hold it in place as this was before sanitary napkins with sticky adhesive backs were being manufactured. Even worse was every time I needed a sanitary napkin, I had to go into my parent's room to get one from my mother's bedroom closet. My mother didn't allow me to keep any supplies in my bedroom in case my brothers found them. Every time I needed to get a sanitary napkin, it was inconvenient, as I had to try to not disturb my parents while also being discreet so my siblings wouldn't notice.

Could life have gotten any more complicated?

Still, the *taboo* zone didn't end there. A little over a year later, a classmate and I went down into the woods to search for specific plants we were studying in our botany class. We had an older Polish housekeeper who came to clean our house once a week. She saw this boy and me going down into the woods and told my mother we were up to no good. It couldn't have been farther from the truth, as we were just carrying out our homework assignment. My mother then had 'the talk' with me.

"There are places that a boy's father can take him if he wants to experiment," she said.

Standing there, my gaping mouth hanging open in shock, I realized she was talking about how fathers could take their sons to prostitutes if they wanted to find out about sex. She also insinuated they shouldn't be trying to find out about it with me. It was incredulous to me that she would say something so extreme when so many ordinary things in her *taboo* zone weren't discussed. I felt left out of the conversation during this talk, as she never asked me anything about what I was doing or if I was fooling around. I couldn't help it that my body stiffened into a defensive mode.

In my mind I was yelling, *Well, what about my feelings?*
What about if, at some point, I want to experience sex?
It's not only boys who have feelings!
But I kept these *taboo* thoughts to myself.

I later came to realize my mother had said this out of her concern that I was down in the woods, fooling around, terrified I would get pregnant. Immensely hurt, my upset wasn't because of lack of information—my friends had thoroughly educated me about everything, but because of the lack of trust, openness, and communication between my mother and me. Isolated and left to my own devices, I realized neither parent could really communicate with me or was someone in whom I could take refuge. There was no safe zone in my family.

Later in life, I came to understand that these *taboo* subjects and lack of acknowledgment were not only a personal matter, but were part of a centuries-old repression and suppression of the feminine voice. For eons, the dictates of women's husbands, the male-dominated society's views, policies, and practices often repressed and subjugated women's feelings, rights and desires. Politically, this started changing when I was a teenager with the Women's Movement and Women's Liberation.

It also became clear to me later in life that these experiences in the *taboo* zone were necessary, and pivotal, to catalyze the deep inner work I would eventually do for myself and facilitate for others to heal and free the judgment and patterns of abuse a vast majority of us carry. As a teenager, even though I understood this *taboo*, I also had a fiercely independent, stubborn streak. Even though I was innocent and may have been naive, I wasn't a total prude. This adventurous, stubborn streak manifested itself in sneaking around in the middle of the night with a group of my friends.

Another girl and a couple of guys who were friends from the neighborhood would sneak down my driveway after midnight, throwing rocks at my bedroom window to wake me up. I would quietly slip out of the house to join them. The four of us would then go dashing around the neighborhood under the cloak of darkness.

Every time a car came close, we would jump on top of each other, forming a misshapen pile of bodies just off the side of the road, hoping the oncoming drivers wouldn't notice us. These risque adventures got our adrenaline pumping.

Perhaps tame by today's standards, but to us it was a walk on the wild side. Sometimes we would go to an unoccupied house up for sale across the street. Trying to sublimate the surges of our adolescent hormones, we'd sit on the ground under the back porch landing, talking mostly about sex. Nobody was doing it, but we were all talking about it.

The middle of the night escapades went on for months, even throughout the winter. One night, after a raging snow-storm cleared, I exited out our front door and trudged through about two feet of pristine new snow under a brilliant moonlit sky. When I returned home, there was mud all over my nightgown. Worried my mother might see it, I tossed my nightgown under my bed, hoping the disaster zone of my bedroom would provide enough distraction so my mother wouldn't find it. In the morning, mortified to see huge deep footprints in the snow leading out from the front door, I was afraid it would be a dead giveaway. There was no way I could explain this away if anyone had asked.

Fortunately, nobody noticed or said a word. I breathed an immense sigh of relief. My mud–caked nightgown disappeared from under my bed. Thankfully, my mother hadn't seemed to notice the mud, as nothing was ever said about it.

During all my nocturnal adventures, fortunately no one ever caught us, so we never got into trouble. It was entirely innocent, as there was no sex, no making out, and no vandalism. We were just a bunch of teenagers talking and dealing with our pent-up adolescent sexual energy, even if it was by jumping on top of each other and hiding from the passing cars in the middle of the night. That was the extent of our risky behavior.

In this *taboo* environment, there was still plenty of irony, like our holiday family dinners. My mother's first cousin, Roland, was a large man with a booming voice. A singer and actor, he was also a flaming queen. Roland and his long-term boyfriend, Scott, lived in Long Beach outside of New York. They would visit us for holiday dinners along with their sidekick, Tim. Even though they were extraordinarily entertaining, there was never any talk about them being gay. However, they were a welcomed change of pace, and an anomaly for us to watch.

Besides Roland and Scott, my father's Aunt Emily, our great aunt, would sometimes visit us with her friend Teresa. Emily was a spinster elementary school teacher, and Teresa was the gym teacher at her school. They had both retired and moved to Florida together. Every once in a while, they would drive up to see us. I remember my then six-year-old sister, Sara, exclaiming that Aunt Emily and Uncle Teresa had arrived. Everyone just took the comment in stride with never any mention of their possible *taboo* relationship. It made things even more confusing for me as a growing teenager. Not that I didn't know about homosexuality, but I didn't know how to act around them or my parents.

After I got my driver's license at seventeen, my father had an invitation to speak at a medical conference in Bogota, Columbia. My parents took all five of us children to Florida to stay at my mother's cousin's house in the Florida Keys. My parents planned I would babysit my younger brothers and sister while they went to Bogota for the week, then we would all stay an additional five days spending time at the Country Club with friends of my parents after they returned from Colombia. We rarely went anywhere at home, so this trip was a big deal for all five of us kids.

My mother had left me enough money to take care of my siblings and eat out most of the time. As a family, we rarely ate out—even going to McDonald's was a rare treat—so my younger siblings didn't understand restaurant etiquette. Every time we went out to eat, my younger brothers would have major food fights in the restaurants. Peas and mashed potatoes would go whizzing over my head to where I wanted to crawl under the table and hide, so nobody could see these hoodlums were my brothers. Even though I was their older sister, they wouldn't listen to me at all. They were totally out of control. I wished I could hide my embarrassment and blend into the woodwork. It was not exactly the ideal vacation I was hoping it would be.

Early one morning, at the end of the week in Florida, I drove from the Keys to the Miami International Airport to pick up my parents at the appointed time. Back in 1969, the only way to check the flight status was by looking at the arrivals board in the airport or phoning the airline directly from a payphone. It was about a three hour round trip to the airport and back, and I had left my fourteen-year-old-brother, John, in charge.

But when I arrived at the airport, I learned the plane would be several hours late. I couldn't trust John to take care of himself and my three younger siblings all day long, so I had no choice but to turn around and drive back to the Keys. Later that same day, armed with the new arrival time for the delayed flight, I again drove back to the airport. But the plane didn't land. The next morning, I was at the airport again with ever-mounting frustration as the gate attendants told me there was yet another delay of at least another twenty-four hours. I had no choice but to get back in the car, preparing to spend yet another day on the road.

As the dutiful daughter, I got up the following morning before dawn and started the long drive yet again, gripping the wheel to keep alert in the predawn grayness for what I hoped would truly be the last time. Leaving before the sun came up, I couldn't even enjoy the spectacular scenery of the azure water along both sides of the causeway on the way to the airport. Arriving at the airport,

Frequency Raising

tired of the long drive and frustrated at the lack of communication, I still had to wait a while longer until my parent's plane landed around 8:30 am.

    My exasperation at this ongoing situation had built up so much by this time, I had reached my absolute limit. My anger and frustration with the repeated long drives and dealing with the out-of-control behavior of my siblings bubbled over. Upon meeting my parents when their plane finally arrived, I had a meltdown and uncharacteristically threw a tantrum in the airport. I needed to escape to a saner environment. I was adamant I wanted to go back to New York to stay with a dancer friend who lived in Manhattan. This meant I would forgo the ritzy Country Club part of the trip I'd been most looking forward to, but that was the last thing on my mind at that point. My parents were so shocked by my uncharacteristic behavior that they immediately booked me on a flight to New York on a different airline, leaving within an hour. I was free, but the troubles for my family didn't end there.

    Later in the week, when my parents and siblings went to fly home, the plane had a double tire blowout on take-off. It was quite a serious, life-threatening problem. Unable to land normally, the aircraft had to keep circling while they sprayed the runway with flame-retardant foam. The plane then returned to the airport and had to make a belly landing on the foamed runway without using landing gear. My mother told me later that at the time they all freaked out. She said if they'd all died, I would have been the only one left in the family. Strange how the only tantrum I've ever thrown in my life got me out of this potentially life-threatening disaster just days earlier.

    It has become very apparent how some unseen force guided and protected me even back when I was seventeen, which caused me to have an uncharacteristic emotional meltdown. I also realize this was the second of my nine lives where I could have faced my mortality had I stayed in Florida. Unknowingly, throwing this tantrum averted me from encountering a potential disaster. Even if I didn't completely understand how or why, it reinforced my sense of being protected and that there's a reason for me being here. I just had to discover it.

    After spending much of life so far making myself scarce to avoid emotional trauma, I realized I also needed to focus on something more positive, something

I was passionate about, to balance out my home life, which luckily, I'd found at an early age.

Chapter 5: Dance to the Rescue

My interest in dance originally started at five years old, watching the young ballerina on the Mickey Mouse Club on television. I wanted to be just like her. Although I went to dance class when I was six, my serious training in ballet began in the fourth grade. By my sophomore year in high school, I was also studying modern dance, jazz, and Haitian dance along with ballet. The dance world became my life, my family, and my reason for being. Finally, I found somewhere where I felt like I fit in.

The summer after eighth grade, at only fourteen, a fellow ballet student and I took the Amtrak train from Connecticut to Washington DC to attend the Washington School of Ballet Summer Program for six weeks—the same place where actress Shirley MacLaine went to high school and received her ballet training. Being away from home for the first time, on our own and dancing, opened the awareness of other possibilities I never knew existed in my thoughts and desires.

As a teenager, I regularly performed with the New Haven Dance Center and also with the Nutmeg Civic Ballet a few times. Along with performing, I also taught adult ballet classes for the New Haven Dance Center. Dance consumed almost all of my life, which fortunately my parents supported. At sixteen, I spent the summer at the Harkness Ballet Summer Program in Watch Hill, Rhode Island, living in an enormous mansion overlooking the ocean owned by the heiress, Rebekah Harkness. In this mansion, which she gave to the Harkness Ballet, they converted the bedrooms into dormitory spaces for the ballet students, having three to four sets of bunk beds in each room. They converted the living room into a studio for jazz dance classes and other events. Harkness Ballet also purchased and converted Watch Hill's firehouse into ballet studios for classes.

I loved living in the Harkness Mansion, as it felt somewhat like home to me. Basking in the sun on its enormous veranda while taking in the stunning panoramic view of the ocean, the gentle salty ocean breeze reminded me of my idyllic childhood in South Portland, Maine. Recently the singer, Taylor Swift, purchased the Harkness Mansion, further linking it to the arts, but this time through music.

After the Harkness Ballet Summer Program, I was more determined than ever to become a professional ballet dancer. I dreamed of moving to New York City in my junior year of high school to attend the Professional Children's School and audition for an apprenticeship with one of its major ballet companies-the New York City Ballet, American Ballet Theater, or the Joffrey Ballet. My parents balked at the possibility of me going to New York, pointing out that attending the Professional Children's School would cost as much as college tuition. I knew, however, if I could pull it off, it was unlikely I'd go to college anyway.

Unfazed by my parent's arguments against this plan, it excited me when one of my dancer friend's colleagues who attended the Professional Children's School offered to show us around. As I was walking out of the house, off to New York to tour the school with my friend and her mom, my mother stopped me.

"Lift your shirt," she asked.

Puzzled at this request, I did as she asked.

Looking down, I saw I had a red rash all over my abdomen.

"You aren't going anywhere but to bed!" my mother exclaimed. "You have the German measles!"

This crushing disappointment was the first turn of fate deciding my future in a different way than I intended.

In my senior year of high school, we moved to Westport, Connecticut, closer to New York City, so I started taking the train into New York on weekends to take ballet classes at the Joffrey Ballet. By this time, the trajectory of my intended life plan to live and study in New York and hopefully to get into a professional ballet company by the time I was seventeen had changed. It was now clear I would end up going to college instead of my once-hoped-for career as a professional ballet dancer in New York. Even though I'd let go of this dream, I still couldn't let go of dance, so I started applying to colleges that had good dance departments.

Sarah Lawrence, a private liberal arts college in Yonkers, NY, was my first choice, but I also applied to others. Not getting into Sarah Lawrence, I settled for attending Connecticut College in New London, Connecticut which was previously an all-girl's college that had just gone co-ed. In those years, they didn't offer a major in dance, but they did host the American Dance Festival each year, where various modern dance and theater companies were in residence for the summer. Debuts of new and avantgarde works abounded, along with plenty of opportunities to study with the movers and shakers of the dance and theater world in the 70s.

During my freshman year at Connecticut College, I came down with some mysterious ailment confining me to the school infirmary for several weeks. They speculated it might have been Rheumatic Fever or Lyme's Disease, however no definitive results showed up other than my blood tests repeatedly came back 'abnormal'. This confinement made completing my classes difficult. It was the only time, other than in Catechism classes in the Catholic Church, that I'd ever received a 'D', in English no less, because of missing most of the required classes for the term. However, in dance, I made up for my missed classes by writing a proposal about why Connecticut College should offer a major in dance. Later in life, after becoming a published author, I found it ironic that my only poor grades were in English and Catechism, which only confirmed to me that my writing ability was an innate talent more than a learned ability.

The highlight of attending Connecticut College was performing in the dance department's productions, along with dancing in the Connecticut College–Wesleyan University Experimental Movement Lab, an improvisational creative movement company. Even though I enjoyed college, I quit school in the middle of my sophomore year as dreams of dancing in a professional ballet or modern dance company in New York continued to spur me on. Eager to make this obsession with dance my career as dance challenged me physically, fed me emotionally, and gave me a chance to express my artistic interpretation and musical abilities, it also was how I proved to myself I was *good enough*. However, fate would soon step in and alter my hoped-for plans once again.

Chapter 6: Thwarted Again

At college, dance wasn't my sole interest. Boys were also important. I wanted to have a boyfriend, someone who genuinely cared about me and wanted to spend time with me. But guys never seemed to be romantically interested in me. They only usually approached me to be their confidant, or to listen to their troubles, which were usually about other girls.

Viewed as a wallflower more than a hot chick, seldom did guys ask me out, so I didn't go to either my junior or senior prom in high school. I never felt sought after, pursued, and only ever dated one guy in my senior year of high school whom my best friend was also dating at the same time. In college, there were a few guys I was mildly interested in, but there was no mutual attraction. Finally, in my sophomore year, someone show me a lot of interest. He pursued me privately, never in public, but I still couldn't believe it. Even though he was a freshman, he was part of the in-crowd, was popular and played in the college blues band; he was the stereotypical kind of guy who had girls throwing themselves at him. He was the beginning of my sexual education.

Even though he often flattered me, I felt torn because he didn't want any emotional involvement or commitment. Right before Christmas break, we were in his bedroom, whom he shared with three other guys. We tried to *go all the way*, but we got interrupted. He pulled the sheets up over my head so his roommates couldn't see who he had in bed with him. Deep down, part of me knew he cared more about me as a sexual conquest than as a relationship. Hardly anyone had ever paid any attention to me throughout high school or college, so in my resulting low self-esteem, I let him get away with that behavior. I figured some action was better than none and I was ready to experience *sex*. But first, I would need to get on birth control.

Not trusting the college infirmary, I asked my mother if I could see her gynecologist in New Haven. When I went, I had my first ever pelvic exam, mainly to get on birth control. But during the exam, the doctor kept hitting something excruciatingly painful, like when the dentist hits a nerve when drilling your tooth. The pain was so intense, at one point I thought I might faint. After the exam, the doctor explained he'd found an ovarian cyst a few centimeters in size. He suggested I go on birth control pills as a treatment method (as it often shrinks cysts) which was serendipitous as I didn't even have to ask him for birth control in that situation. He told me to check back with him in two months.

Meanwhile, having just quit Connecticut College at the end of the first semester of my sophomore year and getting ready to move to New York, I went back to Connecticut College for one last visit before moving into the city. I attended a party in the room of my amorous freshman where everybody was drinking beer, smoking pot, and getting pretty wasted. At the end of the evening, as everybody was leaving, he asked me to stay—finally we *went all the way*. The experience fell way short of my expectations, as there was no tenderness, connection, or love. It didn't even feel good. I wanted to experience sex, and so I'd agreed to it, but it felt degrading and unpleasant.

I remember thinking, *are you kidding? Is that what all this fuss is about?*

The following week I set off for New York driving on the Major Deegan Expressway in the Bronx on my way into Manhattan. I rounded a curve with limited visibility when suddenly I came upon a long pileup of cars right in front of me, which I couldn't avoid. I plowed right into the back of the pileup. In shock, I got out of the car and wondered why my pants were soaking wet, only to realize it was blood from what I later found out was a punctured kneecap. Medics took me to Morrisania Hospital in a terrible section of the Bronx. As I lay dazed on the stretcher in the back of the ambulance, I noticed the railing had smears of dried blood from someone else on it.

Chapter 6: Thwarted Again

When I arrived at the hospital, they deposited me along a wall in some hallway. I waited for hours, receiving no attention. All I could think about besides the lack of care was how was I going to get in touch with my parents? Eventually, a doctor arrived and assessed my condition. He was the only doctor I'd observed all afternoon. No one else in the hospital even asked me if I wanted to notify anyone that I'd been in a car accident, probably because it was a toll call to call Connecticut.

Thankfully, this doctor was so concerned about my punctured knee he took it upon himself to call my parents, who drove in from Connecticut to retrieve me. Later, I learned that at the time I went to the Morrisania hospital's emergency room, the city was investigating the hospital for health violations and considered shutting it down, which I guess never happened.

Back home at my parents' house in Connecticut, while still recovering from my knee injury, I went back to see the New Haven gynecologist to follow-up about my cyst. In two months, it had grown in size so much that it was now the size of a large orange. He referred me to a hotshot gynecologist in New York, also on staff at St. Vincent's Hospital, where my father worked. I went to see this new gynecologist on a Friday afternoon, planning to head back up to Connecticut College after the appointment to visit friends over the weekend since I was now injured. I couldn't move right away, anyway. But the gynecologist's response quickly thwarted my plans.

"You aren't going anywhere—I am admitting you to the hospital on Sunday. You'll have an IVP series on Monday (a series of x-rays on a tilting, turning table with an injection of dye to check kidney function) and then first thing Tuesday morning I am scheduling you for surgery."

I was in shock at this pronouncement. Although I'd just met this gynecologist, I didn't resonate with him at all, and I wasn't sure I even trusted him—he acted far too slick and arrogant. But in those days, and at nineteen, you didn't make waves going against what my parents thought and what was 'best' for me.

I guess the medical urgency was because my cyst had grown so much in such a short time that the doctor feared I had ovarian cancer. Thoughts of illness and death as a young adult had never occurred to me, yet here I faced that precise possibility, the third time I would face my mortality.

After being prepped, they wheeled me into the operating room and hooked me up to all kinds of equipment, blood pressure monitors, sensors, and tubes. Lying naked on the operating table, feeling vulnerable like a bloated fish, swabbed with the Betadine antiseptic, the anesthesiologist started making small talk with me.

He asked, "Where do you go to school?"

"Connecticut College," I murmured as the sedatives took effect.

He piped up again, "I know someone who attends Connecticut College. He's the son of one of my orthopedic surgeon colleagues."

He then told me his name and asked if I knew him.

Knew him?

Are you kidding?

He was the guy I'd just slept with and lost my virginity to a week earlier.

Groggily, I barely murmured, "yes" before the anesthesia fully kicked in.

The last conscious thought I had was of losing my virginity to this guy before I went off to La-La land.

The cyst turned out to be a benign congenital cyst, which I'd supposedly had from birth. They removed it and also did a whole exploratory of my abdomen to make sure there weren't any other *hidden* problems. Relieved that removing the cyst meant I'd only lost the functioning of my left Fallopian tube, I was more than a little upset when I found out the surgeon also removed my healthy appendix at the same time. It had made the surgery more significant than it needed to be. And there had been no discussion of removing my appendix before surgery, nor was my permission given. Livid about this, my initial dislike for this gynecologist now felt justified. Intuitively, I understood we are born with organs for a reason, even if science doesn't know exactly why just yet. I felt betrayed and violated that this arrogant male took it upon himself to *play God* inside my body without my permission.

After staying in the hospital for ten days, I returned to my parent's house in Connecticut for a lengthy recovery. After five months, it was no surprise I got antsy to dance again. So I went back to the Dance Festival at Connecticut

Chapter 6: Thwarted Again

College that next summer and learned they were forming a new repertory company to revive some of Doris Humphrey's choreography. She was a pioneering dancer and choreographer in the 1930s. Still not fully recovered, I auditioned but didn't get into the main cast, but was fortunate to perform in her piece, *With My Red Fires*, along with a handful of other student dancers.

This repertory work was being filmed for the archives of the Lincoln Center Library in New York City. The recording of this is now available in many libraries and is free to view on Facebook. Thrilled to be dancing once again, it turned out I'd pushed myself physically too far, too soon, causing a build-up of scar tissue which caused some more problems further down the line.

After the Dance Festival, I finally made my move to New York City. I shared a loft with five other people on 2nd Avenue above the Naked Grape Clothing store in the lower East Village in Manhattan just up from St. Mark's Place. The loft spanned the whole top floor of the building. In the back of the loft, we erected wallboard partitions to create separate bedroom spaces which weren't very private. Although we couldn't see into each other's bedrooms, the gap between the partition and the ceiling meant we could hear everything that went on with everybody. Having six of us living there with only one bathroom, any sense of modesty or dignity soon went out the window. Often in the morning, three or four of us were simultaneously in the bathroom trying to get ready and get out the door.

My oldest roommate, Tommy, a somewhat solemn but subdued gay dancer and choreographer, managed the loft. He had sectioned off the whole front area to use as a dance performance space. Over the summer we'd often hang out the loft's front room windows so we could watch the never-ending parade of drag queens strutting up and down 2nd Avenue. And then there was flamboyant Keith, a younger gay guy, who was a lot of fun and kept me laughing.

Often in the morning, he'd come running into my cubicle, jump into bed with me, and innocently tickle and snuggle with me. There was also a young Asian dancer who had just gotten into one of the professional modern dance companies—she was the most serious one of them all. And then there was Jamie, a young aspiring, but serious writer. He wrote porn for 42nd Street-type of magazines to earn money to support himself living in Manhattan.

Another dancer, Samantha, and I brought the count up to six roommates. And while we were all doing whatever we could do to make ends meet, Samantha's way of financially coping was even more extreme. She had appeared in pornographic films as a way of earning money and financing her education. Samantha had already starred in several movies, acting with well-known porn stars.

Once, she asked me if I wanted to come with her to a special screening of one of her movies for distributors to decide if they wanted to purchase the film. Curiosity got the better of me, so I went with Samantha. We entered an auditorium filled with men in long black overcoats with little black derby hats—a very creepy atmosphere. While I sort of knew what to expect, I must admit the movie shocked me. I'd never seen *hardcore* porn before. And more shocking still, here was my roommate and friend, doing everything from A to Z in this XXX rated movie, when I had barely lost my virginity. But I didn't judge or fault her for her choice, or for *acting*. It paid her bills and her tuition. We all had to do whatever we could to stay in New York and pursue our dreams.

Years later, when I was in graduate school in Hawaii, the university held a Blue Movie Series at midnight once a month. One month, they played a movie my roommate had starred in, so I went to see it. It was strange to watch my former roommate on the screen after so much time had passed. But her acting choices didn't seem to harm her future career, as she eventually became an acclaimed, award-winning choreographer with her own dance company that toured internationally.

While living with Samantha in the loft, she informed me about a modeling opportunity, posing nude for a guy in the Student Arts League of NY. She had done it a few times and suggested I check it out. It paid $10 an hour, plus extra for cab fare, which was a lot of money back in the early 70s. Partly curious and partly strapped for cash, I eventually mustered up the courage to do it. I nervously arrived at the apartment and sheepishly disrobed. The man posed me on the couch and started painting my likeness on the canvas. Everything seemed okay the first few times—he would make me tea and feed me health food cookies. But I was especially glad his painting style didn't precisely capture reality, so those who saw his paintings would never figure out it was me.

The man was a kind of short, pudgy Italian looking guy with beady little eyes. When he paid me at the end of the session, he would peel bills off a massive wad of cash he kept hidden on the top shelf of his coat closet. I wondered if he might be in the Mafia, but decided it was better not to ask questions. After the sessions, even though it was often nearing midnight, I would save the extra money for the cab fare and take the subway down to Union Square before walking the few blocks to 2nd Avenue. The modeling job continued for about six months, and the man was a perfect gentleman for the longest time. But after several months, he started making advances, and it soon became clear he was becoming more interested in me than in his artistic endeavors. When his advances became more persistent, even though the money was great, I had no choice but to quit.

I agreed to model because I found it challenging to sustain myself financially between the expenses of living in New York City and the tuition I needed for my various dance classes. I studied at the Joffrey Ballet School and the Alvin Ailey School. I took occasional ballet classes with David Howard, Finis Jung, and always intended to study with Maggie Black, but never actually got there. I also studied modern dance with Merce Cunningham and jazz dance classes with Luigi.

Back when I initially started living in New York, I had asked my parents for money. They would only provide financial support if I were back in college, but college wasn't the reason I went to New York. If I wanted financial support, I had to come up with an alternative solution. Besides, studying at the Joffrey Ballet School was not the same thing as being in a college or university to my parents. Regularly, I also, took ballet classes at the Alvin Ailey Dance School with Elizabeth Hodes.

Her husband, Stuart Hodes, was the chair of the dance department at New York University. Because Elizabeth knew me, recognized my talent and ability as a dancer, she vouched for me by letting her husband know this. A few days later, and virtually unheard of, the New York University (NYU) Tisch School of the Arts accepted me for their 1972 fall term without having an audition. Because I was now back in school again, my parents agreed to support me financially once more. So Samantha and I spent the fall term there, which was located almost across the street from our loft on 2nd Avenue. It was the most effortless commute we'd ever had.

Even though my parents relented and agreed to support me because I'd returned to college, I was still restless and discontented. I wanted to be taking classes elsewhere, not only relegated to those classes taught by the faculty of the school.

But even though I was finally living my dream, I still yearned to study with the best dance teachers available in New York who taught outside of the university system. One of these New York teachers had even told me I was so talented that I could do anything I wanted in the dance world—I just needed to lose twenty pounds. And there it was again... even though I knew it would help my career, the childhood struggle not to let my father *win* by getting his way if I lost weight still plagued me.

After that one semester at NYU, I again quit school but stayed in New York. Instead, I got a job in the department store, Bonwit Teller, on 5th Avenue, working in the coat and suit department literally stuffing little old ladies into coats and suits. The pay was minimal, but after a probationary period, you could start working on commission. I soon learned that gaining commissions would be a rather tricky pursuit because of the two crusty-looking older women on the floor. The two women, hardcore New Yorkers, had worked at Bonwit Teller for upwards of thirty years and had their technique down to a fine art. With one ear constantly monitoring the elevators, whenever the elevator stopped at our floor, they would run to make sure they received the arriving customers first. Between them, they snatched up and claimed every potential prospect, swooping down like vultures upon their prey. As an inexperienced young newbie, I didn't have a chance in hell of competing. And I soon learned not to get in their way.

Becoming financially self-sufficient again, I continued my attempt to live my dream of being a dancer in New York City. And I hadn't completely given up on the desire to have a boyfriend, either. Coincidentally, and unbeknownst to me, that was just about to come into play.

Chapter 7: My Major Stumbling Blocks

Men and money have been the major stumbling blocks in my life. From my first boyfriend the end of my senior year in high school who was also dating my best friend, to losing my virginity to someone who only saw me as a sexual conquest, my track record with guys was pretty dismal until I met Jeremy.

My roommate, Tommy, staged a Halloween performance in our 2nd Avenue loft. He invited his friend, Jeremy, to join in the production, casting him in the monster's role. He cast me as Jeremy's dance partner in this performance. Thus was the start of a long karmic relationship between Jeremy and me. When I first met Jeremy, he'd entered a training program to become a certified teacher of the Alexander Technique—a postural movement technique designed to release tension in the body, training the body to move with greater ease and harmony. Many actors, dancers, and musicians find it very helpful with their craft, so it was no surprise he moved in the same circles as me.

When Jeremy and I started dating, he told me upfront that he was bi-sexual. But rather than a turnoff, I was comfortable with his sexuality as he was gentle, and more in touch and expressive of his feminine side without being too effeminate. It was a relief finally to be with someone who showed a genuine interest in me, and someone with whom I could feel safe enough emotionally to let in. But it wasn't easy at first. Even though I'd experienced sex before, sex with Jeremy wasn't like those other times. When we started becoming intimate,

I'd involuntarily start crying and shaking all over. I didn't understand why, however, some emotional, visceral reaction would just take over my body.

At my most vulnerable, Jeremy would just hold me, allowing me to tremble for as long as I needed to. Slowly, I realized it wasn't the sex that I feared, but the emotional intimacy. This physical response of mine went on for months. Slowly, however, my emotional body started opening up in incremental stages to receive the love and attention I'd so deeply craved yet also feared, feelings which I'd shut down up to this point. Eventually, my capacity to receive shifted profoundly. Unexplained things would then sometimes happen like once in the throes of passion I'd suddenly experienced a popping sensation at the top of my head, like a cork popping off a champagne bottle. I guess it must have been my crown chakra opening, even though I didn't know a thing about chakras back then. Because of these experiences, I fell hard for Jeremy.

Our relationship continued moving forward over the next eight months until summer when I again returned to the Connecticut College American Dance Festival, and Jeremy left for the west coast to do some more training there with an Alexander Technique teacher in San Francisco. I was obsessed with thoughts of Jeremy during the entire summer. When I was away from him, I had a hard time getting him out of my mind. Determined to reconnect with Jeremy again after the Dance Festival ended, I headed to the west coast in pursuit of him. I agreed to drive across the country and share expenses with an acquaintance, Mark, whom I'd known from Connecticut College who was moving to Los Angeles to take a job as the lighting designer for a modern dance company.

After driving to LA with Mark, I then intended to take a bus to San Francisco to see Jeremy. Having not been west of New York since living in Minnesota as a young child, I was excited to engage in this adventure! Mark and I set out driving the southern route through Appalachia, eventually connecting with the Old Route 66 to California. As we drove through western Pennsylvania, we couldn't find any restaurants along the Freeway, so we took an exit in search of a place to eat. We drove quite a distance before finally finding a diner in a small rural town. After settling into a booth, our waitress acknowledged us. Middle-aged, short, and squat with a beehive hairdo so high it

Chapter 7: My Major Stumbling Blocks

enhanced her height by at least a foot, it looked like an entire flock of baby birds could nest in that hair. She waddled over to our table to take our order.

Mark and I looked out of place at this diner. We were in 1973 in rural America and I had very short hair cropped close to my head like a little boy's haircut, whilst my driving companion wore sunglasses with bright red lenses. People shamelessly stared at us, which made me squirm with self-consciousness. After ordering some food and an ice tea, I asked if they had any sugar substitute like Sweet-N-Low.

The waitress glared at me. "We ain't got none 'o' that stuff."

"We grow 'em fat' out here," she growled, somewhat annoyed.

And so this was the beginning of encountering different mindsets and attitudes far from the norm of my college friends or New York theatrical and dance circles.

Mark had an acquaintance who had invited us to stay with him for a night in the Appalachian Mountains of West Virginia. After driving through a long winding road of stunning scenery, we arrived to find a ramshackle cabin housing a bunch of people who lived in a self-sustained community far away from any other towns or civilization where they even took the law into their own hands. Almost everyone had a rifle nearby at all times, which made me nervous. I didn't know what I was getting myself into or even if it was safe to stay the night, but happily, the host welcomed us. He led us up a steep ladder into the attic space to our sleeping accommodations for the night, which was a mattress on the floor. There was very little headroom, so we crawled on all fours to get to the bed.

As we made our way over to the bed, the entire floor underneath us shook, bouncing wildly up and down with each movement. It took all of my dancing prowess carefully to navigate the bouncing floor over to the mattress. I barely relaxed enough to sleep, fearing that at any moment the unstable floor might give way and we would end up crashing down into the living room and people below us. It was a night I'll never forget. Relief flooded through me when we could finally move on.

Continuing west, in Oklahoma, we ate steak—the best I'd ever had. However, communicating with the local folk proved to be an exercise of extreme patience. The locals talked in such a slow drawl that understanding even the most straightforward phrases required a significant amount of concentration. I quickly became impatient with the conversation, along with how long our order took to arrive. We moved on, stopping for the night in Flagstaff, AZ, in a funky, flea-bitten motel. In trying to keep our expenses to a minimum, Mark and I usually shared a bed even though we weren't a couple. Mark was all excited about sleeping in the water beds in this motel, but I told Mark a little fib that I hated waterbeds. I didn't dislike them and had even owned one at one point, but lying about not liking the waterbed allowed me to have some private space and sleep in a bed by myself for a change.

Finally arriving in Los Angeles, Mark and I parted ways, and I went to see Keith, one of my former roommates from the loft in New York, who had moved to Los Angeles several months earlier. Keith let me stay with him so I could rest and we could catch up. Eager, however, to get to San Francisco to see Jeremy, a few days later I caught a Greyhound bus for the nine-hour journey up north.

When I reached San Francisco, I called Jeremy, who agreed to meet with me. I'd hoped he'd sweep me up into his arms, joyful to be together again, but rather than being excited to see me, Jeremy in a matter-of-fact way told me he was having a romantic homosexual relationship with his teacher in San Francisco. My heart felt like it shattered into a million pieces and sank back into the deep abyss from where it had risen. Jeremy then said the thing I feared most—he thought it best we didn't keep seeing each other. Shocked at this pronouncement, I didn't know where to turn or what to do. So in San Francisco I found a bedroom to rent in an old Victorian boarding house on Van Ness Avenue, a little way up from the waterfront and Ghirardelli Square.

The other tenants, crotchety old ladies, were unfriendly and miserly. One of them had a fit because I used the sponge which sat by the kitchen sink to wash my dishes. They pointed out that the sponge was not a communal item— each person had to have their separate sponge and dish soap. I tried to spend as little time there as possible since the atmosphere was so unfriendly. In trying to stay away from the house as much as I could, my passion for dance was once again my salvation. With what little money I had, I took some classes at the San Francisco Dance Theater while also looking for jobs. Job hunting proved to be a

Chapter 7: My Major Stumbling Blocks

hopeless endeavor as I stood in line for a receptionist position with almost a hundred applicants in line ahead of me. Despite searching high and low, I kept coming up empty-handed. Finally, in desperation, an acquaintance suggested I sign on with a company that sold encyclopedias door-to-door. Whilst this job only paid commissions, they paid a small stipend for food when we were out in the field.

This would at least handle my basic survival. And so started my brief door-to-door salesperson career being dropped off in neighborhoods in towns up and down the California coast such as Lompoc, Santa Maria, and San Luis Obispo. In scouting out which were the best neighborhoods, we'd look for *baby doos*, houses whose yards had outdoor play equipment showing that young children lived there. They were the perfect target audience for selling the Encyclopedia Britannica.

But once I started the job, the rejection would prove even harder to take. House after house, people slammed doors in my face and hurled nasty insults at me. It was demoralizing. Any self-confidence I had left after Jeremy abandoned me went right out the window. For a seasoned salesperson, all that negativity might be like water off a duck's back, but for me, not knowing I was an Empath made it worse. Desperate to make some money, I pushed on, unconsciously taking on all the surrounding negativity, internalizing it and squishing it tighter and deeper inside.

This, along with still being devastated and distraught over Jeremy ditching me for another relationship with a man, I finally reached my breaking point. One afternoon I knocked on a young Hispanic mother's door, and before I knew it, I was sobbing uncontrollably in her living room. She invited me to stay for the next few hours until my rendezvous pickup-point time.

The woman graciously took care of me, making me tea, feeding me snacks, and comforting me as I told her my story. The whole six weeks I worked for that company, I only sold one set of encyclopedias to a dirt-poor family. They so much wanted to help their children achieve a better life that they committed themselves to buying the Encyclopedia Britannica set and making the payments, even though they couldn't afford it. I left that house feeling guilty for the sale because I knew they needed every cent just to feed their children. It broke my heart. With this, I'd reached the end of the road. I was no longer willing to sacrifice myself for a job that manipulated me into coercing people to buy something they couldn't afford, so I quit.

Still in the predicament of how to survive, I soon ran out of money and food except for one sleeve of saltine crackers, which I ate for a few days. Out of options, I swallowed my pride, made a sign asking for help, and started begging for food and money on a San Francisco Street corner, which I wasn't good at either. It was inconceivable to me I'd sunk to such a low and desperate level. That night, as the rain fell, I prayed for a solution—for my tide to turn.

In the morning I woke up in a sopping wet bed. A couple of inches of water covered my floor. The Victorian house in which I rented a room had survived the 1906 earthquake, but all the windows leaked. Overnight, the gentle rain had turned into a raging storm and now everything I owned was soaking wet.

What on earth do I do now?

Beyond my wit's end, with only one course of action left, I swallowed my pride once again, and called my mother, pleading with her to buy me a plane ticket for a flight the next day back to New York. She agreed. I called Jeremy's brother, who also lived in San Francisco with his girlfriend, and asked him to tell Jeremy I was flying back to New York, praying that Jeremy and this whole terrible ordeal would soon be a distant memory.

Tired, wet and hungry, my last night in San Francisco became bearable only when Jeremy's brother and his girlfriend treated me to a farewell dinner in Chinatown. After several days bordering on starvation, I was thankful to have a delicious meal with two kind and caring souls. As the plane lifted from the runway the following morning, I sobbed.

My first trip to San Francisco was the antithesis of the utopia I'd dreamed it would be. Letting go of my hopes, dreams, and desires particularly with Jeremy was necessary. I knew I just had to put it all behind me. Moving forward-how, when, or where remained a mystery. I hoped when I got back to the east coast I would have some sign of what to do or where to go next.

Chapter 8: The Other Side Beckons

Even though my journey as a dancer kept developing, I never lost sight of wanting to know the *more* of things. When I was in college, my mother loaned me two books, *The Betty Book: Excursions into the World of Other Consciousness* by Stewart Edward White and *Journeys Out of the Body* by Robert Monroe. I didn't quite understand why my mother even had these books, but I was grateful for their impact on my life.

The spring of 1971, during my freshman year in college, a group of friends and I drove to Florida for spring break. The entire drive I sat in the backseat devouring these books, finally finding the answers I'd long sought since I was fourteen.

These books reinforced in me that there was *more* to life than what I'd experienced. *The Betty Book* shared accounts of people who had crossed over who would communicate with the living after death while Robert Monroe's book discussed astral projection, the ability to project one's consciousness and awareness outside the physical body to visit other realms.

Returning to my parents' house in Westport, Connecticut, I reflected on my crushing disappointment I experienced while in San Francisco. Whilst still not sure of what I wanted, what I didn't want had become much clearer. My *soul lesson* was far from being finished but I'd had my first inkling that pinning my hopes on a man rescuing me, taking care of me, and making me happy as my upbringing had led me to believe, was more of a fantasy than a reality for me.

Raising My Frequency

My failure to progress forward in my dance career, find a good job, or a fulfilling relationship meant I was back to square one. I was grateful however that Spirit had gotten me through and that just like the cat, I eventually landed on my feet again. But deep down inside, I just knew there still had to be *more* to life.

After spring break, when we got back to the dorms at Connecticut College, I had a powerful desire to experience astral projection. I set the intention to have something happen, then almost immediately forgot I'd intended it. One night, a short time later, as I was in bed drifting off to sleep, a yellowish luminous hand suddenly appeared, reaching back towards me inviting me to take its hand like an adult would extend a hand to a small child. Suddenly I bolted upright, wide awake and terrified. How could I have thought of asking for an experience like this was alright? My racing mind screamed in my skull,

Who are you?
What do you want?
Is it safe?
Are You going to harm me?
Where are you going to take me?

Fears, I didn't even know I had rushed into my awareness. I jumped out of bed, trying to shake off the experience. No matter what I did, I couldn't get calm enough to lie back down and go to sleep.

First, I started wandering the hallways on the different floors in my dorm. Then I visited people pulling "all-nighters" in the dining room until finally I went over to the vending machines in the Student Union building to keep myself awake. Eventually a few hours later, I returned to my room as I couldn't keep my eyes open any longer and fell into a deep sleep with no more intrusion of apparitions. Even though this apparition scared the bejesus out of me, it didn't alter the fact that *The Betty Book* and *Journeys Out of the Body* just whetted my appetite to know more.

Soon after reading these books, I discovered the *Seth Speaks* and *Seth Material* books by Jane Roberts. This further confirmed my deep inner knowing there was far more than this third-dimensional reality and that life existed way beyond what we thought we knew. Metaphysical books weren't easy to find in the early 70s.

Long before the Internet and Amazon, a limited selection of metaphysical books took up maybe two feet of shelf space in bookstores, as there was not much available. Initially, after starting my relationship with Jeremy, not only did I become his Alexander Technique Guinea pig, but he also started teaching me how to practice the Alexander Technique with clients. Following his instructions, I stood at the end of the table and placed my hands on his head (he was lying face-up on a massage table) when something unexpected, other than what he was teaching me, transpired. Suddenly, I could sense *energy* moving in his body. I intuitively knew the places where the energy flowed in his body and where it had become stuck. Inner pictures of this *energy* flow or lack of flow in my mind showed me what was taking place in his body.

This inner vision reminded me of the old Drano commercials where a clogged section of pipe stops up a sink. Pouring Drano down the sink dissolved the clogged area, allowing the water to flow unhampered again. This same process I witnessed in my inner vision happening in the body. Intuitively, I knew what to do and exactly where to place my hands, both on parts of his body, and in the auric field around the body, to get the *energy* to flow freely once again.

Who knew where this healing modality came from?

I'd had no conscious awareness or training in any of what was spontaneously occurring. Also, I'd never heard of anything like this before, in 1973, when it all began. This process was just there from what I later understood to be *soul memory* and differed significantly from what Jeremy was trying to teach me. This just further catalyzed my quest to understand this experience of *energy*, and to understand its purpose in everyday life.

I kept exploring and expanding this modality through working on various people. Not knowing what to call it, I referred to it merely as hands-on healing. Over the next several years, I developed a small group of clients who would pay me $25 for a session. A short time after regularly conducting these sessions, I noticed I started having what I can only describe as surges of energy, or waves of vibration, a trembling which welled up and threaten to overtake my body. Once this vibration started, it continued to come in waves. I didn't know what it was, but it frightened me. I'd involuntarily clamp down on these waves of energy as best I could, hoping to get them to stop. Fortunately, these alarming surges of energy only happened every once in a while. Then I'd be back to normal.

After my disastrous trip to California, back at my parents' house in Connecticut, a friend invited me to attend a party in Manhattan where, unexpectedly, I again ran into Jeremy. He'd returned to New York to continue his Alexander Certification course. He acted all lovey-dovey and glad to see me, the reaction I'd hoped for when I went chasing after him to San Francisco, but here it was, happening now. Weak willed and vulnerable to his display of desire and affection and not being fully over him yet, I relented. We ended back in bed. Despite the way he had treated me, we picked up our relationship where we'd left off before the summer as if nothing had happened.

Growing up with no model of what being respected and treated well looks like and feels like from men, dysfunction was the unconscious norm for me. It's all I knew. Some karmic relationships, like the one I had with Jeremy, are like an addiction which I wasn't ready to give up yet. I willingly put up with his betrayal and unacceptable behavior to have something rather than nothing. It wasn't like there was physical abuse or anything, just a lack of trust.

Now that Jeremy and I were back together, I moved from my parent's house in Connecticut back into New York again. This time I shared a 5th-floor walk-up apartment with a gay guy named Danny who was friends with my previous roommates from the loft on 2nd Ave. Danny's railroad apartment, on Perry Street in the West Village of Manhattan, had a compact kitchen, a little triangular room at an angle off the kitchen which led into a living room separated by beautiful wooden sliding doors with frosted glass pane windows in them.

Danny slept on the convertible couch in the living room while I slept on the pantry room floor just behind the kitchen. This floor was just big enough to hold a cot-sized mattress underneath the shelves which held our dishes and kitchen utensils. The toilet, a single communal commode with a pull chain to flush it, sat upon a platform in a small enclosure in the hallway outside the apartment. The entrance to the apartment in the kitchen had an array of New

Chapter 8: The Other Side Beckons

York locks, deadbolts, chains, and a security bar. If you had to go to the bathroom badly enough in the middle of the night, you'd have to have enough patience to get through all the locks first, so it was best to try to not have to get up in the middle of the night.

There was no shower in the apartment, only a claw-foot bathtub in the kitchen with a hinged piece of plywood on top of it, which served as our kitchen counter. Danny and I were used to each other and the situation, however there was one time when he arrived home with an entire group of gay male friends accompanying him. They entered the apartment only to find me naked, sitting in the bathtub in the middle of the kitchen. There was nothing I could do other than raise my hand in a gesture of greeting as they all walked past me. Through all these different roommate experiences, being embarrassed had long left the equation. The price was right, however, back then I only paid $55 a month for my share of the rent in this rent-controlled apartment. Prices were a lot cheaper in the early 70s. Financially always trying to "make do" I felt I had little choice other than to find the least expensive options for everything, along with putting up with whatever circumstances surrounded these choices. Rather than reacting to things like I was a victim, often I had to re-frame these challenges and look at them as adventures rather than obstacles in my way.

My relationship with Jeremy continued for the next year. A close friend of my mothers who was an acrylic nail technician in Saks Fifth Avenue Department Store's beauty salon, knew the owner of a high-end specialty shop just off of Madison Avenue who was hiring. A small store with only two clerks, the assistant manager, and the owners, they had top-end sports and safari clothes, elephant's hide luggage and elephant hair jewelry and other exotic items. I didn't agree with the slaughtering of elephants for such merchandise, but it was a job that I desperately needed and the pay was higher than what I received at Bonwit Teller. They had a very elite clientele. Jacqueline Onassis came in to shop one day when I was working there, however, the assistant manager waited on her.

To get the job, I had to go to some office in midtown where they hooked you up to electrodes for a lie detector test, which we were told we had to have every six months if we wanted to stay working there. I wondered why we had to do this twice a year. The answer became obvious a few months later, when a major scandal broke. A Hispanic couple working in the basement managing inventory and shipments apparently for years had been stealing thousands of dollars of merchandise each month. They sent the stolen merchandise out through a Mafia connection in the sanitation department. The payoff for this merchandise was the Mafia supplied this couple with little boys for sex.

Only now, almost fifty years later, do I fully comprehend it was the fringes of the underground sex trafficking world I'd stumbled onto as I was very young, naive, and a bit of a Pollyanna. I didn't quite understand what a puritanical view of the world I'd grown up with until so many of my experiences and adventures in New York showed just how much attaining success depended on engaging the lower frequency aspects of the first three chakras; power, sex, and survival, often trading sex in some form for money and advancement.

By the time summer came, I'd quit my job and again returned to the summer program at the American Dance Festival at Connecticut College, as Jeremy and I were doing well, so I thought. I figured we would just have a long-distance relationship while I was away for the summer. As soon as I left for the dance festival, I found out he was in another relationship, this time with a woman. Angry and hurt by this betrayal yet again, I decided against returning to live in New York at the end of the summer.

Knowing my parents would again support me if I were in school, as they did for the term, I attended NYU (New York University), I applied for a re-admittance to Connecticut College. Already having credits from previous years at Connecticut College, a semester of credits from NYU, and the credits I'd already received from attending three summers at the American Dance Festival, I found out with an additional academic year at Connecticut College along with one additional summer at the American Dance Festival, I could graduate only a year later than my original graduating class.

In a unique situation returning to Connecticut College, I was older than the other students and had gained a lot of world experience. Returning to college, I danced in, and help co-choreograph, a Gershwin musical revue. During a break in the dress rehearsal, I walked out into the auditorium to

Chapter 8: The Other Side Beckons

retrieve my sweater, which I'd left on a seat. This short little guy in saddle shoes walked up onto the stage and shook hands with Jim, the artistic director.

Not knowing who he was, seeing him however stopped me dead in my tracks. As I watched him, I experienced some deep soul recognition which I didn't even know existed. Before school resumed after the Christmas break, I got a call from one of the dance department teachers saying there was an opportunity to co-choreograph an opera at Yale with her for the coming term. She asked if I was interested. I happily responded, "Yes."

While we were still on Christmas break, the first meeting for this upcoming production happened at Yale. I went to the meeting and lo-and-behold there was the short little guy in saddle shoes who turned out to be Bill Harwood, the conductor of the Yale Symphony, and the director of the entire production. So, I started co-choreographing *L'Enfant et Les Sortileges*, a French Maurice Ravel opera about a naughty boy who gets punished for his behavior when all the objects in the room come to life to teach him a lesson.

I needed to be in New Haven for a lot of the rehearsals at Yale, but since I didn't have a place to stay when I was there, Bill Harwood (the conductor) invited me to stay with him in his apartment on the Yale campus. Bill had two twin beds in his room. He slept in one bed and I would sleep in the other one. He was always very gracious and helpful to me. I felt such a powerful soul connection between us, not a romantic attraction because he was gay, just some deep soul recognition that I hadn't experienced before. Maybe it was because of this intense soul connection that I felt seen, acknowledged, and empowered in a way that supported and nurtured my creativity to flow. It was one of the first times I felt acknowledged and seen for who I really was, not so much because of my technical ability, but also for my creativity. I could finally be fully myself without holding back. The opera was a great hit and the highlight of my college senior year.

Completing my last summer of credits at the American Dance Festival in 1975, I took part in a collaboration program between dancers and people filming dance for television. Someone in the program heard that the National Theater of the Deaf in residence at the Eugene O'Neill Theater in Waterford, Connecticut, next door to New London where Connecticut College was located, was looking for someone to teach the Alexander Technique. They'd suggested to their director that he should talk to me. When I met with the company director, I argued against them hiring me because I wasn't a certified Alexander Teacher as Jeremy had trained me privately, but it wasn't official. They weren't at all concerned about credentials or having the certification, so I lost the argument and won the job agreeing to have them hire me to teach Alexander Technique for the National Theater of the Deaf company that summer.

While teaching there, I attended a special dinner one evening for the faculty and staff. I sat next to this very engaging man, Lee Kalcheim, who was a playwright at Eugene O'Neill Theater that summer. I don't remember exactly how it started, but I believe he initially came to me as a client for Alexander Technique, which quickly morphed into my other hands-on healing work. Somewhere along the line, we started dating. He was thirty-seven, an accomplished playwright and successful TV writer, having already written episodes for *All in the Family, The Alfred Hitchcock Hour, The ABC After School Special*, and other shows. He was also fourteen years older than me, which isn't unheard of, but I was a very young twenty-three and felt like I was about twelve years old most of the time. I didn't even feel like a grown-up yet. Here I was dating this very accomplished well-off, kind, and generous older man who had an apartment in Manhattan, a country house in Connecticut, a small convertible sports car, and who treated me like a Queen.

This was every girl's dream, right?

However, it was a far cry from what was familiar to me, from the relationships I'd had with other men and with my father growing up. Lee and I enjoyed each other's company and had fun dating maybe for about six months. One morning, while at his house in Connecticut, I woke up and looked over at Lee. He was peacefully sleeping. Rather than feeling peaceful myself, I felt ready to jump out of my skin. I was so uncomfortable. Feeling smothered and claustrophobic, all I could think about was getting away. It had nothing to do with anything Lee was doing, or not doing, at all. All of my unconscious insecurities and past trauma had come to the surface, warning me it was too good to be true and that I'd better get out of the relationship before the 'other shoe' dropped where I would get hurt again.

These fears, unfounded in reality, were very real to me. I was unaware of it possibly being self-sabotage, nor did I know I could get help with this. Decades later when I carried through the process suggested by my psychic friend, Cynthia, of going back through all my romantic male relationships giving back any dysfunctional energy which may have originated with these partners, to my surprise Lee was the only person who seemed to be free of this dysfunctional energy.

For the last few years in my workshops and events, I'd been telling the story I had been living Plan (B) for my life because Plan (A) never happened. Plan (A) was foremost about finding a partner (my soulmate) and having a family. I always assumed it would happen, but it didn't.

In going back through journal entries, letters, and cards getting ready to write this memoir, I had a moment of revelation. Lee had offered me a Plan (A) but I didn't recognize it. Lee represented all I had been asking for as he was intelligent, accomplished, well to do, generous, nurturing, and more or less in the same field of work as me. If I hadn't baled on him, who knows if he and I would have continued to date, taking our relationship to a more serious commitment level, or not? God, the Universe, Source—or whatever you want to call it, had offered me Plan (A) but I said, "No." It wasn't clear whether this decision to reject Plan (A) was out of my fear, insecurity, and self-sabotage or whether Plan (B) was always the plan from my Higher Self's perspective. I suspect my soul opted for Plan (B) all along.

Finally, after decades of never finding the right partner to marry, failed relationships, sorrow, and immense frustration, when I was fifty-five, I had a reading with someone who explained it all to me. In this reading, I was told in my present life I'd created a very narrow window for relationships because in all of my other previous lives obligations to spouses, children, relatives, and my religion held me back. Never free before to go when and where Spirit called, I decided in this current life I'd agreed to be available for whatever spirit wanted me to do. I wasn't at all happy to find out I had a narrow window for relationships. However, I knew it was true. Since the relationship I so desired wasn't happening, I kept opting for the path of spiritual awakening and the adventure of Plan (B) whose directive I now follow.

That year after I graduated from college, I went back to teaching dance for children and adults in New Haven. I was also part of a dance company who spent two weeks performing Modern and Haitian Dance in Port-Au-Prince, Haiti. I was sure they would laugh us off the stage as we were a racially mixed group of women from Connecticut performing Haitian Dance in Haiti. However, they loved it! Even though it was quite an adventure performing in Haiti, it became clear my life was going nowhere. After graduating from college and spending this next year teaching dance in New Haven, I knew I needed to move forward differently with other goals in mind, so I was ready for a whole new chapter to unfold in my life.

Chapter 9: Opting for a Career Path

Dance was all I knew. I decided applying to graduate school programs offering Master's Degrees in Dance would keep me connected to the dance world and would provide me with great teaching credentials. Reasoning I was now getting too old to gain admittance into a professional dance company, I could at least get a Master's Degree qualifying me to teach dance as a university or college faculty member.

I couldn't have been more surprised and elated at the response to my applications. Again, I applied to Sarah Lawrence, my first choice of colleges five years earlier, who had rejected my application. And I applied to the University of Hawaii because they also had a teaching assistantship position for which I could apply. To my surprise, Sarah Lawrence invited me to visit their campus and audition for entry into their graduate dance program. Miraculously, I was one of only three people in the country accepted into their graduate program in dance that year.

Sarah Lawrence topped my list of where I wanted to go. However, my hopes of attending school there soon faded when my father said he wouldn't pay for graduate school. He said I would have to foot the bill for the rest of my education. The tuition and living expenses at Sarah Lawrence were among the highest in the country, and I didn't know how I'd manage paying Sarah Lawrence's tuition even with partial funding from student loans. So, at the very last moment, I changed my mind from having my heart set on attending Sarah

Lawrence to accepting admission into the University of Hawaii's dance program instead.

The University of Hawaii, a state school, had much cheaper tuition even for out-of-state residents. My justification for going there was mainly economic. I reasoned that if I lived in Hawaii for a year, I could then declare residency, which meant in my second year of school, I'd only have to pay the in-state tuition of a few hundred dollars instead of thousands of dollars each semester. The University of Hawaii had posted a job announcement for the teaching assistant position in the dance department, which I also applied for when I applied for admission to the university. Even though the University didn't hire me for the teaching position, they admitted me into their Graduate Program.

Taking out one $2500 student loan got me started. With this student loan, I paid tuition for the fall semester and moved into a roommate situation with two guys who shared a house off-campus, walking distance from my classes. Besides offering the teaching assistant-ship position, each semester the university also offered two full-tuition scholarships, one in the dance department and one in the theater department. I was very fortunate to receive the dance department's full scholarship award for the second semester of my first year of graduate school, and I could stretch my student loan to cover living expenses for the spring term.

Hawaii was a wonderful paradise in which to live. I had to rely on the tropical breezes and heavenly scents of plumeria, jasmine, white ginger, and other flowers in abundance which were everywhere to give me the laid-back feeling of living in Hawaii as my course load was intense, and I barely had time to enjoy the beach. Besides our dance department courses, each semester we also had to choose an elective course as part of our curriculum. As an outgrowth of my hands-on healing work and interest in science, I opted for the advanced premed anatomy and physiology as my elective course. If I hadn't devoted my life to dance, I probably would have become a doctor like other members of my family.

Entrance into this elective course required college biology and physics as prerequisite courses, which I didn't have. The professor permitted me to take the class as my elective course only if I took it pass/fail instead of for a grade.

He said I had until the last day of class to drop the course if I got in trouble. Not only did I pass, but I would have received an 'A' if I hadn't taken it for a pass/fail grade. The second term continuation of this class, I took it for a grade, this time receiving an "A." The dance department staff thought I was crazy for taking this heavy-duty premed course as my elective. I felt this study was constructive, as it helped me have a deeper understanding of the mechanics of the human body, both for my hands-on-healing and for understanding and teaching the mechanics of movement to my students.

As always, my spiritual interests and larger questions regarding life and our place in the universe continued to be an underlying current in my life. Every morning on my way to dance class, I would pass through the gate across from our house and walk through the pasture to the dance studio. As I walked, I would mull over certain things as I sought clarity and understanding of who we are as both physical beings and spiritual beings. Passing through this gate each morning turned out to be very symbolic of the awakening process in which I'd found myself.

For about a two-week period, I felt like I'd come to a life–and–death decision point. I agonized over whether there really was any truth to the belief that life went on beyond the physical body, as there was no proof of anything.

Did consciousness continue on after death, or not?

Having ditched religion by quitting the Catholic Church when I went away to college, many would think the issue would be the fear of going to hell. That wasn't it. It was much more basic than that.

After about ten days of being in this crucible of indecision and mental torture, I finally decided I may as well live my life "as if" it was all true: that life, energy, self-awareness, and consciousness exist beyond the death of the physical body. I finally reasoned if it weren't true, if some awareness didn't continue after death, once I died, then I wouldn't know the difference, anyway. Long ago, I had let go of the Christian belief in heaven and hell with Jesus up on a cloud in the sky. Making this deliberate, conscious decision to live my life as if it was true finally gave me peace of mind and allowed me to move forward on my quest to further understand *energy*, frequency, and spirit.

I also started a relationship with this guy Dan, whom I'd met in a vision workshop. During one of the school vacations, Dan and I went to Kauai, where we hiked the trail into Kalalau Valley. I didn't understand what I was getting myself into, nor did I have any idea that the death-defying challenges of the fourth, fifth and sixth of my nine lives were barreling down on me in rapid succession. On this hike, I only wore tennis shoes as I had no hiking boots or poles, which later I realized was my first huge mistake. The trekking was arduous, made even more challenging by us having to carry rather hefty packs on our backs containing our tent, sleeping bags, clothes, food, supplies, and other incidentals for several days of camping in the wilderness.

Enthusiastically, we started up the trail, moving along at a nice clip. After hiking for only about forty-five minutes, suddenly I found myself pretty severely challenged as the only way to proceed forward was to claw the earth with my fingertips hoisting myself up the almost vertical embankment. I should have realized right then this would be a hike like no other hike I'd ever done. My previous hiking experience was pretty much in the hills of Connecticut while attending Girl Scout camp as a kid. Here there were no gentle slopes, no guardrails, and nothing to hold on to, and soon I realized this Kalalau Valley Trail was a different league of hiking altogether, which I was unprepared for on all levels physically, mentally and emotionally.

The hike followed the path along the Na Pali Coast of Kauai. As we trudged along, the path meandered through tropical forests of lush ferns and guava groves, passing trees and bushes of exotic flowers with sweet fragrances. We traipsed across gentle streams and listened to the cooing of the birds. Then suddenly, we'd emerge out of the dense coolness of the tropical jungle foliage into harsh glaring sunlight beating down on the dry crumbly dirt path which hugged the Na Pali Coast cliffs.

To even glance down was dizzying and disconcerting as the ocean waves crashed upon the rocky coastline hundreds of feet beneath us. As we kept trekking, we soon discovered this trail was seemingly a never-ending series of walking through the forest, then out again, onto the bare cliffs which went on and on.

After hoisting myself up, clawing the earth with my fingernails within the first forty-five minutes of the hike, my next major challenge came when we encountered about a six to eight-foot section of the trail in one of the forested sections, which had fallen away from a sheer rock wall. We had to pick our way across this gap using handholds and footholds on the rock wall face wherever we could find them, all with a fifty-pound pack on our backs!

By this time, I was wondering what on earth I'd gotten myself into, as this was not at all what I'd expected the hike would be like. However, I felt immensely pleased with myself, successfully bridging the gap in the trail despite my extreme apprehension. Landing on my feet on solid ground, I'd thwarted the possibility of death yet again in what I've identified as the fourth of my nine lives. We continued on with the hike.

The most terrifying moment came, however, when we were on one of the outer cliff sections. We were traversing a path on a steep sideways incline. The path tilted sharply downward to the right, only about a foot away from where the cliff dropped off hundreds of feet to the rocks and ocean below. Walking out onto this unleveled, precarious section of the path, I only made it about fifty feet when suddenly I couldn't get any firm footing. Wearing only my worn tennis shoes, not hiking boots, it felt like a thousand tiny ants were under my shoes ever so slowly and relentlessly rolling me towards the edge of the cliff where I wouldn't be able to stop myself!

My worn tennis shoes had terrible traction on the loose, parched, gravelly dirt. Panicked beyond panicked, silently hysterical and frozen in fear, I tried not to slip anymore.

This is it!
If I keep slipping, I would fall hundreds of feet to my death.
My life now, at this moment, will be over.
I have to do something, but what?

My boyfriend who had on sturdy hiking boots with good traction had gone ahead of me unfazed. He eventually turned back toward me when he realized I wasn't behind him and saw I was in trouble. Stuck in absolute terror, riveted to this spot, trying so hard not to slip, I couldn't move forward, nor could I move backward. Reasoning with myself that I couldn't stand on this spot forever, I had to do something, so I prayed for help.

The thought came to me to just look down at my shoelaces and put one foot in front of the other.

Focus only on your shoe laces.

Still overcome with immense fear, it took all the courage I had to lift my foot up off the sun-baked sloped path, hoping I wasn't heading towards my death sentence. As I put each foot down, one in front of the other, I "heard" a suggestion in my mind:

"Visualize a string from the bottom of each of your feet extending down all the way to the core of the earth anchoring you to the planet."

With each step, I knew I was to only focus on these imaginary strings extending down to the core of the earth to keep me from slipping. I kept being reminded I was to only look at my shoelaces, nothing else, ensuring I would not fall.

Finally, I made it through this harrowing section and could let my guard down a bit. Although still shaken and trembling, I breathed a gigantic sigh of relief as I'd successfully navigated the challenge of what I later realized was the fifth of my nine lives.

We camped out for the night along the trail as it was a two-day hike into Kalalau Valley. On the second day of trekking, as we came close to the valley, our next challenge was to make our way across a raging river holding our packs high above our heads. It was tricky navigating through a riverbed of immense boulders while all of this rushing water was coming at you as you tried to keep your balance. Finally, we made it across to the other side of the river and entered the mile-long Kalalau Valley beach. It was gorgeous, like being in a fairy tale. The first thing we came to was a high waterfall with an ancient Hawaiian burial ground at the top. The high waterfall cascades down into a pool at the bottom where people placed their beer to keep it cold. This pool was a kind of social gathering place, the natural 'happy hour' spot. Beyond the far end of the beach was an amazing, immense natural stone arch that led to another beach where they filmed the movie "King Kong," starring Jessica Lange.

There were probably about thirty to forty people just visiting or living in the valley who had dropped out of society. Some more permanent residents lived up in the hills where the foliage could mask their marijuana growing operations. In the mid-70s, it was not unusual for the narcotics helicopters to fly regularly over the area looking for marijuana crops.

We made our way down the beach, found a spot to pitch our tent, and shed our clothes like the rest of the valley inhabitants. Almost no one in the valley wore clothes during the day. We spent the next couple of days connecting with people, swimming, and exploring the long beach. This guy Charlie, whom we became friendly with, insisted we go around the point to the other beach where you had a much better view of the natural arch used in the King Kong movie. Charlie led the way, swimming around the point so we would know what to aim for.

Stark naked, I was wearing only swim fins and Dan was paddling on a yellow blow-up raft. There were big stinging jellyfish in the water which you had to stay clear of, but we finally made it around the point to the other beach unscathed where we spent a few hours exploring the stone arch and the beach. Charlie even taught us how to eat mollusks off the rocks. I never thought I would ever do something like that in a million years. We just rinsed them off in the saltwater and popped them in our mouths, alive. They were kind of sweet tasting. But after eating only two, it was all I could handle as eating something alive freaked me out. I found it interesting how my preconception and judgment about eating something alive far outweighed my experience of eating it, which really wasn't that bad, however I just couldn't let go of my preconception about it. At least I tried it!

It was getting late in the day and time for us to head back to the Kalalau Valley Beach. We started swimming back around the point, but no matter how hard we tried, we virtually could make no headway. We didn't know the current had changed direction, going against us, and the wind had picked up, causing rough seas and whitecaps to come up. Trying to stay in sight of Charlie, I followed him the best I could in those rough ocean conditions.

I was an experienced swimmer and had the advantage of wearing swim fins, but it was too far to make it around the point in these conditions. So,

Charlie motioned to me to follow him towards this cave at the end of the point jutting out. Exhausted, I finally made it to the mouth of the cave. Charlie told me to stay in the cave while he went for help. In the back of the cave was a little opening where he could climb out and get back to the Kalalau Valley Beach to look for help. I sat there crying as the cave gradually started filling up with water. I just kept looking out, scanning the ocean and the horizon to see if I could see any sign of Dan. There was no sign of him at all. Hysterical, I kept trying to banish the thought of having to call his parents in Oklahoma to tell them he had drowned off the coast of Kauai.

Finally, about forty-five minutes later, Charlie reappeared through the little hole in the back of the cave. He'd found two surfers who agreed to go out on their boards to look for Dan.

He warned me, "It's already almost too late!"

To get out alive and not drown in the rising ocean water in the cave meant we had to go right then. It was like a scene in a movie. After climbing through the little opening in the back of the cave, we then had to scramble up onto a narrow ledge. This long, narrow ledge was at the end of a point of land jutting out into the ocean from the beach. The tide was coming in quickly.

We repeatedly had to turn our heads towards the rock ledge and hold steady as gigantic waves crashed over our heads. The powerful undertow would then pull the water back away from the ledge. Several waves crashed over our heads while we figured out how, and when, to jump away from the ledge so we wouldn't get crushed against the side of the rocks.

Miraculously, we timed it right, both of us jumping off the ledge without getting smashed back onto the rocks or being dragged underwater by the powerful undertow. Exhausted, we slogged our way through the water back to the beach. The sun was setting. Still, there was no sign of Dan. Even though I'd felt lonely before, this feeling of "alone" without Dan there with me came out of my fear he'd perished rather than through his choice to not be with me.

My feelings of loneliness usually stemmed from an underlying belief that I didn't matter, or I wasn't good enough, however this time was different. I tried not to give up hope. Finally, about an hour later, the surfers came back with Dan on one of their surfboards. I was never so glad to see anybody in my entire life. Dan wasn't much of a swimmer, so when he couldn't make any headway swimming against the current, he let go of the raft and just drifted back to the beach we had just come from, where he fell asleep.

After this ordeal, another of my nine lives, I decided I'd had enough. There were only three ways you could get in, or out, of Kalalau Valley. One was the two-day hike on the precarious trail, which I refused to do again. The second was getting booked onto one of the large zodiac rubber rafts propelled by an outboard motor which we hadn't prearranged, and the third was securing passage on the helicopter which brought supplies. There was no set schedule, however, for the helicopter's arrival, but we heard you could illegally get out of Kalalau Valley on the helicopter by paying something like 40 bucks a person. You had to pay cash or they wouldn't let you out of there. Since there was no schedule, you never knew when the helicopter would suddenly show up. There was a little mound of grass where the helicopter would usually land, so we hung around this spot from sunrise to sunset for two days, hoping the helicopter would show up. It could be days or weeks before it came.

The third morning that we were hanging out close to the mound of grass where the helicopter landed, we had gone down to the stream to wash out our camping dishes and utensils when suddenly we heard the helicopter approaching. We went running back up to the mound, leaving our dishes at the stream. Collecting our things, we paid our money and got on the helicopter. As the helicopter lifted into the air, we saw a couple looking up at us in the helicopter, holding up our dishes.

They mouthed to us, "You forgot these."

We mouthed back, "Keep the dishes," we just shrugged it off and let it go.

The helicopter airlifted us out of the valley to the Kauai airport. Grateful to be out of there, intact, in only about six minutes, I realized I didn't care how much it had cost us. Amazed at myself at how well I'd kept up only wearing worn-out Keds sneakers, hiking with an unbalanced pack on my back, and having absolutely no experience navigating difficult level hikes, I believe it was a miracle we both survived to tell the tale.

As I keep reviewing the trajectory of my life experiences and life choices in this awakening process, it is becoming more apparent to me how perfectly guided we are by Spirit when we listen and take heed of what is being impressed upon us. I was so set on attending Sarah Lawrence yet ended up at the University of Hawaii ostensibly for economic reasons which turned out to be the perfect place for me as it offered me tuition scholarship and a teaching position which ensured I left graduate school with very little debt. If I'd gone to Sarah Lawrence, I don't know how I could have paid back my student loans with what was on the horizon in my life, which didn't turn out to be the future I'd envisioned.

I recently looked up the Kalalau Valley Trail on the Internet, only to discover that it's listed as one of the twenty most dangerous hikes in the world. The trail has claimed dozens of lives and over one hundred people have drowned in the powerful surf. Had I known this ahead of time, I probably never would have agreed to this adventure. Also, it never even dawned on me when we set out on this hike that I should have expected more consideration from my boyfriend. I believe he knew how difficult the trail was, that I had no real hiking experience, and was ill-prepared. At the very least, he should have made sure I had good sturdy hiking boots, as well as a balanced pack before embarking on this hike.

This was just another example of settling for dysfunctional behavior, as I didn't know any better or didn't realize, or even had a clue, I deserved more. These emotional and psychological issues I'd always either pushed down or didn't even recognize when people did not have my best interests or safety at heart, but the perfect opportunity for addressing them was just around the corner.

Chapter 10: Elevating My Career Prospects

My second year of graduate school turned out to be a great blessing. Linda Jahnke, who'd received the teaching assistantship position in the dance department at the University of Hawaii, took a leave of absence to follow her husband, Roger Jahnke, to California, where he was starting training in Acupuncture and Chinese Medicine. In her absence, the university awarded me the teaching assistantship position, teaching five beginning ballet classes for the university along with my other course work and performance schedule.

Being awarded this teaching assistantship, after receiving the dance department scholarship the previous year, I finally felt I was receiving the recognition I deserved for my talent and abilities. With this teaching assistantship award, the University of Hawaii gave me a full-tuition scholarship along with a $4000 stipend, which helped me make it through my entire two years of graduate school by taking out only one $2500 student loan. I doubt anything like this would have happened if I'd gone to graduate school at Sarah Lawrence.

During this second year of graduate school my schedule got even busier. Carrying a heavy load of courses, teaching five ballet classes a week for the university, and putting together my half of a full evening concert which I was staging along with another Master of Fine Arts candidate, there was very little room for personal time or for going to the beach. We devoted all of our time to staging this concert. The other MFA candidate choreographed half of the evening concert, and I choreographed two pieces and reconstructed a third dance piece from Labanotation (dance notation) as part of the required elements for our Master's thesis. People loved our dance concert, and we also received favorable reviews in the Honolulu newspaper.

Besides my course curriculum, teaching responsibilities and Thesis concert, I also became very involved with an off-campus group, Re-Evaluation Co-Counseling. This group interested me because for years I'd realized I needed psychological help to get past my childhood trauma in regaining my connection to my true core self.

In the fall of 1972, when I first moved to New York, I felt emotionally numb. A therapist in New York who treated a close dancer friend of mine suggested psychotherapy might help me. I asked my mother for money to do this, but she evaded my request and told me to ask my father.

Really?

I'd spent years avoiding interacting with him at all costs, but I knew I needed help, so I asked if he would meet with me. Meeting him at his office at the hospital took everything in me to muster the courage to face him. After taking a deep breath, I blurted out my concerns. I shared how unhappy and emotionally numb I felt, and that it frightened me because I didn't experience any emotions anymore. I asked him for financial help to see a therapist. An epic tirade followed.

My father just stood there yelling at me, "You are perfectly happy!" as he berated me for thinking I needed help.

He pontificated how psychiatry and psychology were in the dark ages and they didn't understand what they were doing. I stood there dumbfounded.

This interaction, although more dramatic than usual, ended up being the epitome of all the exchanges I'd ever had with him.

It was always all about him. He extended his own inflated ego to everyone and everything around him, showing no empathy, compassion, or an ability to even perceive me as a separate person from him. Determined not to "let him win" meant preserving my identity as a unique separate self from him. I would not let him destroy me–that essence that made me, me. This is what was unique and precious about me.

Chapter 10: Elevating My Career Prospects

Stunned at this tirade, I asked him, "Why are you crying?" Tears streamed down his face and dripped off his chin. He flatly denied he was crying.

Talk about ultimate denial and lying!

I vowed I'd never put myself in that position with him ever again. Years later, doctors diagnosed him as being bipolar. Fortunately, my mother scraped up some money for me to at least attend the group therapy sessions, which helped.

I remember in the group session one day; the therapist turned to me and asked, "What part do you play in all that has happened?"

Wait, what do you mean, what part did I play?

Hey, I'm the victim here! I thought to myself.

It was the first time someone confronted me about the part I played in the situation. Contemplating this spurred me on to delve further into understanding the dynamics of oppressor/victim patterning. If I could understand this and take responsibility for healing my own messed up internal state, maybe my world could also change for the better. Thus began a lifelong endeavor of investigating and healing these dysfunctional patterns, starting with seeing the therapist in New York and taking part in the Honolulu Re-Evaluation Counseling Community when I was in graduate school.

During my second year of graduate school, things were finally going along really well for me when out of the blue, an alarming weird thing started happening. While standing upon a low table being measured for a costume in the props department the first term of my second year, this inner movie scene started playing out in my head, uninvited. It wasn't something I was consciously thinking about at all. In this inner scene, I saw myself driving in the car, when suddenly it appeared I was heading towards the windshield in slow motion.

I knew I was about to be in an accident. This premonition freaked me out so much I felt the blood drain from my face as I tried to stay focused, conscious, and not faint. I tried to dismiss it as just a fluke, however the following month the same thing happened again. In vain, I tried to stop worrying about it and just let it go, but it started becoming a regular occurrence, happening every few weeks, then progressed to every week, eventually progressing to becoming almost a daily occurrence over the ensuing six months. It creeped me out even further by this point.

Even weirder during my second year of graduate school was my compulsion to fly back to Connecticut for Easter vacation. Flying back to Connecticut at the end of March didn't make logical sense, as I'd most likely return to Connecticut two months later, anyway, when I finished graduate school. However, the compulsion was so strong I just had to follow it.

After flying back to Connecticut for Easter break, the first thing I tried to do was to renew my recently expired Hawaii driver's license at the Connecticut DMV since I figured I'd be returning to live in Connecticut after completing my graduate studies until I found a teaching position. However, the Connecticut DMV office had closed for the Easter holiday weekend. For years, every time I went back to Connecticut, I'd drive up to Connecticut College to see my friends still in college there. A few years earlier, when I'd attended Connecticut College, I'd bought a used, dented, three-year-old Ford Maverick from one of the dance teachers there. My father's college graduation present to me was fixing the dent in my car. When I left for graduate school, I signed the car over to my parents for $5. This way they would pay the car insurance and also have it available for my siblings to use while I was away at graduate school.

On this Easter vacation trip to Connecticut College in New London, I'd just come out of the Madison tollbooths on I-95 when they still had toll booths. Suddenly, the car careened erratically all over the road completely out of control. It felt like I'd hit something huge in the road, but saw nothing. Next thing I knew, people were standing over me, asking me if I was okay. I'd completely blacked out and lost consciousness when my car crashed into the center median. It's unclear how long I'd lost consciousness, but it was long enough, however, for an entire group of people to see what happened, pull over, get out of their cars and open my car door to see if I was alright.

Apparently, the entire front right wheel just fell off my car as I was driving about fifty-five to sixty miles per hour, which caused the accident. Later investigation determined there was a defect in the axle which had rusted through, causing the wheel to fall off the car on the freeway, surprising, since the car was only six years old.

Chapter 10: Elevating My Career Prospects

Once I regained consciousness, my very first thought was, thank God it finally happened! The accident, which I'd kept seeing play out in my mind for so long, finally occurred. Now I didn't have to be fearful about this almost daily premonition coming true anymore. Thankfully, my seat belt prevented me from going through the windshield, but I hit my chin hard on the steering wheel. This impact ripped all the flesh of my chin inside my mouth, away from the bone. The police officer who arrived on the scene said, "I'm amazed the accident didn't kill you."

Because I had a recently expired license from Hawaii, fortunately he didn't give me a ticket. But I explained to him I tried to renew my license before taking this trip, but the DMV was closed. He told me if my expired driver's license had been from Connecticut instead of Hawaii, he'd have to arrest me. I knew how lucky I was. Refusing to go in the ambulance, the police let me call my mother to tell her what happened. I told her I planned to take the train back to Westport so she could take me for medical help. I asked the police to give me a ride to the train station. Shaken and sore with a gaping serious wound in my mouth, I must have been numb and in shock to endure long enough to get back to my parents for the medical help I needed.

Taking the next train back to Westport, my mother picked me up at the station and took me straight away to the children's dentist. He treated the injury, putting clay packing in my mouth since I didn't even have enough intact flesh left to suture it. The clay packing had to stay in my mouth for about two weeks, so I couldn't eat solid food, only liquids.

Returning to Hawaii a little later than the end of the Easter break after the initial injury healed enough, I still needed to finish out the rest of the school term.

Prior to the Easter break, the US Army at Schofield Barracks in Hawaii hired me and several other dancers to perform in a spring talent show competition they were putting on against other army barracks after the Easter break. To be ready to perform, I went to a chiropractor for the first time in my life, hoping for relief from an immovable stiff neck which had suddenly become stuck over my right shoulder.

"You look like a Mack truck hit you!" he exclaimed.

You'd think it would have registered that I'd been in this car accident about six weeks earlier, but it didn't occur to me then. He adjusted me so I could perform in this Army production coming up in a few days. What I didn't realize was I was exhibiting a classic pattern of injuries, which sometimes appear several weeks after an accident.

Even though I'd gotten through this one performance with help from the chiropractor, I soon started having such chronic severe sciatica, the pain forced me to stop dancing. It got to the point I couldn't even walk without severe chronic pain. Fortunately, I'd completed all of my graduate school credits, so I received my Master's Degree even though for the last couple weeks of the term I could only watch the dance classes because of my injury. At the time the accident occurred, I was in the middle of applying for dance department faculty positions in colleges and universities. I hoped my teaching assistantship at the University of Hawaii would further enhance my chances of getting hired by some institution. Since I could barely walk, more or less dance, everything came to a halt because of this car accident.

My father, who carried the insurance policy for my car while I was in graduate school, closed out the medical claims for the accident without consulting me. Right after the accident happened, I talked to my father about suing Ford because the accident resulted from a defect in the car's axle. He didn't want to bother suing Ford, saying we would get nowhere suing a company like Ford. People didn't readily file lawsuits in the 70s, anyway.

Twenty years later, when having recurring neck pain, an MRI showed I was suffering from herniated discs in my cervical spine from the impact of the accident. Also, around this same time, I ended up having two root canals done, which puzzled the dentist why I needed root canals on virgin teeth. He asked if my mouth had ever received a blow or impact. So, years after this accident, I also ended up paying outright for these root canals and crowns.

I assumed after a short length of time I would heal enough from the effects of the accident that I could resume my applications for faculty teaching positions and return to my life as a dancer. This was not to be as I ended up suffering with long-term chronic sciatica for years thereafter, way beyond the time window for my dance career. As it became apparent this career was over, my world and identity as a dancer collapsed.

Dance had been my entire life and focus since childhood. Fellow dancers were my tribe, and choreographing, teaching dance, and being a dancer were the only things I knew how to do well. Now I would have to find other things to focus on and also be a means of financial support. I thought maybe there would be a way of getting compensation for the accident, but that was in my father's hands who refused to do anything about it. Over the next ten years, I read accounts of two other cases which involved the same make and model car, also with a similar defect in the axle resulting in the wheel falling off. Both people received multi-million-dollar settlements from Ford. So, this accident, which caused me years of pain, cost me my career, and years of out-of-pocket medical and dental expenses was yet another issue I had with my father, which made me unhappy and kept me struggling. But just blaming my father wasn't helping anything.

The other ironic thing in all of this was that during my second year of graduate school, I finally took steps to lose twenty pounds of extra weight by joining Weight Watchers. I'd lost some weight when I went back to Connecticut for Easter. After the accident happened, because I couldn't eat solid food for a long time, I dropped even more weight to where my mother said to me, "I never thought I would ever say this to you, but you are too skinny!" For the first time in my life, I'd finally achieved my goal weight as a dancer, except now any potential career as a dancer was out the window.

Many decades later, after doing a lot of inner work, I came to realize these premonitions I'd had for six months before the accident occurred were preparing me to undergo a major shift in my life. When the accident happened, I absolutely knew Divine Intervention took place protecting me from losing my life, but I didn't know why it happened. The harm I experienced proved to be purposeful in the larger picture.

The trajectory of my life needed to change for fulfilling my soul's purpose, which meant my dance career needed to end. Looking back, I see how every time I tried to achieve a major goal in my life, or recognition in my dance career, something always thwarted these desires.

Eventually I came to understand I wouldn't be doing what I came here to do if I'd kept on with dance as my career. It took this car accident and the six months of premonitions to prepare me to handle it. I came to realize it was my Higher Self orchestrating these things, not my father's actions, nor some outside malevolent force. This accident was my Higher Self's way of getting me back on the path of awakening so I could be of the greatest service, although I knew nothing about awakening or being of service at the time of this accident. The only thing I consciously knew, for the first time, was that some kind of Divine Intervention and protection had occurred which I couldn't explain.

Stuart Hodes, who was the chair of the dance department at New York University when I attended school there for a semester, received the Martha Hill Lifetime Achievement Award at age ninety-six.

In his acceptance speech, he described dance in this way:

"Dance is magic time. When you go onstage, magic happens and we become something else, an intensification of life where you're completely absorbed in what you are doing." The magic he described in this quote is what I perceived *energy* to be. Now my quest became how to understand and experience this *energy* in other ways than through dance.

Chapter 11: Becoming More Conscious

Glimpses of this *energy*, when magic happens, I realized, had been going on with me since childhood. I'd just taken it in stride; rarely questioning my intuition, the synchronicity that happened in my life, or insights I'd had about people or situations. I thought everyone else also experienced these things too. I was wrong.

Soon I discovered that most people didn't have a clue what I was talking about, or experiencing. Where I started finding confirmation of my experiences was from those people who were writing, speaking and sharing their experiences, not necessarily from religion, but from their own experience in the spiritual realms. In college, I started exploring the spiritual realms as best I could with what was then available.

Continuing with this exploration in graduate school, one of my RC (Re-Evaluation Counseling) partners, a professional astrologer, prompted a surge of new interest by teaching me the basics of astrology. I viewed this as yet another tool to help me understand the influences and patterns of *energy* and how it affects people's lives. Since college, even though I'd devoured whatever metaphysical or spiritual books I could find, I never felt comfortable discussing this with anybody.

This was my own very private, very personal, clandestine pursuit. Even though I'd read and absorbed information the best I could, no way was I ready to engage in a conversation or interaction with anyone else about it. That was way too threatening. No one needed to know about it. One day while looking for an astrology book in the Ala Moana Shopping Center bookstore in Honolulu, I reached for a book and simultaneously this man also reached for the same book. He stepped back, bowed, apologized, and said I should take the book. Then he turned to me out of the blue and started giving me a mini-reading on the spot. No one had ever "tuned" into me before, nor had I asked that he do this.

At that moment, it proved to be very helpful, as I was wrestling with a big decision of whether to stay in Hawaii or go back to Connecticut when graduate school finished in a couple of months. He told me when I got back to the mainland, I'd know what to do. He told me he taught metaphysics and then asked me for my phone number just in case there was more information for me. Usually, if people are promoting themselves, they want to give you their phone number instead of asking for mine. I felt uncomfortable handing over my phone number. I wondered if he was just 'hitting' on me. Despite the red flag and my discomfort with doing this, something came over me and I hesitantly handed him my phone number.

A few days later, the guy called saying he had information for me. Reluctantly, I agreed to meet him, suggesting we go to the shopping center's very public cafeteria, as I felt this would be a safe place to meet. Rather than looking forward to this encounter, I found myself in abject terror at the thought of meeting with him. I didn't understand why. Suddenly, all these irrational fears welled up within me of being physically or psychically raped, attacked, or having put myself in danger where all kinds of tortuous things could happen.

Overwhelmed with fear, I told myself to "get a grip."

Later, when thinking about the choice I made to meet with him, I noticed how mustering the courage to disrobe and model naked for the artist in New York didn't bring up nearly as much fear as agreeing to meet with this Asian man in a public place. The thought of speaking to anyone about spiritual things raised some deep primal fear in me like I might lose my soul.

Still feeling very agitated on my way to meet with him, I parked the car and started walking towards the cafeteria. However, as soon as I saw him sitting on a bench with his back to me, a wave of calm, centered *energy* washed over me. I instantly knew it would be all right. There was nothing to fear. He was a small

Asian man who had a slight limp and a lisp. This was the first time I'd ever talked to someone else about spiritual things.

We talked for about six hours that first day we met. During our second meeting, he told me the reason I intrigued him was because I had the largest, most exquisite being of light with me he'd ever seen. He was in awe of this being and wanted to know who it was and its connection to me. This was news to me. Thus, my friendship with Bill Nakagawa began. He became a mentor, teaching me the ways of Zen. We met several more times in person, had amazing exchanges, before I moved back to the mainland after graduate school, as he said I would. Bill continued to mentor me for the next few years through letters in which he taught me metaphysical principles and Zen types of contemplation. These had no answers the mind could satisfy; they just deepened the contemplation process. He never charged me any money nor asked me for anything in return.

Moving back to the mainland from Hawaii, I again settled in Manhattan, since I still had many friends there. A short time after my arrival back in New York, who do I run into there? Jeremy! We had previously split up four years before, but I guess we had more to complete with each other. Fortunately, this time, the relationship with Jeremy didn't have so much of the intense, addictive, romantic pull on me as the previous times we were together. I got together with Jeremy for one more round, partly because I knew Jeremy could help me physically through his Alexander Technique work, as I still had a lot of chronic pain from the car accident.

After resuming our romantic relationship for the third time around, Jeremy started intensively working with me using the Alexander Technique to help my body gradually unwind from the trauma and realign itself so it could heal faster. I ended up moving into his tiny, but cute studio apartment. It was only about eight feet by ten feet with a working fireplace and French windows which opened up overlooking the courtyard. At one time, it had been the carriage house for the main house in front, but it was eventually converted into six apartments.

I don't know how we amicably survived in such a small space. There was a cot size bed with a trundle bed underneath which we would pull out at night to make a double bed. There was also a tiny kitchenette with a small sink, two metal cabinets, two burners that sat on top of a half-size refrigerator, and a minuscule closet. In the bathroom, a dresser barely fit between the end of the claw-foot bathtub and the wall. It was hard for the two of us to move around the cramped space, but somehow, we made it work. At least it wasn't a fifth floor-walk up this time. Fortunately, Jeremy wasn't there a lot as he was remodeling a space uptown to turn into a living loft and work space so he could do his Alexander Technique work there.

Jeremy now had become the executive director of the American Alexander Technique Center and got me the job of being the Administrator of the center, as I again needed a job. My duties included that of receptionist, bookkeeper, and scheduler for teachers booking rooms, along with the administrative work for the teacher training program. It thrilled me to have this job as I met a lot of interesting people. I was thankful I no longer had to work in retail.

While working at the Alexander Center, I became friendly with Amy, a woman in the teacher training program. She told me about a light work school she attended and facilitated an introductory process for me. This was my first experience working in my body with a 'white light' guided meditation. I knew right away I wanted to attend the Actualism School, so I joined their introductory course. The Actualism School taught Russell Paul Schofield's processes of using inner light-fire energy tools for awakening more joy and greater well-being. I didn't realize it at the time that these processes we were being taught were tools to help me raise my frequency. I was part of the school, advancing through the upper training levels for the next four years, from 1978 to 1982.

Amy also was a channel. I'd read about channeling in the *Seth Speaks* books but had never experienced it myself. Amy invited me over to her apartment in Brooklyn Heights to experience this phenomenon. She had recently started channeling and wanted to do it for groups. She asked me to coordinate asking questions and working the tape recorder during the sessions as when she was in a full-trance channeling state; she remembered nothing that transpired.

The entity she channeled called herself She-Lah. Amy's entire demeanor changed when She-Lah came through. Her voice became much stronger and louder when She-Lah was speaking. The voice was so loud that someone said they could even clearly hear it three floors down on the street level.

This entity, She-Lah, mostly spoke about bringing light to the planet. However, she did not want to sound religious or scare us off. This was 1979, when rarely were these types of things talked about. She-Lah was most disturbed by the disregard humanity exhibited for the care and maintenance of the planet.

The satellite Skylab was falling out of orbit in 1979. No one knew where it would land or if it would fall into a populated area, causing damage or not. She-Lah expressed dismay that humanity was so oblivious and insensitive to the burden the planet must bear, and the atrocities the fish and the oceans must take on because of what we've imposed on them. This being was a compassionate presence, offering nothing but kindness and love. There was nothing to fear, I realized. We started scheduling group sessions in order for She-Lah to speak with people.

My mother, who loaned me her metaphysical books several years earlier, which started me on my path, was still somewhat curious about spiritual things. She agreed to take the six-month Actualism School Introductory course and had met Amy while at the Actualism School. I convinced my mother to come to one of She-Lah's group channeling sessions.

When She-Lah spoke to my mother, she addressed her as "Mother in the Corner." She said to my mother, "You need to get about your spiritual business!"

She-Lah continued, "You've been a high priestess many times in other lives."

However, my mother wasn't having any of it. She just said she wanted everything handed to her on a silver platter. She didn't want to have to work for it. It doesn't work that way. So that was the end of that. No longer did I try to include my mother in anything after that.

Woven throughout my life, I've also had moments of coincidence, or synchronicity, as we all have. One day after leaving Amy's apartment in Brooklyn Heights, I was walking to the subway when I passed a man whom I thought I knew. About twenty paces after passing by him, I stopped and turned around to look back at him. He stopped at the same moment and gazed back towards me. We both laughed as we caught each other, sizing each other up. Coming together, we introduced ourselves, trying to figure out how we knew each other. He introduced himself as the actor and theater director, Andre Gregory. I thought at first, I must have known him because he was a faculty member at the NYU School of the Arts when I attended school there for that one semester in 1973. But that wasn't it.

It was only after we ended our brief conversation and I continued walking towards the subway when I realized it was from regularly going swimming at Miller's Pond in New London, Connecticut, during the 1974 American Dance Festival. Several experimental theater companies, including Andre Gregory and his company, were in residence that summer. Many of the actors and us dancers would regularly go skinny dipping together at Miller's Pond. He and I hadn't recognized each other in our clothes. We had only known each other from skinny dipping. A few years after we ran into each other his film, *My Dinner with Andre*, came out in which he and actor Wallace Shawn shared anecdotes of their experiences with each other during a dinner meeting.

In my job as the administrator of the Alexander Technique Center I'd also hear about all the projects and endeavors in which the students and teachers were taking part. One of the Alexander Technique Teachers taught sessions for the International Primal Therapy Association. Through her, I found out the office of the Primal Therapy Association was looking for someone to work part-time, taking care of voice mail messages and returning phone calls. When I told them I was interested in the job, they hired me. I'd go to the International Primal Therapy Association office in a therapist's apartment, work a few hours, then leave. Other than a few weekend events, their big focus was a week-long summer conference held each year at a children's camp, which they rented for the conference.

Being their secretary, they invited me to attend the conference if I wanted to go. Although Primal Scream Therapy was not my thing, I thought it would be fun to attend as I imagined it would be like summer camp, only for adults. When I went, I planned to do only the fun, frivolous, foo-foo stuff they offered, nothing heavy. I took part in trust exercises, floating each other in the pool and a chair massage class and something else called Dynamic Meditation.

I thought meditation was for relaxation, right?

Well, this Dynamic Meditation, or Chaotic Meditation, as they sometimes called it, was anything but relaxing. Bhagwan Shree Rajneesh (who later went by the name Osho) originally taught this meditation process to his disciples. Osho was the Guru who owned dozens of Rolls Royce cars in his compound in Antelope, Oregon.

One of his disciples taught us this meditation. We started this Dynamic Meditation by bending over with our hands on our knees, hyperventilating (fast breathing) for ten minutes, followed by jumping, screaming, rhythmic movement or whatever your body wanted you to do for ten minutes, then with arms raised above our heads jumping up and down for another ten minutes shouting, "Hoo Hoo."

Finally, we'd freeze in a pose for fifteen minutes without moving, followed by dancing or celebrating. This was the first time I'd done this meditation, or anything else like it. In the middle of the meditation, the powerful waves of energy I'd periodically experienced years before threatened to overtake my body. The force of these waves of energy felt so intense, I feared I'd splinter into a million pieces and would never come back together coherently again.

The only thing which mitigated the intensity of this harrowing experience was when I started violently, repeatedly vomiting. I purged everything out of my system until it was only dry heaves. Very fragile, I still felt like I could psychologically or physically splinter at any second. Lying down on the floor, I knew I needed to ask everyone to put their hands on me to help me stay in cohesion. People asked what was happening to me and I shared what I was experiencing. Years later, I came to understand I needed their hands on me to help me become grounded. These waves of energy were apparently a spontaneous rising of Kundalini energy, which I didn't have any clue about then.

Later, I found out Kundalini energy is a life force energy usually dormant, coiled at the base of one's spine. When it becomes activated, possibly stimulated by something such as this meditation or sometimes just spontaneously, it can rise upwards through the spinal column. When the Kundalini energy spirals fully up the spine and reaches the level of the Pituitary and Pineal glands in the brain, one may experience a state of bliss, or Nirvana. With the full ascension of the Kundalini up the spine and into the centers in the brain, one's frequency is raised and one may transition into the stage of becoming an enlightened Guru, which often takes years, if not lifetimes, to achieve.

People explained the Kundalini energy to me and said that was what had happened to me. The extreme discomfort, fear, and other emotions I'd experienced, along with the vomiting, was because as the Kundalini rose upwards through the spine, it activated each chakra (energy center) along the way. It was like a deep cleansing process, sometimes very painful and disconcerting, as the rising Kundalini hit all the energy blocks stored in the chakras. This was apparently what happened to me.

While holding their hands on me, one person said to me they were envious of my experience. They'd wanted what happened to me to happen to them.

Are you kidding?

I wouldn't wish this on my worst enemy, as it was painful and terrifying.

This wasn't to be my only occasion of a spontaneous Kundalini awakening, however. Years later, I would have another one, which resulted in a much different outcome. So much for thinking I was only opting to do the tame foo-foo stuff at this conference!

After returning from the conference, Jeremy and I finally parted ways as I wanted to go on a much more spiritually focused path, which made him uncomfortable. He had also completed his uptown loft enough and could move into it while still working on the finishing touches. Graciously, he agreed to keep subletting his little rent-controlled studio apartment to me where I continued to live until I left New York.

By the end of this third time around with each other, my experience in this relationship was now exactly opposite to the intensity and addictive quality of the first time Jeremy and I were together. We had come full circle and had worked through our karma from this life and our past lives. I knew our relationship was finally complete. We had finished what we came to do and were now free to go our separate ways. I had learned a lot about what I would

Chapter 11: Becoming More Conscious

and wouldn't accept in a relationship, yet I would have more lessons on this again, yet to come.

I was still trying to figure out what I wanted to be when I grew up. Life as a dancer was now out of the question. I needed a new direction. I decided I wanted to go through the training class to become a certified Alexander Technique Teacher, however, they wouldn't accept me into the program. I guess they didn't want to lose their office person and administrator. With this rejection and my split with Jeremy, it was a little awkward still working at the Alexander Technique Center with him as my boss. It was clear it was now time to leave, so I quit my job at the center.

Fortunately, I found another job in a small company office, Liberty Petroleum, on 5th Avenue and 42nd Street. This was a basic entry level position where I learned while I was on the job. Even though I didn't have experience in this work arena before, I knew I was smart and could figure out what I needed to do for the job.

It was also my first introduction to computers and the challenges they present as computers were just now becoming more commonplace in business settings in the early 1980s. Only two of us worked there, along with the owner. What I remember most was all the hours of trial and error, trying to figure out how to get the computer, printer, and the monitor to work together. This was well before the use of personal computers for business. The owner had gotten great deals on all these separate components. What he didn't understand was that these components weren't compatible. They wouldn't work together easily unless the parts were specifically designed to work together. It was our job to make them work. Again, I was *flying by the seat of my pants*. The other employee and I finally figured out how to Jerry-rig something so we could get on with compiling the database and mailing lists.

Even though this job was short-lived, it gave me enough experience with computers for being hired at my next job. It would take another couple of decades before I would come to understand fully how these various and random jobs provided me with the exact experience, I would need for what my soul's plan was for me.

87

Chapter 12: Meeting the Masters

My accommodation at the Primal Therapy Conference was in a twenty-cot co-ed dormitory room. The guy sleeping in the bed next to me, Barry Levin, was at the conference to learn more about primal therapy, as he'd been a Primal Therapy client for a while. In bed at night, Barry and I started conversing, finding out we had things in common and similar interests.

When he told me about his spiritual interests, I shared with him I was an Actualism student. I led him through the Actualism Introduction a few days later. After the conference Barry also enrolled in the Actualism School. He ended up being a year behind me in the classes. We started dating. One day we got together with a group of his Primal Therapy friends. One of his friend's girlfriends shared that she worked in a Wall Street insurance company's accounting department and that they were looking to hire somebody else for their department. Because of my previous job experience using computers, I felt I might qualify for this job, so I applied.

Unione Italiana Reinsurance hired me to work as part of a three-woman team running their accounting department. Amazed that I not only got the job but also became part of the team of women running the entire accounting department, was almost unheard of in the male-dominated insurance industry in the early 1980s. This was a great boost to my self-confidence, as often in my mind I had a subliminal internal dialogue running of how incompetent I was (courtesy of my father). Even though I was now working at this job on Wall

Street, I still kept my part-time hours working for the International Primal Therapy Association. Especially since pursuing dance was no longer an option in my life, spiritual endeavors and exploration took up that space and focus in my life. Jill Adams, a friend in my Actualism class, told me about audiences with an Ascended Master named Ramtha.

Channeled by JZ Knight, in 1977, in Tacoma, Washington, Ramtha spontaneously appeared in front of JZ and her husband. Ramtha introduced himself, explained who he was, and started working with JZ to prepare her to become a full-bodied trance channel for Ramtha. Once she accomplished this, JZ started traveling to different cities around the country, conducting Ramtha Dialogues.

When JZ channels Ramtha, her body puffs up, expanding into a more impressive size. Her voice completely changes. Everything about JZ transforms into a distinctly more masculine, unique, personality and presence as Ramtha. Ramtha appears in the movie *What the Bleep Do We Know* which came out in 2004. This movie postulates spiritual connections between quantum physics and consciousness. I started attending *Master's Meetings* in the summer of 1980 held at Dean Thompson and Thomas Sharkey's apartment on Manhattan's upper west side. These *Master's Meetings* were for people to review and put into practice the information and processes Ramtha taught in his dialogues.

Because I had to save up the money to attend a Ramtha Dialogue in person, I had to make do with just attending the *Master's meetings* for about six months. Finally, in January 1981, my boyfriend Barry, Jill, and I attended our first Ramtha Dialogue in New York City. By this time JZ had been traveling around the country for about two years doing Ramtha Dialogues in California, Alabama, New York, and the Pacific Northwest. Thirty-five of us first-timers were at the New York dialogue. People who'd seen Ramtha before could attend for a nominal fee, but only as observers. They could not speak to Ramtha or take part in the dialogue. They were only there to listen. Ramtha divided the dialogue into three sections. In the first section Ramtha greeted people and gave each person a message.

Following the initial greetings, he shared his story of how he became the ascended Master known as "Ramtha the Enlightened One." He continued on with the story of his life as the "Ram," a 35,000-year-old magnificent warrior and conqueror in ancient Persia, who conquered two-thirds of the known world in his time. In Hindu literature he is the entity referred to as the Ram. Run through by a sword and gravely injured, he did not die. He spent many years healing his body, mind, and soul from the brink of death as he learned to observe and contemplate life. Through an alignment of peace and profound love, he came to love himself so fully that he sped up the vibratory rate of his body. The frequency of his consciousness and his body quickened so much that his body ascended. He ascended from form, from density, back into the light and then back into pure thought.

Ramtha's teachings were the first time I'd heard about the concept of ascension. Ascension is all about raising your frequency. Throughout history, certain people have been able to achieve this. He taught us that once you've mastered this physical plane and moved beyond death through ascension; you were now free to go anywhere you wanted in the universe. You were no longer bound to the endless karmic cycles of death and rebirth on Earth. Even though this was the first I'd heard of ascension in this lifetime, something resonated deep within my soul that I'd encountered this teaching in previous lives.

In this first Ramtha Dialogue session, Ramtha greeted us one-by-one. All of my friends received either past life readings or detailed information to aid them with their current challenges. When Ramtha approached me, he looked deep into my eyes and my soul.

His exact words were, "This (pausing) what you need to know are in your questions. We will speak evenly, perfectly..." and other words I didn't hear.

This was because my perceptual awareness of the room and the surrounding people in my peripheral vision faded out and disappeared completely as he addressed me. I was locked into a tunnel of timelessness and infinite space with Ramtha. I sensed I received a massive download. I knew something profound had happened but I didn't comprehend it. After a while, my peripheral vision gradually started fading back in as the room and people in the chairs took form again in my visual field.

He then said to me, "I love you. You will come again unto me."

Afterwards, I questioned whether I should be happy with this exchange or disappointed. I didn't receive tangible information as the rest of my friends had received which my mind wanted to hear. Instead, his intense gaze had pieced through my ego directly to my soul. I have yet to fully unpack all that took place in that exchange.

The question-and-answer period with Ramtha took place in the afternoon session. When my turn came, I shared my biggest concerns with Ramtha. I feared I'd miss the signs and signals from Spirit which would show me how to perceive, receive, and follow the awakening journey. He said he'd send a *runner* to me. *Runners* were his term for sending the exact people, experiences, or events as unmistakable demonstrations of proof which would answer their questions. I'd just have to wait for the 'runner' hoping I'd recognize it when it came along.

The evening session with Ramtha was called the Christ-Raising or opening of the seven seals. This was one of the last times he did this individually with people instead of all together as a group. Ramtha went from person to person touching each of their chakras (seals) with one hand while simultaneously touching the same chakra on JZ's body with the other hand, thus activating and opening the seven seals. I expected to have a tremendous change after this, but life returned to normal. Nothing much appeared to have changed on the surface but subtle changes started happening.

Approximately fifteen months after our Dialogue 1 with Ramtha, I experienced an outrageous occurrence of synchronicity because of a wrong phone number. This experience was so far beyond coincidence, I knew it was the *runner*. I couldn't have missed the sign. Going to my Primal Therapy Association job one evening after dinner to get the books ready for an audit the next day, the phone rang. The phone seldom rang unless it was my boyfriend Barry asking when I'd be finished with my work. I was usually there just to collect the messages from voicemail. I answered the call.

The person on the other end of the line said, "I'm looking for Lance Thompson."

"I'm sorry you must have the wrong number." I replied. "There's no Lance Thompson here."

I was just about to hang up when I heard the caller ask, "Then, is Thomas Sharkey there?"

I piped up, "I know someone named Thomas Sharkey, a Ramtha student. Is this who you are looking for?"

"Yes," was the reply.

Now these were the two guys who hosted the *Master's Meetings* I went to before going to my first Ramtha Dialogue. As we talked further, I found out that Lance was really Dean Thompson's first name, which I didn't know as he never used it.

Dean and Thomas had moved to the Pacific Northwest. They were just back in New York visiting their friend Ginny before going to the Boston Ramtha Dialogue the following week. The woman on the phone turned out to be a relative of Dean's calling from somewhere in the Midwest trying to locate him. I gave her their friend Ginny's phone number where they were staying. Later, I got a call from Dean thanking me for facilitating his relative getting in touch with him. The funny thing was, I apparently gave the woman the wrong phone number for Ginny. It was off by one digit; however, the call still went through, miraculously!

After this happened, I remember sitting on the floor in immense gratitude, saying to Ramtha (in my head)

I get it!

I get it!

This was the *runner* Ramtha promised he would send to me. This incident helped me experience a greater level of trust that I wouldn't miss the signs and signals Spirit was sending me. It helped me see how reality could be more fluid and malleable than the hard linear box I thought it was.

Shortly after this occurrence I had a private reading with Ramtha. I shared with him that I had a desire to move out of New York, but I didn't have any idea where I wanted to be. Two pictures came to my mind: one was the ocean surrounded by a landscape of thick forests of evergreen trees, while the other was the southwest desert landscape. Ramtha suggested I move to Oregon, saying he was sending Masters there. Masters was the term he used for his students. He had his staff put me in touch with a Master who had just moved to Florence, Oregon, from Alabama.

I called this woman and asked her if I could come visit her. A couple of weeks later I flew to Oregon to meet with her and discuss the possibility of moving there. We agreed moving there would be a positive step. She offered to let me move in with her. I returned to New York and gave notice at both my jobs. After giving notice at my job at Unione Italiana Reinsurance, I got called into my boss's office. Instinctively bracing for confrontation, as was my usual reaction to male authority, I needn't have worried.

He said, "I am sorry to see you go. I have been very pleased with your work. If you ever decide to return to New York and need a job, we would love to have you back. There will always be a job here for you if you want it."

Not at all what I expected to hear. This was a new experience for me being praised by male authority instead of feeling attacked.

The last thing Ramtha said to me in my private reading as I was getting up to leave was that someday I'd do things I didn't even yet have the mind with which to conceive it. Now that was a mystery to ponder.

A short time later, Barry, my friend Mark whom I had known from college (not the one I drove cross-country with), and I went to a Ramtha Dialogue in Boston. Dean and Thomas were there along with the actress Shirley MacLaine. Thomas had become Shirley's personal assistant and was now living with her in a house she bought in Graham, Washington. During a break, Barry, Mark, and I went outside to take a walk.

We were waiting for the traffic light to change so we could cross a large eight-lane street. Facing us on the opposite side of the street in the oncoming direction was a group of Ramtha Dialogue attendees, including Dean, Thomas, and Shirley MacLaine, along with another woman named Shirley. They were all looking and waving towards our direction. I looked behind me to see who they were waving at. No one was there. It took me a few moments to realize they were waving at me!

Sheepishly; I shrugged my shoulders and tentatively waved back. The news of my *runner* had apparently circulated throughout the group. The story that

Dean's relative had successfully reached him was way beyond coincidence. It proved I wasn't as invisible as I thought I was.

During a break in the morning Ramtha Dialogue session, my guides prompted me to get up and go talk to Shirley MacLaine even though I was shy. Approaching people, I didn't know, especially celebrities, wasn't easy for me to do. The overwhelming feeling of *energy* directing me to do this was like a volcano under my rear end, which was so intense I couldn't hold myself back from speaking to her. I willed myself to get up out of my chair and walk down the side isle to the front where she was standing so I could introduce myself.

"I am Catherine Ann Clemett. I went to the Washington, DC, summer program at the Washington School of Ballet in 1966." (This is where Shirley had gone to high school and received her ballet training.)

Looking for common ground, I shared, "We had the school's director, Mary Day, as our teacher. Mary would give us corrections by sticking her long, red fingernails into your ankle as she's pushing your leg higher and higher way above your head. Meanwhile, I thought I'd die any minute if she didn't let go of my leg." Shirley could relate.

In the morning session, Shirley had discussed her apprehension with Ramtha about publishing her manuscript, *Out on A Limb*. She was concerned how publishing it might affect her reputation and career. Compelled by my guides to express my opinion on how important I thought it was for her to go ahead with publishing it, I continued.

"I want to let you know how impressed I am by your commitment, your books, and your travel. I love that you have the courage to face the unknown and move forward with a sense of adventure. This is inspiring to me as I am getting ready to move across the country to Oregon. I feel it's really important that you go forth with publishing *Out on A Limb*. The world needs what you have to share."

Who was I to say this to Shirley MacLaine? However, my guides would not leave me alone until I had done it. Shirley just listened.

The rest of the morning Ramtha discussed *bumdum*, as he called it. He talked at length about how bums (homeless people) were among the most enlightened beings on the planet because they're not bound by society's rules as much as most other people were. Ramtha told us he and other ascended beings had appeared in their physical embodiments to all of us.

Rhetorically, he asked, "How many of you knew you'd encountered an ascended master who may have appeared to you perhaps as a bum? "

"How do you suppose you acted around them in your ignorance?"

It sank in that one never knows *who* one might meet. I realized on a deeper level how important it was to release automatic judgment about people and treat everyone I encountered as if they were God, the Christ, or an ascended being, for you never knew if they could be a Master in disguise. Little did I realize at that moment this was the ultimate setup. My friends and I went to lunch and then returned to the dialogue for the afternoon session. The staff asked us to come back a little later as JZ was doing private readings, so Mark, Barry, and I took our tea out to the Boston Commons where we sat down on a park bench. An asphalt sidewalk separated us from an identical bench facing us. There sat a bum, a homeless person, on the bench opposite us. He acted nuts. He gyrated all around in an agitated way talking to himself. I just figured he must be one of the mentally ill people who lived on the streets. As I paid closer attention to his gibberish, he kept going on about some object in the sky. I wondered if he was referring to UFOs, perhaps?

As I continued to watch him, it felt like my heart and soul started doing exuberant flips and somersaults in my chest. Never had I felt anything like that before. Crazy thoughts surfaced as I questioned this bizarre reaction occurring within me. Trying to put it into some kind of context in my mind, I started silently voicing internal questions:

Could this homeless person be my soulmate?

I'd always wanted to be with my soulmate.

Could this strange visceral reaction I was having be because he could be my soulmate?

How crazy was that thought?

As I was engaged in this internal debate, I realized the light in my peripheral vision was so bright I had to squint in order to keep looking at him.

Who is this?

Who is this bum, really?

Chapter 12: Meeting the Masters

The bum was actually quite handsome with curly brown hair, a beard, fine-boned features, and the most piercing light blue eyes I'd ever seen. However, in scrutinizing him, something was wrong with this picture. He looked like he was a big kid dressed up for Halloween who'd taken charcoal and rubbed it all over his face and clothes to make himself look dirty to convince us he was a bum. Yet he didn't smell bad or feel dirty when you were near him. He just looked the part.

Careening his neck as he alternated between looking up to the sky, and then contorting his body as he looked back around himself talking gibberish, I found myself much to my utter surprise, asking him the question out loud.

"What object?"

Immediately, he zeroed in on me.

His blue eyes pierced right through to my soul as he said, "Wouldn't it be nice to hang upside down and swing like a bat?"

Whaaaaat?

Okay then. I'm thinking to myself, you probably are just a crazy homeless guy.

Suddenly, he became lucid and coherent. He started telling us about all the restaurants around the park, informing us where we could get good muffins in one place and great coffee in another. He then asked us where we lived. Barry and I shared that we lived in New York City. Mark said that he lived in Connecticut. He then asked me where I lived in New York.

My first thought was, "Uh, I don't think I want to tell you where I live."

But then I relented, saying, "I live on 15th Street close to Sixth Avenue."

To which he replied, "Oh, I've been on that corner!"

Barry, who was a computer programmer, explained where he lived and that he worked in Manhattan and Long Island. Again, the bum piped up, saying he had also been in the vicinity where Barry lived and also where he worked.

I then told the bum I was getting ready to move to Oregon.

He gave me advice.

"You need to travel light. All you'll need is a little bug and a sleeping bag." I wondered what he meant by that. He continued talking on and on about several places in Washington State—the Olympic Peninsula, Hurricane Ridge, and Mount Rainier. Through it all, I still kept wondering, "Who is this guy?"

This encounter took place on a Sunday afternoon in the park. A family walked down the sidewalk between our two benches. I assumed they had just come from church as they were all dressed up. They were a sizable family group: mother, father, a baby in the stroller, older children, and grandparents in tow. After passing by us, the family's father hung back to yell at the bum.

He exclaimed, "You shouldn't be here. Why aren't you working down in the steel yards?"

The bum just gave him a quizzical look with a glint in his eye.

He shrugged his shoulders and said, "I'm a bum. I enjoy being a bum!"

The man finally realized he wasn't getting anywhere with this bum so he and the family continued on strolling down the sidewalk. Our verbal interaction with the bum resumed. Mark noticed the bum was drinking a rare beer only bottled in one particular plant in Rhode Island.

"Where did you get that beer?" Mark asked the bum.

Pointing to one of the garbage bins in the park he answered, "Got it out of there."

"I'm drinking the water from there!" He pointed to a decorative fountain with water spouting out of the mouth of the cement statue.

He then extended his arm towards me, offering me a sip from his beer bottle.

I was pretty convinced at this point that this bum was an ascended master, as Ramtha had just been talking about in the morning session. There had been too many strange feelings and weird occurrences pointing to this as a possibility.

I kept thinking I should've taken a sip out of the beer bottle he offered to me. Who knows? It could be something miraculous, similar to when Jesus turned the water into wine. However, inside my mind an overwhelming battle of indecision raged. Even though I considered taking a sip from the bottle he offered me, I was in an endless ping-pong game in my mind, alternating between a *yes* and *no* decision.

I knew he was witnessing the dilemma going on in my head. My dualistic mind kept vacillating between the thought of the beer bottle being snatched

Chapter 12: Meeting the Masters

from the public garbage bin containing potentially who knows what contaminated, germ-laden water to the other possibility of being offered potentially some miracle elixir. I knew my discernment was being tested. If he really was an ascended Master, I believe he'd have raised the frequency of what was in the bottle transmuting any germs, negativity or whatever wasn't safe to ingest. My mind hit the wall. I couldn't vacillate forever. I concluded I just couldn't go there accepting a drink from the bottle he offered me. Finally, ending this stand-off in my mind, I thanked him.

"I am not thirsty. I just finished my tea," was my response.

I had to say something to him. I also realized that by refusing to take him up on his offer, I would never know what was really in that beer bottle.

We had to get back. As I stood up to leave, the bum stood up and came over right in front of my face.

He innocently interrogated me. "Did you kill someone?"

In the way he asked, there was no hint of judgment or accusation. The question confused me as it felt so open-ended.

"I don't think so," I responded.

It was such a bizarre thing to ask. At the moment he asked me if I'd killed someone, all of my doubts came up. There was no way to discern if he really was an ascended Master or just some crazy bum. I walked away and didn't look back.

This encounter would have great significance in changing the direction of my life. However, it wouldn't be until twenty-five years later that all the pieces would come together for this understanding. Everything the bum said to me in that encounter, which sounded crazy at the time, turned out to be clues and markers on my timeline over those next twenty-five years of my life.

After the Boston dialogue, I only had a few weeks to move out of my apartment sublet and get ready to move to Oregon. In the last few days, I was in New York I stayed with my friend Jill on the Upper West Side. She lived in an upscale apartment building on Riverside Avenue. I had just been shopping, getting all kinds of supplies for cleaning and moving. Laden with bags and packages, I went into the lobby of her building to wait for the elevator.

As I entered her foyer, a well-dressed black man pressed the buzzer of someone in the building. I continued on into the lobby. As I walked towards the elevator I realized I hadn't heard the buzzer ring allowing him to come in the front door, nor had I heard the front door click shut. I usually wouldn't pay attention to this but for some reason this time, I did. The man entered the lobby after me.

At that moment, I heard a loud male voice in my head, command me to take the stairs. I hesitated because Jill lived on the third floor which was a long walk up the stairs with so many packages. Just then, the elevator door opened. I got in. The man quickly crossed the lobby and followed me into the elevator. The elevator started its ascent. He stood quietly with his hands folded and his chin bowed to his chest. Concerned when I got on the elevator, I now thought to myself, maybe I was wrong about this person. Suddenly just before we reached the 3rd floor where I was getting off, he reached out past me and pressed the stop button on the elevator, stopping it between the 2nd and 3rd floor.

He demanded all my money, jewelry, whatever I had. I froze, paralyzed with shock.

He screamed, "Are you resisting me?"

Then he pulled a switchblade out of his pocket. In my momentary stupor it took my brain a couple of seconds to register that the sharp blade of a death weapon was pressed against my throat. Terrified and immovable, my bladder involuntarily let go, sending a river of hot pee gushing down my legs. I fumbled through my purse and gave him all my money, about $60, and whatever else he asked for. He got off on the third floor and barked at me not to follow him.

I continued going up and got off the elevator on a higher floor, waited a few minutes until I thought it was safe, then went back down to Jill's apartment totally shaken up. I tried to file a police report. The police wouldn't even take a report from me as this was such a common occurrence in New York.

The gift of this experience, I later realized, was the release of any lingering doubt about receiving and perceiving guidance from the other side. This was the first time I unmistakably and loudly heard guidance from the *other side* rather than it being just a vague feeling. That still small voice inside had become a shouted command, which unfortunately I didn't follow. Next time I would know better.

This was also definitely a sign it was time for me to leave New York. Days later, my cat and I boarded the plane to Oregon, starting a whole new chapter on the West Coast.

Chapter 13: Mystery Solved, Yet Deepens

My Siamese cat, Angel, and I arrived in Oregon. We made our way down to the town of Florence about halfway down the Oregon coast. Here we met up with Linda, the woman whom I had visited in Oregon. Linda had a Ph.D. in Education; however, there weren't any jobs for people with her qualifications in this sleepy little coastal town. So, she did the next best thing; she opened a daycare center. I moved in with her and helped her run the Rainbow Winds Daycare Center. My job was to make the lunches and snacks for the kids and help with the daily activities while Linda focused on running the daily day care center operation.

Living in Florence, Oregon was a far cry from where I had been living. Living in Florence turned into an experience of decompressing from years of living a fast-paced, overstimulated existence in New York City. However, there wasn't much to do in Florence. We could only go out to eat at Mo's Chowder or Abbey's Pizza so many times a week. The movie theater in town was only open on Saturdays and Sundays, so with few options of things to do, Linda and I took to roaming the aisles of the Safeway Supermarket to entertain ourselves in the evenings.

The most exciting times were when people came to stay with us. Ramtha started sending dozens of his students to check out the possibility of moving to the Pacific Northwest. In the summer of 1982, we must have had about sixty or more Ramtha people pass through Florence. During the day, we used the house for the daycare center. But at night our house became a dormitory for all the people passing through. We would invite them to spend the night sleeping in their sleeping bags on the living room floor.

Often in the evenings we would go down to the beach at South Jetty to watch the skies for signs of UFOs, as Ramtha talked about them frequently. During weekends, we went to Ramtha Dialogue if one was scheduled in either Seattle or San Francisco, we and whoever was visiting us would all pile into the daycare van. We'd leave late on a Friday afternoon and drive the long distance to the event. We would also have social gatherings of friends we knew from Ramtha events, and other like-minded people, who lived in the area at our house. During one of these gatherings, an acquaintance named Bob invited me to stop by and visit him at his apartment in Depoe Bay if I was ever passing through. Since I had no plans to drive up to Lincoln City, passing through Depoe Bay, I just tucked this invitation away in the back recesses of my mind.

After living and working with Linda at the day care center for about nine months, I wanted to be closer to the Ramtha happenings. I moved up to Tumwater, Washington, into a house owned by this woman, Elizabeth, JZ Knight's secretary. She was at full capacity for the number of roommates who could live in the house, so I ended up moving out into the garage. Putting plywood down on the garage floor, covering it with rugs, and bringing a bed and bureau out of the house I was able to make it into my bedroom space. It was okay for a while since I was there during the warm weather months.

Meanwhile, I reconnected with Dean Thompson and Thomas Sharkey, who had moved to Washington State. Dean channeled this entity named Solano. When I went to one of the Solano channeling events, I asked Solano about the experience I'd had with the bum in Boston the previous year.

"Was the bum I met last year in the Boston Commons an ascended Master? Was that his body?"

Solano replied, "He is one who has seen the folly of this plane and no longer lives by its rules. Yes, that was his body. You drew him to you. It was your experience and you will see him again."

See him again!

How could that happen I wondered?

Chapter 13: Mystery Solved, Yet Deepens

I didn't know how I felt about seeing this bum again. Events surrounding the first meeting with him were confusing enough! It served to only deepen the mystery. After a few months of living in Washington State, when the weather turned colder, I went back to Oregon to live. This time I lived with a friend and her family, whom I had met at a Ramtha Dialogue. They lived in Tillamook, further up the Oregon coast from where I had lived before. One day while driving along the Oregon Coast, I remembered my acquaintance Bob's invitation from two years before to stop and visit him in Depoe Bay. It seemed like a good time to take him up on his offer. I arrived at his small apartment, with its gigantic picture windows offering a gorgeous panoramic view of Depoe Bay. The view was spectacular! He invited me in. Although happy to see me, he was even more excited to show me something.

I had barely entered the apartment when he exclaimed, "Here, you've gotta try this! You must try this!"

Sitting me down on the couch, he had me remove my shoes. Then he put these massive fiberglass boots with big hooks on the back on my feet. I wasn't sure what this was about yet. He had me help him move his bureau over to his bedroom doorway so we could pull the drawers out for me to use them like a stepladder. This enabled me to climb up and hook the boots on the metal bar spanning the width of his bedroom doorway. He then moved the bureau away from me and helped me straighten myself out. I was now hanging down, facing into his bedroom.

He gave me a gentle push. I found myself upside down, swinging in the doorway staring at a large four-to five-foot poster on his bedroom wall opposite the doorway. It was obviously some Ascended Master.

I asked, "Who's the Master?"

He said, "St. Germain."

This was the first time I'd ever heard this Master's name or seen his image in this life that I was aware of.

It took me until the next morning to finally realize there I was, *hanging upside down and swinging like a bat!* That was the very first thing the crazy bum in the Boston Common said to me two years earlier. It then occurred to me that the bum in Boston must have been the Ascended Master, St. Germain.

Raising My Frequency

Even though I now knew this Master's name, I knew nothing about him, so I had to research who he was and why he was important. I could only find this out through books, as this experience happened in 1984, well before being able to us the Internet for research. Over the next few years, I learned a lot about St. Germain. I eventually bought a laminated picture of him at a metaphysical bookstore in Mt. Shasta many years later.

Shocked to see that this picture of him looked almost exactly how he had appeared to me other than, in person, his hair was curly in ringlets rather than being wavy. His eyes were a lighter, more piercing blue color than the image which I bought of him portrayed. An attractive, rather fine-boned man, it was unmistakably him!

After staying with this family in Tillamook for a while, I again knew it was time to find a new living situation. I saw an ad for a roommate on a bulletin board at the Post Office in Oceanside, Oregon, a little coastal town outside of Tillamook. What I hadn't noticed on the ad was that the guy was looking for another guy to move in. Somehow, I skipped that fact. He agreed to let me move in as his roommate anyway, since most of the time he stayed with his girlfriend in Tillamook. He was rarely at his house. I loved his house. It was high on a hill overlooking the ocean and beach at Oceanside. Often hang gliders would launch from the hills above and soar down over the house.

The Cape Meares Lighthouse was just down the road from his house. I would often go there to meditate and hang out at the Octopus Tree. For years, I had been searching the skies, hoping to see a UFO not realizing I'd already seen one when I lived in Hawaii in the 70's. It hadn't registered at that time that the faint speck I had watched while I was lying in the grass outside the cafeteria in the middle of the day was a UFO. For several minutes it zigzagged through the sunlit sky at right angles.

I still, however, had a strong desire to see a UFO, one that I absolutely knew was a UFO. One evening at dusk, I went down to Cape Meares. I sat on a mound of grass next to the parking area. It was getting dark. Suddenly, I got scared. All these terrifying thoughts went running through my head.

What if one really came?

What if one landed?

Chapter 13: Mystery Solved, Yet Deepens

It would freak me out!
What would I do?

Nothing happened, or so I thought. As I was driving back up the hill to the house, high over the tree line, I saw this bright shooting star move horizontally along the horizon line with the largest tail I'd ever seen. I remember thinking to myself, *that's not a shooting star!*

That night I had this day-glow lucid dream. I rarely remember my dreams, but this was different and very detailed. In the dream, a giant mother ship came over the house like the mother ship in the movie *Close Encounters of the Third Kind*. It beamed me aboard like the 'beam me up Scotty' command in Star Trek. In the dream, I sat on the floor in a semicircle with five other people. Three tall opaque extra-terrestrial beings with large black almond-shaped eyes were instructing us how to project peace from the region of our solar plexus. I noticed a metal staircase leading up to a balcony surrounding the room in which I found myself. There were all kinds of different alien species and people everywhere. I saw human children hanging on the banisters, along with military people up on the balcony. There was a lot of activity going on. It reminded me a little bit of the bar scene in Star Wars.

Next, a being had me follow them as they ushered me through a maze of corridors towards the outside wall of the spaceship. They beckoned me into a compact room filled with shelves with what looked like dozens of egg carton crates filled with soil.

The beings had these huge hypodermic-needle-looking devices that worked with pneumatic air pressure to inject seeds into the soil of the egg-crate-looking containers. It amazed me to witness how the seeds germinated and grew into fully mature plants before one's eyes in a matter of minutes. Fifteen years later, I read a specific, very detailed, channeled account which shared the same information regarding how extra-terrestrials grew food on their ships.

Whoa!

Now I believed this experience truly happened and wasn't just a dream.

I led a simple life in Oceanside. I would spend time on the beach and hike along the coastal trails nearby. By this time, my injuries from the car accident which ended my dance career several years earlier had healed enough so I could at least teach preschool-age children to dance in Tillamook and Netarts. I also helped another friend run a daycare center in Tillamook.

Easter Sunday was coming up. I was looking forward to spending it with friends who had invited me to a gathering in Lincoln City. The day before Easter, however, I woke up sick with a bad sore throat. I realized I should stay home and not go anywhere. Disappointed, I was trying to think of what I could do to feel less lonely having to stay home by myself.

Since Ramtha had talked about how the Masters have taken bodies and appeared to all of us, I came up with the idea to invite the Masters I knew to celebrate Easter with me. So, I invited Jesus, Ramtha, and St. Germain, as those were the only Masters who I knew of at that point to come and eat Easter dinner with me.

Writing out an invitation card addressed to each one of them, I burned them in the fireplace. I prepared dinner as if they would show up physically at my doorstep, making enough food for a special dinner to feed all of us. After that, I took a bath and got dressed up in my good clothes like I would for a dinner party.

Who knows?

I had to allow for the remote possibility they could show up in the flesh. I didn't think they would, but I wanted to be ready in case they did show up. Even though they did not physically show up, energetically, I knew they were there.

The next several hours were amazing. I was in some of the highest, most altered states of consciousness and *energy*, I've ever experienced. I knew they had facilitated raising my frequency, my vibration, so I could experience a much more expanded awareness, understanding, and experience of reality beyond my usual level of consciousness. For instance, they had me focus my attention on a tree.

When I was really being fully present with the tree, they would say, "I am that."

Then they would direct my focus to the next thing, and the next after that.

As I could be fully present with each thing presented to me, repeatedly I kept being told, "I am that. I am that. I am that."

Chapter 13: Mystery Solved, Yet Deepens

This was years before I came across a book titled, *I Am That*.

All the time I was living in Tillamook and in Oceanside, I was still attending Ramtha events. The last full weekend event I went to was the *Soulmate Intensive* in Seattle in January 1986. The members of the large audience attending this event were all whistling, catcalling, and acting like Ramtha was Michael Jackson or something. It had gotten too large for it to be an intimate back-and-forth exchange with Ramtha like it was in the earlier years of the Ramtha Dialogues. I knew I didn't need to go anymore. It wasn't Ramtha that put me off, but his followers who were acting more like a fan club than serious seekers of the wisdom and truth he offered. I couldn't handle or didn't want to be part of it anymore. I didn't feel like I was leaving Ramtha, as I knew he was still with me.

When the Ramtha School of Enlightenment, officially founded in 1988, asked if I wanted to attend the school, I rejected the offer. As tempting as it was, I had to follow my greater knowing, which was that I felt I was complete with Ramtha. However, Barry, my boyfriend that I had when I was in New York, who eventually moved to Washington State a few years after I moved to Oregon, joined the Ramtha School when it started. He was a student there for the next twenty years.

Later, in 1986 I met another channel, Penny Torres Rubin, who channeled an entity called Mafu, which was very similar to how JZ channeled Ramtha. Mafu said he was an incarnation of the Pharaoh Akhenaton. I loved Mafu. He referred to himself as the comforter. During one Mafu event which I attended, I was sitting in a seat at the end of a row in the auditorium. Mafu, and entity being channeled through Penny's body, came up to me and put his (Penny, the channel's) hand on my heart. Immediately, out of nowhere, I broke down in heaving sobs.

He asked, "Why is this (gesturing towards my heart) breaking?"

I hadn't any idea why.

Mafu continued addressing me, "The biggest thing holding you back from knowing you are God, and from going home (ascending), is the judgment you placed on yourself and held in your soul for murdering a baby of yours. It is like a giant timber in your eye."

Then he related the story of how I had once lived in a time and a place where men would use children, particularly little girls, to fight. Today in certain countries they do this with roosters-cock fighting or dog fighting, but in that life, they used children. Mafu said the men placed bets on these children forcing them to fight. If these young girls survived childhood without dying in these fights, upon childbearing age, men then took these girls as mates. This had happened to me. In this other life, I became pregnant and gave birth to a baby girl. It was only out of my great love for her and my overwhelming fear that she was doomed to suffer the same fate that I had endured that I took her life. I murdered her!

He said the horror of it was so beyond what I could cope with that I went numb in my soul and was never being able to forgive myself for it. He said that all of my physical problems, my pelvic pain and surgery, my diseased conditions, my inability to have satisfying love relationships, my money difficulties and my not feeling successful in this life, all stemmed from this incident.

Overtime, as I did the deep inner work on healing this incident, I came to understand how I, in that lifetime, was only a child severely traumatized and abused from a very early age. When I gave birth I was no older than twelve or thirteen years old. Abuse, pain, and suffering were all I'd ever known in that lifetime.

How could I truly forgive myself for this?
How could I know if it is true?
If I forgave myself, will this get rid of all the pain, fear, and doubt in my life?
How can I even connect with the memory of this?

In retrospect, these questions were the entry point for me to understand and re-assemble the jigsaw puzzle of my shattered self, which I'd always tried to figure out. This missing piece was the key for me in putting myself back together in wholeness. I saw how the challenges and patterns in my life were not only a result of living a blueprint that wasn't mine in this lifetime, but these challenges also came from a deeper energetic disturbance from this other lifetime. Awakening isn't always about reaching bliss and the heights of consciousness. It is being able to face and forgive the darkest shadows within one's self so the truth can set you free. At age fourteen I asked to understand and know what *energy* meant. As bits of information about my soul's journey started falling into place, I realized I was receiving cosmic lessons about *energy*.

Energy exists in a frequency range from negative low frequency states of fear, hatred, blame, greed, and self-serving attitudes to that of high vibrational *energy* states of love, bliss, insight, and selfless service. I was being shown the imprints of my lower frequency states of *energy* to prepare for the next stage of my journey of learning how to shift and heal these debilitating negative states. I share the full story of this in my book, Soulweaving, Return to the Heart of the Mother.

The very last thing that the bum in Boston asked me was, "Did you kill somebody?"

The clue was there all along.

Shortly after receiving this information from Mafu, I was at work one day running the restaurant part of a health food store On Bainbridge Island when one of the regular customers walked in. Upon seeing her, my entire body went into goosebumps. In that moment, I absolutely knew she had been the baby in that lifetime whom I'd murdered. Even though we were only casual acquaintances, I told her what I had been told by Mafu. I share with her that I knew she had been my baby. Rather than thinking I was a total crackpot, this acquaintance agreed that it also felt true for her. She had no residual energy of blame, judgment, or accusation; nothing but love was present.

The only place there was still residual *energy* around this still existing, was within me. I had to figure out how to deal with it in a way which would truly shift the frequency of this negative imprint within me. I started by writing a forgiveness letter to the baby I'd murdered, which I called *love no matter what*. Then my guides had me re-script the whole situation. For 30 days they had me do a meditation every day where rather than the baby dying, I was to take her and heal her from the brink of death in my mind. Then I was to care for her and raise her just like I was scripting a movie. Slowly by doing this process, the negative imprint, emotional trauma, and deep grief within my soul around this began to ease up.

During the couple of years, I attended Mafu events, I had another one of my thirty-second experiences where it felt like the veil to experiencing beyond ordinary reality suddenly and unexpectedly opened. At a Mafu event in Seattle after our lunch break, I was hiking back up to the event from eating lunch down on the waterfront. As I placed one foot in front of the other while climbing up the hill, with each step I took it felt like the sidewalk lovingly rushed up to cradle my foot with the most exquisite sensation.

The sidewalk gently greeted each of my footsteps, cushioning my foot with love. Even though it was only a brief experience, it was a profound moment of connection in a way I'd never felt before. It amazed me that this feeling came from a sidewalk, of all things, an inanimate object! It further reminded me that everything, even inanimate objects, have a "heart," a frequency range, and have not only a connection to Source, but actually are an emanation of Source. It was an example of how divine reflection is present in relation to everything if I but allow it.

Chapter 14: Men, Money, and Miracles

In dealing with certain soul lessons and themes in this book, the chapters are not always in strict chronological order. In the summer of 1984, I got a job working for Guest Services up at Mt. Rainier in Washington State. My assigned job was to run the rural Post Office in the lodge at Paradise Inn. We usually worked six days a week with one day off which for me was always on Sunday because it corresponded to the United States Postal Service's schedule. Most of the time on my day off I would drive my old beater Ford Pinto car down the mountain to see friends in Purdy, Washington, near Gig Harbor.

My car's ugly appearance, more indicative of low lifers than someone like me, didn't fit my image at all. But it was cheap! My plan was to drive it for perhaps six months and then trade it in for a better car. However, my financial life never got upgraded enough. I ended up driving that car, aptly named Little Red Dent, for the next six years instead of only for the next six months as I'd planned. The driver's door eventually became sprung and was unusable, forcing me to get in and out of the car through the passenger side. I struggled to climb over the stick shift until I could finally plop down in the driver's seat. It all got old after a few years.

While visiting my friend on my day off, I would sometimes go to this beautiful park about a fifteen—or twenty-minute drive down this spur on the peninsula before heading back up the mountain. One gorgeous late August afternoon, I spent an hour by myself with no one else around in this wonderful park. I needed to start heading back to Paradise on Mt. Rainier before it got too dark to drive up the mountain. When I went to start my car—no such luck. Repeatedly, I tried to start the car, but the motor just wouldn't turn over. Utterly alone, what was I to do? I had seen no one. This was 1984, way before cell phones. It would've taken me hours to walk back up the road in the dark to get help. I just sat there trying to remain calm and not let my fears overtake me as I faced this dilemma.

My now dead car was in a little parking area just off the road into the park. Suddenly, out of nowhere, a man wearing coveralls came strolling around the bend into the turnoff for the parking lot. No one else was around. I saw no other cars, nor had I heard any cars or heard anyone. I didn't know how he got there; but he just stood in front of me asking me if I needed help. I did.

Fortunately, I didn't feel any trepidation during this encounter. He had me pop open the hood so he could see if he could find the problem. He started tinkering, all the while pulling out various tools from the recesses of the deep pockets of his coveralls. It seemed something had clogged up the carburetor along with flooding it with my repeated tries at getting the engine started. He did something to the carburetor which unclogged it. Finally, after being patient for a little while, the motor started. I thanked the man and offered to pay him something for his trouble, which he wouldn't accept. He just wished me a pleasant day and then disappeared as mysteriously as he arrived. There was no logical explanation for this. The whole afternoon I had not seen or heard anyone other than him.

Who was this guy?
Where did he come from?
Could he possibly be a Master who had materialized just to help me out?
Was his spontaneous appearance similar to St. Germain's years before?

These weren't questions that had a logical, reasonable, answer, so I didn't dwell on it. I was just so grateful to have his help in getting me out of that predicament.

While working up at Mt. Rainier, in my off hours I also resumed experimenting with automatic writing. For many years, I had attempted to do this but often felt frustrated. Most of the time all my hand wanted to do was to draw circles, shapes and sigils, more so than words. Far from being secure with

Chapter 14: Men, Money, and Miracles

the process, I was always too self-critical. Eventually, I realized that my hand wasn't going to write words by itself without some involvement from my mind's participation. I had been trying to disassociate my mind from the process of my hand writing words or drawing pictures. Finally, I had to give myself permission to let the words tumble into my mind without censoring them. I didn't know what to make of it when I scribbled a sentence, *as to your lover...*

My lover?

What?

What lover?

Ever hopeful that an amazing relationship would show-up, I was more than a little surprised. The automatic writing message said this lover would be considerably different from anyone I'd been with before, so I needed to be open and prepared for that possibility.

What did that mean?

After receiving this message, I kept my eyes peeled for this lover to show up.

Week after week, as the summer up at Paradise flew by, no one even remotely interesting to me showed up. Disappointed like usual, I figured I just must have made this message up because I wanted it to happen so much. It was hard to distinguish and trust whether the message was coming from some kind of intuition, foretelling of a real possibility, or not.

About six weeks into the season at Mt. Rainier, I heard through the grapevine that management had fired someone from the front desk team and then hired a guy from Wales to replace them. This new hire had been visiting Paradise Inn as a tourist, accompanied by a friend of his mother's whom he had been visiting. While at Paradise Inn, he'd heard there was a job opening, so he applied. In the back of my mind, I wondered if he could be the person referred to in the automatic writing message.

The next morning, I finally saw this new hire for the first time. Bounding down the stairs, looking somewhat like an overgrown adolescent who appeared way too juvenile for me, I said to myself,

"No way. That can't be the person referred to in the automatic writing."

So, I wrote him off and didn't even think about it again. Several days later, he took notice of me when we both shared a table in the employee cafeteria. We struck up an interesting conversation. A few days after that he came into the Post Office to buy some international stamps. However, he came in the back door of my post office cubicle only accessible from the front desk area rather than coming around the front to the customer window. Sidling up to me, invading my personal space, he stood so close to me he was practically breathing down my neck. I was instantly on alert that something more was going on here.

This new hire, Geoffrey, was twenty-three years old, while I was thirty-two. The automatic writing message miraculously turned out to be right. Despite our age difference, we eventually became lovers. Almost everybody working up on the mountain for the season had been pairing off. I lived in the girl's dorm, which was on the top floor of the Mountaineering Guide house building across from Paradise Inn. My eighteen-year-old roommate had already moved in with a guy in the boy's dorm, which was down past the Visitor Center.

Since I no longer had a roommate, Geoffrey moved into my room with me. We took the bunk beds apart and pushed them together into one double bed, our home for the rest of summer up at Paradise. It was great to have a hiking buddy, a lover, and a companion up on the mountain. I also met another person who was to become important in my life, my friend Kay. She was a few years older than me. Kay and I were the only thirty-some things working for Guest Services among a sea of mostly eighteen-year-old kids working up at Mt Rainier that summer.

Near the end of the season, Geoffrey and I took off a little early from our contracts to travel around a bit until it was time for his return flight to Wales. Before coming to the States, he had bought a round-trip airline ticket, arriving in May and leaving in September. When Geoffrey flew back to Wales, I wasn't quite ready to let go of the relationship yet, so I entered a hard transition period once again.

After leaving Mt. Rainier, I returned to the Portland area but had a hard time finding work. Finally, in desperation I ended up taking a job delivering Domino's Pizza in a bad section of Portland for a brief time. Depressed about Geoffrey leaving and also heartbroken that I'd had to surrender my cat to the

Chapter 14: Men, Money, and Miracles

humane society when I couldn't find anyone to care for her when I went to work at Mt. Rainier, I entered a period of the dark night of the soul.

Nothing was working in my life. Besides my heartbreak over Geoffrey's leaving and having to give up my cat, I wasn't making enough money. I was in a dead-end, going-nowhere, job. A series of challenges hit me all at once. My car had mechanical problems which I didn't have the money to fix. Then, my roommate informed me I would need to find another place to live by the end of the month. It seemed things couldn't have gotten any worse.

During this challenging time, all I kept thinking about was how Ramtha had taught us that we were great creator beings, even though I didn't feel like one at that moment. Feeling like I was in a straitjacket with nowhere to turn, nor any idea how to fix the problems in my life, I shut myself away in my bedroom for the next thirty-six hours. All of my emotions of frustration, anger, and fear poured out of me as I pounded pillows, cried and exhausted myself. Throughout it all, I kept dwelling on the thought of what a powerful Creator God I was.

But what was I truly creating?

I reasoned I was such a powerful Creator God that all I seemed to create was darkness, which obliterated everything I wanted in my life.

Throughout this thirty-six-hour period, I kept affirming and thanking the universe for me for being such a powerful Creator God that all I was creating was darkness. That was what was in the space. I kept thanking the universe all night like it was a mantra. I was in absolute gratitude, acknowledging my power for what was showing up in my life, even if it was negative. I realized how powerful I was to create such darkness, challenge, and misery in my life. Rather than in any way trying to change the circumstances, I just kept acknowledging the tremendous power I had to create such darkness and despair in my life. After falling asleep for a while, I awoke to the sensation of light flooding my room. It was like it was coming from under the bedroom door from the bottom up. The most miraculous aspect of this experience was that my entire life shifted in the next thirty-six hours without me doing one external thing! Everything just magically fell into my lap. Somehow, I had gotten out of the way of myself. I realize now that despite the appearances, the victimization, despair and negativity expressing in my life what I had really done was to shift my automatic response of contraction and fear to a conscious and deliberate action to raise my frequency through gratitude for these experiences showing me how much of a powerful creator God I was.

Geoffrey phoned me from Wales, saying he missed me. He asked if he could come back and live with me for a year.

I said, "Yes."

My uncle's brother whom I'd only met once before who lived in the area called me up out of the blue. I told him about my car problems, and he offered to fix my car in his garage if I could get it over to his house. Also, an acquaintance who lived on Mercer Island in the Seattle area called me to say she was getting together a household of Ramtha people. She asked if I wanted to come live there. I asked her if Geoffrey could come too. So, when Geoffrey came back to live with me, we moved into this Ramtha household on Mercer Island and found work in Seattle. We went on with our lives. This experience was to be a forerunner of an intense experience which would take place later in my life, giving me a deeper understanding of what it means to be in non-resistance.

One evening after moving to Mercer Island, everyone had left the house. I was there alone. Cleaning up the dining room table after dinner, absentmindedly standing there with the sponge in my hand, the veils of consciousness again momentarily parted. My perception of reality suddenly shifted into such a feeling of bliss and completeness; I didn't even need to take a next breath.

Overtaken by absolute peace, cohesion, oneness, and wholeness which engulfed me to such a degree, I didn't even have a hint of any struggle, doubt or want. Nothing was lacking or needed. Eventually, my perceptual of reality again returned to its usual state.

What on earth was that?

Was this an experience of what it feels like to be in unity consciousness?

Being back in my questioning mind took me out of this exalted frequency. Even though it was a fleeting experience, the experience was so profound, I realized I could go back and relive it at any time. Whenever I am fearful or

Chapter 14: Men, Money, and Miracles

distressed, going back to it would help me get back into a state of more perfect balance and harmony. As with my other brief moments of spontaneously altered states, this experience just furthered my quest to understand and know more.

Eventually, Geoffrey and I left the Ramtha household on Mercer Island. We moved into a house with another group of friends on Bainbridge Island across Puget Sound from Seattle. This group of friends also included our friend Kay, whom we'd met while working up at Paradise Inn on Mt. Rainier. I had been working for a temp agency, Manpower, in Seattle. I would go to different job sites for a few weeks, then was off to the next assignment. Manpower had job contracts with various companies who paid Manpower for contract labor, and then Manpower paid us.

One of my jobs through Manpower was to package up the initial release of the Windows Operating System Program over at Microsoft. However, this still wasn't my idea of a career. Now that we were living on Bainbridge Island, it became inconvenient, tiring, and expensive to commute on the ferry every day to Seattle. Sometimes I would even have to take my car on the ferry if the job wasn't right in downtown Seattle.

Although grateful to have a job and income, I still wondered where my life was going and what my purpose was. I felt like I did when I was fourteen. I still felt there had to be *more* to life, which I'd somehow missed. Now, however, I felt like I was just marking time. One day while commuting from Seattle, I remember being on the top of the ferry deck, alone in the rain. Sobbing, I shouted out to the universe and to God. I pleaded to be used to make a difference somehow, to be of service. However, it would take over twenty-plus years until God granted my plea and that path of service came fully into view.

I started looking for a job on Bainbridge Island. Fortunately, I had a friend who cooked and ran the restaurant part of the Natural Gourmet, a health food store located down behind the island's Town and Country Grocery store who was looking for a replacement. I applied for the job and got hired. My friend Valerie trained me for a few weeks, then I took over running the cafe.

Getting to work about 5 am each morning, I'd make a daily soup, and several daily deli salads similar to ones you would find at Whole Foods today.

I'd also make green salads with tahini dressing, as well as pesto, croutons, and sushi which we sold in the deli case each day. Prepping everything for making sandwiches, green salads, and a hot special every day, I had to complete it all well before the lunch crowd arrived as I also served as the waitress for the lunch customers. Having this job was fortunate in that I got to meet several of the local people. By this time, Geoffrey, who had been back living with me for a year, decided he was ready to return home to Wales. It shouldn't have surprised me since he'd been sending all of his money, other than what he contributed for food, home to Wales during this entire time.

He'd contributed nothing towards building a stronger relationship and future with me. Also, he would get phone calls all the time from his former high school girlfriend. Even when I answered the phone, she was rude to me, pretending I didn't exist. Geoffrey was true to his word. When he came back to live with me, he only lived with me for a year. He actually left on my birthday to fly back to Wales. I was devastated yet again. A short time after Geoffrey left, my previous boyfriend, Barry, finally made the move out of New York to the west coast.

He came to live in the house with us as a roommate on Bainbridge Island. Barry and I were no longer romantically involved, just wonderful friends. It was nice to have him living on Bainbridge Island. His moving into the household also helped me get over the heartbreak I felt from Geoffrey leaving me. Within a short time after returning to Wales, Geoffrey married his former high school sweetheart.

Despite all of this, a bright spot showed up among all of the drama. I bought a pair of cowboy type boots at a Track-N-Trail shoe store in Silverdale, WA. When I went to pay, there was a shoe box on the counter announcing contests for winning walking tours of Tibet, Nepal, or Machu Picchu in Peru. I've always wanted to go to the Himalayas, so I entered my name, address, and phone number in the entry form. About three months later, a miracle happened. I received a certified letter in the mail announcing that my entry was the first place drawing out of twenty-nine stores on the west coast. I had won the trip to Machu Picchu. Mountain Travel in San Francisco and Rockport

Shoes sponsored the contest. I'd won one spot on a Mountain Travel Tour to Peru along with a professional camera, airfare and all expenses paid.

Told I'd receive a call from a sales rep with all the details, I kept waiting, but the call never came. Wondering if the trip was real or a hoax, I called Mountain Travel to find out. I explained that I'd received notification about winning a trip but hadn't received any information about it yet. They transferred me to someone named Dick McGowan to answer my questions about winning the trip. He assured me it was legit. I found out he used to run the Guide Service up at Mountain Rainier at one point, so I shared that I ran the Post Office at Paradise Inn one season and that my dorm room had been on the top floor of the Guide Service building. What synchronicity!

I then told him I had looked up the Peru trips in the Mountain Travel Brochure but didn't know which one I'd won–if it was the eight-day trip or the twelve-day trip. He told me if I preferred the twelve-day trip to the eight-day trip, it didn't make any difference to them. He said when the salesperson called me to set up the trip to just tell them that Dick McGowan said choosing the twelve-day trip was fine. Later, I found out he was the Vice President of Mountain Travel. Of course, I chose the twelve-day trip which included two days in Lima, two days in Cuzco, two days of river rafting on the Urubamba River, two days in the jungle canopy of the Amazon at Puerto Maldonado, and four days hiking the Inca Trail to Machu Picchu. I knew I would need to get myself physically into shape to do this trip. I started walking up and down the hills in this park on Bainbridge Island almost every day for the next five months, getting myself prepared.

There were sixteen of us on the tour. Most of the people on the tour were senior citizens from a hiking club in New Zealand. They were in much better physical shape than any of the rest of us younger folks. One of my favorite parts of the trip was the two days of river rafting, even the part where we had to navigate a class-three rapids. Mostly, we floated serenely by little Peruvian villages where we watched the villagers performed their daily chores: washing their clothes in the river and drying them on rocks. Life appeared to be simple and idyllic here. Hotels outside of the larger cities were a little sketchy, however. The hotel we stayed in near the area where the boats launched onto the river was an ornate building with a beautiful courtyard, but few other desirable features.

Hot water for guests was only available for about an hour early in the morning, and again for an hour in the evening. The reoccurring decor seemed to be a multitude of electrical boxes hanging down from the walls, suspended from a few wires. You couldn't even flush any toilet paper down the toilets. Everything had to go into a receptacle next to the toilet. Such was part of the education of traveling in a third-world country.

After completing our river rafting part of the trip, we next went to stay in the jungle canopy outside of Puerto Maldonado. To get there, we had to travel at night for several hours on a covered canoe in the dark. The helmsman knew every bend of the river and navigated it by feel instead of through visual cues, as it was pitch black and we couldn't see a thing. We had no choice but to trust him.

Finally, we arrived at a little compound of thatched roofed huts up on stilts lit only by kerosene lamps as there was no electricity there. We had to abide by certain rules to stay safe, including brushing our teeth with Coca-Cola or Inca Cola which resembled orange soda We couldn't even risk putting any local water into our mouths for fear of getting nasty parasites.

A whole cacophony of noises greeted us in the morning from the lush tropical jungle teeming with everything from exotic colorful birds and other animals to silent piranha in the ponds and streams. Despite the primitive conditions, the staff took good care of us. For breakfast they made us gigantic pancakes. However, after a few bites, they settled like cement in our stomachs. Unfortunately, the pancakes were the mainstay of the breakfast menu for the next couple of days.

Each morning, much to our dismay, there were these giant pancakes greeting us, yet again. In the afternoon of our last day in Puerto Maldonado, a couple was celebrating their fiftieth wedding anniversary. The kitchen staff brought out this enormous cake, all frosted and beautifully decorated. We were all looking forward to eating it. It was only when they cut into the cake that we realized they'd made it with about ten layers of the dreaded pancakes with jam spread between the layers. We couldn't believe it. It made us laugh, however.

Chapter 14: Men, Money, and Miracles

The four days of trekking the Inca Trail were both breathtaking and terrifying. We hiked through magnificent scenery of mountains, valleys, and ruins along the way. The downside, however, was that we each got sick somewhere along the trek. My roommate got sick the first night. The porters took her out on a pack mule. Fortunately, my wave of dysentery didn't hit until we were back at the hotel in Cusco. I was lucky to be in my hotel room with a bathroom while I was losing it at both ends. Many participants got sick while still on the trail, so I was fortunate that the only hardship I suffered through this illness was a lost shopping day in Cusco because of it.

The second day trekking up the mountain we came across a thriving little business in which a woman living in a hut along the trail sold ice-cold Coca-Cola and Inca Cola to trekkers hiking the Inca trail. She must have kept the sodas buried in the earth somehow or had some other way of keeping them cold, as there was no electricity in her hut. The second night I was by myself in the tent since they had already packed my roommate out by mule.

When I woke up the next morning, something very large was firmly pressing up against the top of my head on the other side of the large canvas tent. I couldn't imagine what it could be. I gingerly ventured out of the tent only to discover it was the back end of a cow which had been lying up against my head. We had camped in the center of a tiny village. All the animals—cows, chickens, pigs, donkeys, and dogs—freely roamed wherever they wanted to go.

The four days of trekking were strenuous as we had to go through two mountain passes, one twelve thousand feet high and the other one fourteen thousand feet high. Our guides gave us big wads of cocoa leaves to chew on to help us adjust to the altitude. Cocoa leaves have all kinds of other elements in them besides cocaine derivatives. All of these elements in the cocoa leaves were meant to help with the altitude, preventing us from getting high altitude sickness.

The day we navigated the fourteen-thousand-foot pass, we started climbing uphill as soon as we stepped out of our tents. We climbed steadily for eight hours except for one flat stretch of about fifty feet where we stopped to eat our lunch and rest. Nearing the top of the pass, I could only take about two steps before having to bend over, heaving, trying to catch my breath and not faint. So light-headed the entire time I was trekking through the pass, it felt like I was in an altered reality. We all moved at a snail's pace as we continually had to alternate between taking two or three steps and then stopping to heave for several minutes until we could catch our breath again enough to continue on. After moving at this snail's pace for the longest time, we finally made it down the other side of the pass. Eventually we entered through the Inti Punku Sun Gate and we descended into Machu Picchu.

Machu Picchu which lay below us was a citadel of terraced stone ruins which were mysteriously created with no mortar. The stones all fit together so tightly and perfectly you couldn't even insert a sheet of paper between any of the stones. High up, far above the Urubamba River, Machu Picchu holds magnificence, mystery, and history. It was amazing how an entire civilization could have existed and flourished there so remotely high on a self-contained plateau. We'd hoped to stay at the five-star hotel in Machu Picchu, but it was on a first-come, first-serve basis, as they didn't accept room reservations. The hotel was already full so we ended up staying in our tents again down by the river.

Grubby after four days of strenuous trekking, we desperately needed to bathe. During our trek, the Peruvian porters would bring us a plastic bowl of lukewarm water and a washcloth each morning so we could at least wash our faces and brush our teeth. Since staying at the hotel wasn't an option, our only other option for bathing was to walk to Aguas Calientes, the next town over, to bathe in their public hot spring pool in the middle of the town. This was where all the locals went. However, the only way to get to Aguas Calientes from Machu Picchu was by walking along the railroad tracks as there was no road which connected the two places.

The railroad tracks passed through two medium length tunnels. The track between the tunnels had a steep mountain wall on one side and a small two-and-a-half-foot high embankment with a drop-off many feet down to the river below on the other side. I was nervous about walking along the train tracks. But if I wanted to go bathe at the hot springs, there was no alternative way to get there. Also, the bad blisters on my feet from hiking needed cleaning and treatment. So, I agreed to walk along the tracks with our group members and the dozens of Peruvian Indians who also walked along the tracks as their means of travel.

We set out later in the afternoon after waiting for the local train to pull out of the station at Machu Picchu. The overcrowded local train was a typical scene of a sea of humanity stuffed into the cars like sardines. People were hanging off the sides of the train clutching chickens, birdcages, and an assortment of other animals and parcels. I felt **extremely** nervous about another train coming along as we were walking along the tracks. I couldn't discern whether it was my intuition kicking in or just plain old paranoia.

We made it through the first tunnel, but I was still overly paranoid. If a train came by while you were walking in a tunnel, you'd have to take your pack off your back and find a crevice where you could nestle yourself into the rock wall hoping there was enough room for the train to clear your body. Even though Carlos, our trip leader, had assured us there would be no more trains that evening, I was still ultra-alert to the potential that a train might come. Suddenly, I could have sworn I felt the tracks vibrate. With my fear escalating, I kept turning around to peer down the tracks behind me. Eventually, there was no mistaking it. There was definitely a light way in the distance coming towards us. As the train barreled down the tracks towards us, all of the Indians started flat out running, yelling in Spanish that we were in danger. Four of us were walking together at this point.

One Indian saw our predicament that we didn't know what to do. He motioned for us to follow him. We all started flat out running behind him when I tripped and fell face down on the railroad ties. Fortunately, one guy in our group walking next to me hauled me up by the back of my jacket like I was a cat being picked up by the nape of the neck. Blood streamed down onto the tracks from the cut I sustained on my leg. In a flash, the Indian hopped up into a little opening in the foliage on top of the hip-high embankment. We all followed suit, squeezing ourselves together in a huddle in this slight space. About twenty seconds later, the train passed by us. It was so large and so close to us I could see up the nostrils of the people sitting in the window seats. Carlos had forgotten about the tourist train when he assured us no more trains were coming. I later learned that people lost their lives on these tracks all the time.

I had beaten the possibility of death one more time, another of my nine lives. It also confirmed to me, once again, it was my intuition that kicked in, not unfounded paranoia. It helped me know I could and should trust my instincts over what authorities or other people were telling to me. It was to realize although they were the authority, there weren't always right.

We made it to the hot spring pool in the center of town It was a small, in-ground, cement pool filled with lukewarm mineral water. The water was such a murky, opaque grayish chalky color I wondered how anyone could get clean. Dozens of people packed the pool, mostly locals. I hoped I wouldn't pick up any disease from being in that murky water. After so many days of trekking, it was nice to at least rinse the grime off.

It was also interesting walking through the town to the hot springs. We passed by a well-to-do area of town because it had a six-to the eight-inch-high sidewalk. The higher the sidewalk was, meant that you were more affluent. The hovels here had a single electric light bulb hanging down on a wire down from the ceiling, also showing that they were more affluent. Fortunately, the walk back to Machu Picchu along the tracks in the dark was uneventful.

After Machu Picchu we returned to Lima where we finished our tour with a celebratory dinner at the Rosa Nautica Restaurant on a pier jutting out into the ocean. It was a magnificent setting for our last dinner. It was wonderful ending listening to a musician play a grand piano along with the sound of the gently lapping waves beneath the pier and the restaurant floor.

Chapter 15: The Cult Years

When I returned to my home and job on Bainbridge Island after Peru, I started talking about Mafu's teachings to Daryl, a customer who regularly came to eat lunch at the Natural Gourmet. I loaned him audio tapes from several of the events. He was excited to have this information as it was in line with the training, he'd received at the Monroe Institute in Virginia.

Robert Monroe was the author of *Journeys Out of the Body*. This was one of the books that my mother had loaned me many years previously which launched me onto this path. Robert Monroe founded this institute. Daryl and I became closer friends. We also eventually started dating. He invited me to go out sailing one afternoon in Puget Sound, so I met him down at the dock.

Wearing a skirt with my purse on my shoulder as I had just walked directly down to the dock from work, he over-confidently thought he could just sail up to the dock long enough for me to get on board. He planned to pick me up from the dock without stopping to tie the boat up. Gigantic mistake! As I was stepping onto the boat with one foot on the boat and the other foot still on the dock, the inevitable happened.

Suddenly the wind shifted pulling the boat away from the dock. There was nothing I could do but fall into the water, purse and all! He fished me out of the harbor and onto the boat. We still went sailing although I was sopping wet, cold, and exceedingly uncomfortable the entire time while still wearing my work clothes. I should have paid more attention to this red flag, but I didn't.

There was a three-day event with Mafu happening in northern California, so Daryl and I registered and drove his car from Bainbridge Island down to the workshop. I was so happy to be starting a relationship with someone who shared the same interests as me. The week before we drove down to this event, Daryl and I had slept together for the first time. I thought we were in the blossoming stages of a new relationship, so it was only natural that Daryl and I shared a room at this event. Everything changed the next day, however.

As soon as the workshop started, Daryl met this young, petite, younger blond woman whom he believed to be his soulmate. With barely a word to me at lunchtime the next day, he moved his things out of the room we'd shared and moved in with her for the rest of the event. Shocked and devastated that someone would do this, it was hard for me to even concentrate and stay present for the rest of the event as I was so upset. There was no way I was going to drive an eight-hour trip back to Seattle in the car with him, so I found transportation to the local airport and purchased an expensive one-way plane ticket back to Seattle.

Adding to the upset of him ditching me, he and his recently found lady-love became part of Mafu's yearlong healing program in Eagle Point, Oregon. They both were going to be part of the training program and the community, which I so longed to join even before I met Daryl but couldn't afford. Not only were Daryl and his new love now a couple, they were also living my dream. It took the better part of a year for me to get over this devastating occurrence which left me in a vulnerable state.

In trying to move on from this bitter disappointment, I needed a new area in which to focus my attention. In the mid-eighties, my friend Barry and I had a friend who wanted to have a TV show on the Seattle Public Access TV station. The public access TV station's crew would film your first pilot show. However, if the station decided to pick up your pilot for airing as a regular program, the host then had to supply their own TV crew for taping the shows.

Our friend Uriah's pilot show, Universal Contact, interviewing different healers, authors, channels, and New Age people was a great success. Uriah recruited Barry and me to be her TV crew. After training and getting certified working the cameras at the public access TV studio, we then started taping scheduled shows every week, mostly in the TV studio with some shows occasionally being taped on location over the next year.

We taped shows with both well-known people such as author Dorothy Maclean, one of the co-founders of Findhorn Garden in Scotland and many unknowns. Several of the shows were with channels and psychics, including Penny Torres Rubin who channeled Mafu and another channel who claimed to channel an entity called Zanzoona whom I'll call Z.

Z announced he was the third ascended master after Ramtha and Mafu who had come here to teach. He claimed his teaching was the straight-up path to ascension. In meeting Ramtha and Mafu, I was on board with them right away. However, from the beginning I had mixed feelings regarding Z and Guru Padma who channeled him. I was hesitant. I may not even have gotten involved with Z if Barry hadn't paid for me to have a private reading with him.

After the reading, his channel invited me to come to Z's events. I didn't understand at the time that she'd begun wooing me. I was naive, too trusting of people, and took people at face-value. Usually I'd felt ignored, overlooked and invisible in situations. But being wooed, I felt seen, welcomed, important and acknowledged.

Eventually after attending every event when the channel and her husband would come up to the Federal Way, Washington area, I started getting more and more involved, not only with Z's teaching but also with the people attending these events. For a long time, I'd been searching for where I belonged. I'd had my heart set on studying with Mafu and being part of his healing program and community, but that hadn't worked out. Here was another opportunity presenting itself.

Although I was interested in the teachings my real desire was to become closer with the people in this group. I moved from Bainbridge Island south to Vancouver, Washington where Z's channel lived across the river from Portland, Oregon. At first, I lived with roommates in both Portland, Oregon and in Vancouver, Washington who were part of the group. And then I ended up living in each of the three additional houses at different times which the channel had purchased in her neighborhood. Through all of these living situations I couldn't help developing an emotional closeness with people in the group.

They became like family. People in the group became even closer and more important to me than my biological family was. We were all convinced we'd found our tribe and our home. I had searched for this for many years.

I belonged.

I mattered.

I felt loved and cared for by the people in this group–at least in the beginning.

Never had I experienced this before. I didn't trust that anyone could love me, or be there for me, without strings attached or wanting something from me except for my brief time dating Lee.

Much later, in retrospect, I saw that the Guru, the title the channel insisted we use in addressing her, wooed us over a long period of time. She was like a spider wooing her prey into her spider web further and further until she could pounce. Then she had you. The Guru brainwashed us. She told us that what we were doing in the group was our soul's purpose and the reason for this life's incarnation. If we didn't follow along and do everything we were told, then we wouldn't be fulfilling what our soul came here to do.

At first, I believed it. It was a little like being told you were going to Hell in the Catholic Church if you didn't obey the rules. Coming out of the other side of my time in the cult, I saw more clearly the energetic pattern at play. The Guru was a brilliant manipulator and a classic narcissist. This was the same dynamic and emotional patterning I'd experienced growing up with my bipolar father. It was familiar to me. Actually, it was as all I knew. I'd developed no boundaries. I didn't even know what it was to have boundaries, or that I had a right and a duty to stand up for myself.

Growing up, I was so intimidated by authority and my father, I avoided confrontation at all costs. It took me until age fifty to have the courage to stand up to my father for the unacceptable behavior he displayed towards me. Usually, I was too afraid of him, not of physical abuse, which rarely happened, but of the emotional and psychological abuse I'd suffered my entire life. I was super-sensitive, highly emotional, psychic, and an Empath which I didn't understand until much later in my life.

My father was always ridiculing and making fun of me, trying to get me to do things his way, to develop a thick skin, become ego-driven, and ruthless in some ways. This just crushed me. He was a classic narcissist, just as the cult leader was. Narcissists often seek Empaths. Empaths are the ones who want to help everyone and will sacrifice themselves for another. Narcissists want power and control over everything. If they see you have an open heart and desire to help people, you're seen as weak and a suitable target for them. If they successfully impose their power over you, they own you. They'll use your gifts and kindheartedness for their particular ends. Narcissists know exactly who to target and how to take advantage of you as their prey.

In the beginning the teachings with Guru Padma and Zanzoona were exciting. We became closer as a group. Working on many creative projects, each of us contributed our talents and strengths. A highlight each year were all of the group camp-outs we had several times each summer receiving teachings but also having fun. It felt like we were a litter of puppies, engaging in a level of involvement and camaraderie I'd never experienced when growing up.

We carried out many positive projects for the betterment of the community, which also helped us to feel empowered in making a difference. As good as it was in the beginning, questionable things began happening as time went on. The Guru, as a master manipulator, started pitting people against one another. She would tell things to some people and not to others, so people started harboring secrets. This resulted in some people feeling entitled to and acting superior to others.

It came to where inevitably, as part of this one-upmanship, someone would tattle on you getting you into trouble. Like prey, the Guru would draw us further and further into the center of her web, where she exerted absolute control over us ostensibly because we weren't capable of managing our own lives —classic cult programming. She gradually isolated us more and more from outside friends and family members, often forbidding us to attend family events and social functions. This wooing escalated into a push-pull process which took place over years until she trapped and controlled us in almost every aspect of our lives.

Even from the early days of my eight years in the cult, I was always in trouble for asking too many questions. There were times I would have to not only bow down to the Guru, but lie prostrate on the floor before her, as I always wanted to understand the reasoning behind why we had to do certain things. My most serious infraction of the *rules* happened when one December my friend Barry came from Bainbridge Island to Vancouver to visit me to take me out to dinner for my birthday.

Members of the group often went on trips with the Guru and her husband to places like Las Vegas, Hawaii, and Europe. Most of the time I didn't have the money to go on the trips so the Guru would have me stay at her and her husband's house to take care of their menagerie of dogs while they were away. When Barry came to visit, I planned for him to sleep in my bed back in the apartment I shared with a roommate. However, he didn't like that idea as he'd never met my roommate. After pleading and pleading with me to let him sleep on the living room floor of the Guru's house in his sleep bag, he finally wore me down. I relented despite the Guru having left explicit instructions to not let anyone in the house for any reason. So, I let Barry sleep on the living room floor in his sleeping bag for that one night, spending no other time at the house. I didn't want anyone to see Barry was there.

When the Guru got back, all hell broke loose. Somehow, she got wind of what happened. Maybe it was Z who informed her. I don't know. She was so angry she threw a small wooden footstool across the room at me, just missing my head. Although I admitted I disobeyed her instructions, I didn't understand why this was such an enormous deal other than I'd undermined her authority. I don't do well with confrontation. However, I knew myself, and I also knew I wouldn't let anything happen to her property or do anything inappropriate in her house.

After she threw the stool at me, she told me to report to their house before dawn on Saturday. When I arrived predawn on Saturday, she assigned me the job of picking up all the wet decomposing leaves in their whole back yard. It was the week before Christmas. In Vancouver it had already been raining for weeks. It was back-breaking work. Throughout the day, she only gave me one glass of water and no other food or water.

After filling seventy-two of those giant lawn and leaf bags full of the soggy wet decomposing leaves, I was told this wasn't being done as a punishment. It was a lesson I was receiving. It beats me what the lesson was other than her trying to break me so I'd yield to her authority. Finishing well after dark, I'd been outside working in the damp chilly December weather for over nine hours. I wasn't allowed to go inside until I finished. That was not the end of the repercussions because of this incident, however. Knowing about my recurring bouts with sciatica from my car accident years before, the Guru knew how attached I was to sitting on comfortable furniture.

She decided sitting on furniture was a privilege which she stripped from me, handing me an edict that I no longer was to sit on any furniture for ninety days. If I defied this order, I knew there would be more consequences. I also knew if I was caught sitting on any chairs or couches, that someone would tattle on me. One time I was out to dinner at a local Vancouver restaurant with several other members of the group. I sat on the floor of the restaurant complying with the Guru's edict. The Fire Marshall came over and made me leave the restaurant as sitting on the floor blocked fire access and was against the law. I left the restaurant rather than taking the chance of defying the Guru's orders.

This was part of the many ways I felt I was being taught to distrust myself. We were being brainwashed and manipulated. We were being taught we could only trust the Guru to know what was good for us, not our own innate wisdom or common sense. When we took it upon ourselves to do something, or take action on anything without permission from the Guru, we were told we were in our ego. This implied that our spiritual development was being set back when we disagreed with or rebelled against her. I know others in the group may not agree with me, but this was how I felt. Sometimes the Guru was right, but many times she was also wrong.

Life was miserable for the next several months. Earlier in the year, the Guru had me go to work for one of the other people in the group who owned a truck dispatch company. Her company put oversize freight from different vendors together with trucking companies to haul the freight. It was not my thing. I soon discovered how corrupt the industry was as everybody lied! For instance, you had to lie and say your truck would arrive within a certain time frame when you knew all along it got stuck in a snowstorm in Colorado. I was repeatedly told to lie. I was terrible at lying. It went against the very fabric of my being.

I was working for this dispatch company when I received the edict of not sitting on any furniture for three months. I had to do my job sitting on a dirty, frigid floor made of unfinished plywood in a funky mobile home. For three months, I sat on the floor using a cardboard box as my desk for my notes and my landline phone.

One day one of my roommates tattled on me telling the Guru that I didn't take a shower every single day. I didn't realize this was anyone's business but mine. I've never usually showered every single day, as my abnormally dry skin would get too dry with daily showers. The Guru told me to shower every day. To prove it, I had to take my wet towel to work to show my boss I'd taken a shower that day. I was beyond humiliated for no good reason.

There were all kinds of rules. When the Guru called over to our house, we had to pick up the phone by the third ring no matter if we were sleeping or what we were doing. I hated it. When cell phones first came out, the Guru required me to purchase one, of course on my dime. We all had to be available to her at all times no matter what time of the day or night it was, or whether we were at work or not. If she wanted something from one of us, we got into trouble if we weren't available. Because of this, I resented having to have a cell phone for the longest time.

There were so many other rules we had to abide by. As women, we couldn't go out anywhere after dark unless a man from the group accompanied us. This was ostensibly because our neighborhood was unsafe. As there were only a few men in the group, most of them married or with partners, it was virtually impossible to find someone to go with you. This pretty much curtailed any activity for us woman after dark. Going outside, down the road to the Guru's classes, however, was an exception.

Even though we lived in one of the more dangerous neighborhoods in Vancouver, to me, this was just an escalating implementation of her control. We were told it was for our own good. Here I was, almost forty years old, having been self-reliant, single, and independent for most of my life, often having lived in questionable areas, now being treated as if I was a young child who didn't know better. I just saw it as more and more ways to break our will and our spirit.

We, fortunately, all had jobs outside the cult, as we needed to pay our bills. Soon I came to realize our jobs were a necessity for not only supporting ourselves, but for subsidizing the cult. Rarely did we have the time, or opportunity, to spend our money on ourselves, anyway. The Guru required us to pay rent for our housing, all weekend workshops fees (mandatory, not voluntary) and several evening classes during the week. Eventually, as we were all drawn further into the web of the Guru, if you didn't show up to a class or a workshop, you'd better have an outstanding excuse. Increasingly, more and more money was being squeezed out of us. Eventually, we even had to pay the Guru to meditate for us, which I resented, as I wasn't sure if it ever really took place. I couldn't see that it did anything for me.

Beyond being increasingly controlled, we also had a lot of adventures which balanced things out, especially in the early days of the cult. Otherwise, I probably would have left sooner. One of these adventures was going to Area 51 in the Nevada desert. Area 51 is the top-secret classified United States Air Force base said to have captured UFOs. I don't remember the exact year we were there, but it was probably in the early 90s. Maybe ten of us went to Area 51. We went as far as we could go right up to the sign threatening our arrest if we went any further. Security forces descended upon us. A sheriff's vehicle came racing across the desert towards us from one direction and a military camouflaged jeep came racing towards us from the other direction. Then we became aware there were eight to ten sharpshooters positioned on their bellies along a nearby ridge, aiming their assault weapons at us. The Guru said as long as we didn't trespass beyond the sign, we were doing nothing wrong and to stand our ground.

If asked what we were doing there, she told us to say we were picking up garbage along the road even though the road at this point was just a dirt track. Going there, we hoped to get a view or some sense of UFO activity, however that didn't happen. The sheriff and military personnel kept trying to get us to leave. We just persisted in a stand-off with them. After a while, it became clear we were at an impasse. We finally backed down and went to eat dinner at the Alien Cafe.

We never knew what adventures or encounters were in store for us. Another time with the group, while waiting for a flight from Portland to Las Vegas, the pilot exited the plane during pre-check and came and sat next to me. I guess I looked like a safe person to interrogate. This was one of the rare times I'd come up with the money to attend a trip. The Guru was in a phase, emulating teachings of other Gurus, in which she dictated we were to wear only orange or red clothes for months. Someone in the group had a cold, so we were also instructed to wear face masks. This was almost thirty years before the COVID-19 Pandemic, when it was rare to see a group of people wearing face masks. So here we were, fifteen people, all wearing orange or red clothing, wearing face masks in the waiting area, getting ready to board our plane.

After sitting down next to me, the pilot turned to me and asked, "Is there something I need to know here?"

"No," I replied.

"Someone in our group has a cold."

We were wearing masks to prevent anyone from spreading germs in case they were getting sick, but didn't know it. I guess that satisfied him as he went back on the plane, leaving us alone. It's no wonder the pilot interrogated me, as we certainly looked like a suspicious lot.

On the positive side, amazing things occasionally happened. During a Kundalini workshop with Z, I asked a question regarding the occasional waves of energy I'd experienced in my body, causing me fear. Just as I posed the question, coincidentally, a wave of this energy overtook me. Z guided me through the experience, asking that I allow it to do what it wanted to do without clamping down on it, or resisting it.

This time the Kundalini energy kept advancing upwards without hitting blocks in my chakras, as happened the first time I'd experienced it. I didn't need to throw up or try to stop it out of fear. With this guidance, I felt safe for the first time in letting it progress. As these waves of energy overtook me, I started having euphoric feelings, coupled with a sense of having no edges or boundaries where I couldn't feel where my body ended. Emotionally, I felt only bliss.

However, my entire body felt numb, like how your mouth feels after receiving Novocaine shots at the dentist. I was "everywhere."

The next thing I was down lying on the floor. After I went "down" it was like dominoes, as person after person after me in the workshop also went "down." This reminded me of seeing people slain in the spirit which I'd seen on TV evangelical events. It was way more blissful than scary, as I feared it would be. It took a few hours for my normal self-perception and awareness of the boundaries of my body to return. Afterward, several people commented on how my lips had turned a purple-blue color while this experience took place. This certainly was another shift of perception out of my normal reality, opening me up further to awakening. However, the honeymoon phase of being in the group for me was long over. Trouble was brewing.

Chapter 16: Seeds of Discontent

Throughout the years, even though there were occasionally some amazing teachings and experiences, these became fewer and fewer and farther and farther apart, I was becoming increasingly unhappy. Negative experiences began far outweighing the positive aspects. When I left the truck dispatch job, I started a catering company called Terra's Bounty. It was a portable version of a food truck. I convinced my friend Kay, who'd also joined the cult because I had joined it, to go into business with me making lunchtime food, which we sold in business parks, medical offices, and car dealerships.

Kay had one route. I had another route. We prepared all the food from scratch and kept it in large coolers in our cars when we were on our routes. Carrying our offerings around in enormous wicker baskets, eventually our customers started referring to us as the *basket ladies*. It was a lot of work as Kay and I did everything ourselves: food purchasing, planning, preparation, selling, clean-up and accounting. After trying out work spaces in a few locations such as senior centers and church kitchens which weren't ideal, I finally found the perfect location for prepping our food in a storage room in a local restaurant. I rented the use of this room from the restaurant. Fortunately, we also had the use of their large commercial kitchen between 5 and 8 AM in the mornings. It was ideal in that it also met all the health department code requirements.

To keep the business going, I ended up working about eighty hours a week, making very little profit as I didn't charge enough for the food. The upside of this was it kept me out of being pulled into nefarious activities of the

Guru's, such as spying on neighbors whom she thought were dealing drugs, or whom she didn't like for whatever reason. Lots of strange things were going on which I didn't want to be any part of. Working eighty hours a week meant I usually wasn't available for her to enlist me into taking part in any of her schemes or shenanigans.

Six people and six animals lived in Lotus house where I lived. The other two single women in the house each had their own bedroom. A couple shared a third bedroom upstairs, and I had to share the fourth bedroom in the basement with the gay guy. Even though this arrangement had been going on for quite a while, I still wasn't happy about it. The gay guy would drive me crazy, especially at bedtime, when he would tease the dogs and get them all cranked up so they wouldn't settle down. I tried putting a small bookshelf at the head of my bed to at least block my view of this mayhem, but it didn't help much.

A lot of things had been building up within me for a long time. Finally, after years of feeling like I was always in trouble or being picked on, I reached my limit one day. I couldn't head it off anymore. I was beyond being angry. As I sat on the steps leading down to the basement, my psyche felt ripped, like when ripping off a piece of Velcro. Instead of feeling cohesive with my emotions and the spatial sense of the front of my body and my face being what was authentically presented to the world, it was gone! Where my face and the front of my body had been, it just now felt like a plastic shell. It felt like the "real me" somehow pulled way back, about three feet back from my body as a necessary form of protection. At that moment, when this "ripping" sensation took place, a shift took place within me. I didn't care anymore! I knew then that I would do whatever I had to do or say, which I thought the Guru wanted to hear even if I had to lie for self-preservation, which, as I've said, was totally against the fabric of my being. This worked for a while until my best friend Kay left the group.

Kay finally knew she had to leave the group, so some of her friends and I concocted an escape plan for her. She had a friend from outside the group who planned to meet her at her house (a different house than I lived in also owned by the Guru and her husband) while the rest of us were at Monday Night Meditation.

Chapter 16: Seeds of Discontent

We told the Guru Kay wasn't at meditation because she wasn't feeling well. After meditation ended, her roommates came home to find she'd gone, calling the Guru to report this right away. Since the Guru knew Kay was my best friend, the Guru immediately called me over to her house demanding to know what was going on. Denying that I knew anything about it, I was terrible at telling lies, as people usually could see right through me. Arriving at the Guru's bedroom at about 9:30 PM, I stood at the end of her gigantic king-size bed being interrogated until well past 3 AM when I finally cracked. Exhausted after the interrogation and standing for nearly six hours, I finally broke down and confessed that I knew where Kay was. Knowing I needed to leave for work in a few hours, I just couldn't hold out any longer, so I caved.

The Guru kept going on and on about how concerned she was for Kay's safety, which I knew was a lie. I said not only did I know where Kay was, but told the Guru, I wouldn't tell her where she was staying because if I ever left the group; I was going to the same location. No way was I telling her where that was! She was just mad she wasn't able to control her or the situation. Sharing that I'd been unhappy for a long time, I confessed to her how living in the same bedroom with the gay guy who cranked up the dogs all the time drove me crazy. I didn't want to be in that situation anymore.

Much to my utter amazement, standing up for myself resulted in a better outcome than I imagined for once. I was always fearful that if I were to go against the Guru or stand up for myself, I would need to be ready to leave the group immediately no matter what time of the day or night it was, which was something I knew I couldn't handle. The amazing upshot of this excruciating night was that the Guru took me seriously about not wanting to room with the gay guy any longer.

Her solution was to let me move into the meditation room in the attic where we did puja–a devotional ritual every night. She allowed me to move the altar forward enough into the room so there was just enough space to place a cot-size mattress on the floor next to a small dresser. Other than doing puja every evening, this now was to be my private sleeping space.

This arrangement worked well for me until the Guru started having an affair with a biker dude who was part of the Gypsy Joker motorcycle gang whom she had known since she was in elementary school. Whenever they wanted to have sex, I was told to make myself scarce or they would just lock the door to the upstairs meditation room so I couldn't get in. They would use my bed when they had sex. There was nothing I could say or do about it. Even before their affair began, the Guru had been having me and one other roommate in the house do what amounted to "remote viewing" sessions where we had to tune in to this biker dude reporting everything we psychically saw about where he lived and what he was doing.

My big ah-ha moment came when I realized here was the Guru, the supposed "big cheese psychic," relying on me and my other roommate to supply her with information. I'd never thought of myself as being psychic or having any abilities before this. As a master manipulator, she knew how to draw out and capitalize on the strengths and abilities you didn't even know you possessed to satisfy her agenda. She inserted herself into every situation in your life until nothing was yours. If you didn't voluntarily give it up, she would intimidate you until you did as I was soon to find out.

When I went on the trip with the group to Las Vegas, we stayed at the Excalibur Hotel and Casino. I played Keno for the first time and lost. One of my friends said you could enter a contest to win a car by writing your name and address on the back of the losing Keno ticket. After writing your information on the back of the Keno ticket, you would then drop it into the big Plexiglas container with the Miata sports car sitting on top of it. Dropping my losing ticket into the container, I thought *I couldn't care less if I ever won that car.*

Three months later, I received a certified letter in the mail for the second time in my life announcing I was the first-place winner of the car out of one hundred and fifty thousand entries. I had to be back in Vegas by the end of the month to claim it. Since I'd been dating someone in the group for a while, he and I flew to Vegas. The Excalibur Hotel put us up and gave us vouchers for free meals for the weekend. All I had to do was pose for publicity photos.

A few years earlier, when Little Red Dent, my old beater car, was running on sheer will-power, I knew I needed to get another car. For months I'd passionately entered every car contest I could find, determined to win because I couldn't see how I could get a car any other way. Finally, when winning a car didn't happen, I let it go and ended up going to the Honda dealership where I bought a new Honda Civic, never thinking Honda would approve me for a car loan, but they did.

A few years after buying the Honda Civic, when I needed a bigger car for my catering business, I traded it in for a Ford Escort Wagon. I had only owned the Ford Escort for about six months when I won the Miata. If I'd taken the Miata, I'd have to pay the sales tax, registration fees, and insurance, none of which I could afford. I asked the contest officials at the Excalibur if I could take a cash payment instead. Since it was a new contest for them, they agreed to give me a $14000 check instead of the car, worth about $17000, so I opted for the check.

After paying off my credit cards, using some money to get Terra's Bounty off the ground, and putting some aside for taxes, I had about $6000 left. One day I needed something, so I took $200 from the remaining balance. The Guru somehow heard about it and decided I wasn't trustworthy with money, so she forced me to sign over the remaining $5800 to her husband, theoretically for safekeeping, which wasn't a shared account to which I would have access. I felt backed into a corner and didn't want to do it. However, I knew I wasn't ready to walk away from the group at the moment, since I was unprepared to leave. Even though I was livid, I agreed.

Stressed from working long hours in my food business along with Siva work (free labor) required by the Guru, she decided I needed to quit my food business immediately. She wouldn't even allow me to do my food route the next day. Closing a business takes strategy and planning, which I didn't have the luxury of doing. With hundreds of dollars of food prepped for our routes for the next day, along with hundreds of dollars of inventory stored back in the kitchen space we rented, I lost all the revenue I would've received over the next couple of days, along with all my inventory. After insisting I quit my food business overnight, the Guru quarantined me in my bedroom for the next two weeks, allowing me only to leave the bedroom to go to the bathroom. Subsequently, when it came time to pay my rent to the Guru, I had no money. I told the Guru's husband to take it out of the money he was supposedly safeguarding for me, which felt like a minor victory.

I needed to find a job again. Fortunately, Pam, the woman whom my friend Kay had moved in with, worked at Portland Community College. Pam was searching for a temporary replacement to fill in her administrative position in the building she worked in while it was being remodeled, as she had severe allergies and couldn't be there during the remodeling. The counseling department hired me as her temporary fill-in.

While in this job, I found out the department was also looking for someone temporarily to fill in as the GED Testing examiner. When Pam returned to her regular job, I offered to fill in for the GED Testing position until they found a permanent hire for the position. When the job listing for a permanent GED Examiner came open, I applied and got the job as I'd already gone through training at the state office in Salem and had six months' experience doing it temporarily. The funny thing which no one knew was my boss Sandra, an administrator at the Portland Community College Cascade Campus, who oversaw the GED Testing Program, was also in the cult with me and was a close friend of mine.

For the next few years, I ran the GED Testing program first at the Cascade Campus, then oversaw the program at two other Portland Community College campuses along with the Portland jails. Even though my responsibilities kept expanding, I still was being paid only a clerk's salary. Over the next few years, I kept telling the Guru's husband to keep taking my rent out of the money he was safekeeping for me, even though I now had money to pay for rent. I was trying to get the sum he was supposedly safekeeping for me dwindled down as much as possible. We both knew that was what I was doing, but I didn't care. We never spoke of it. There was no way I'd continue to let them get away with having all that money.

The Guru also confiscated all my boxes of audiotapes and videos I had of teachings with Ramtha and Mafu. Those were more important to me than anything, but I just had to surrender them over to the Guru as I was told I could only serve one Master at a time, meaning Z. I was getting so fed up with how I was being treated-abused really-along with longtime disillusionment with the teachings, I knew it was time to think seriously about leaving. I would literally pray to get any value out of the classes for which the Guru required us

Chapter 16: Seeds of Discontent

to pay and attend. The classes had mostly turned into the Guru carrying on with endless stories about herself and her dogs rather than any real teachings. That was just not right. Change was in the wind.

Chapter 17: Freedom

Each year, the GED testing program required that my supervisor Sandra and I attend a state-sponsored GED Testing Conference. Even though we had a choice to attend a conference scheduled closer to Portland, we opted to attend the one being held on the Oregon coast instead. I just refrained from telling the Guru that there was also a conference being held in the Portland area. Attending the conference was mandatory for my job, so the Guru couldn't prevent us from going.

Because the conference we were attending was at the coast, we had to stay overnight. We drove to the coast in my car. Sandra was driving the speed limit at 55 mph on the two-lane highway when we noticed there was a seagull standing in the middle of the road up ahead. Birds are savvy and always get out of the way. However, this bird just stood there making no move to get out of the way. It was impossible to brake and not hit it.

The forceful impact was so strong; it decapitated the bird. The body flew off in one direction and the head flew over the top of the car. Everything became slow motion for me at that point. It was like I was in the middle of a vision quest. I knew this decapitated bird was a sign that if I didn't leave the cult, that bird's fate would be my fate. My spirit would irretrievably break.

Now I knew without a doubt it was time to leave. Sandra and I concocted a plan. We barely even paid attention to the conference that weekend as we were engaged in crafting this escape plan. We stopped at a souvenir shop where I bought a Myrtle Wood cutting board to symbolize my freedom when I would have a place to live outside of the cult. I planned to leave quietly. Sandra and I decided I would ask my friend, the other woman my age who took dance classes at Jefferson High School with me, to come with her husband and their truck to move me out of the house during a weekday in early June. The plan was to do this when everyone was at work so hopefully no one would notice or interfere with the plan. Even though we thought we'd come up with a solid plan down to the last detail, it didn't happen that way.

As part of our siva work (unpaid work for the Guru), in our house we would rotate whose duty it was to do the Guru's laundry. I hated being saddled with this task because if it were just washing a light and dark load of clothes that wouldn't be so bad. But she insisted certain items had to hand-washed and then sometimes also ironed. The only available time to do it was after midnight when our 11 PM puja finished. This meant staying until 1:30 or 2 AM to get all the laundry done. Then I'd have to get up early in the morning to go to work. Usually, having to do this task triggered a lot of resentment in me. But after deciding I would leave the group; I saw how I could use it to my advantage.

While being up late doing the Guru's laundry as the rest of the house was asleep, I started smuggling my possessions out bit-by-bit, loading them under my Ford Escort hatchback cover so no one could see anything. Each day I would bring them to Pam's house, the woman whose job I filled temporarily when I first went to work for PCC (Portland Community College). When Kay left the group, I'd helped her move to Pam's house the previous year. Now I was getting ready to move there as well when I'd successfully escaped the group.

While sneaking things out to my car in the middle of the night, I kept hearing a message in my head from my guides saying, "You've graduated."

I heard it again.

"You've graduated."

It was not a message warning me I had to leave, but a calm message of acknowledgment letting me know I'd completed the soul lessons I came to experience from this group. It was now over and done with. I could move on.

The other stroke of luck which worked to my advantage was the Guru was going to have me move out of Dragon Island, the house I had been living in for a few years to move back into Lotus House, another house the Guru owned on a side street several blocks down the street from where I currently had been living. With this directive, I could now publicly move things without it raising questions. I would move a few things at a time to Lotus House to make it appear I was moving there, and then I would take some of what I'd hidden in my car to work to give to Pam to store at her house. This plan worked great until Memorial Day Weekend.

Saturday morning of the Memorial Day Weekend, I got a call from the Guru. She cornered me, saying, "I know what you are doing. I've already got people in their cars to help you retrieve your things wherever you've stashed them."

She said that I've moved so much in my life, *which was true*, I needed to be with all my belongings under one roof at Lotus House. How she knew this, I don't know. I told no one within the group about my plans other than my boss, Sandra. Busted, the thing I'd feared the most throughout all my years of being in the group happened.

I knew I had to leave at that moment, ready or not! Fortunately, I had already moved a lot of my things, which made the process easier. However, I hadn't planned to go quite yet. I expected I'd have another week to complete my packing for the move. Guru Padma demanded I go get my things. I told her I needed to get in touch with the people with whom I had stored most of my stuff and that I would get back to her.

Panicked, I called Sandra who also lived in a house in the neighborhood which she and her partner owned. Her partner had been part of the cult for about a year and a half but had left the group several months earlier. I stored some of my larger things in their garage, so what I told the Guru wasn't a lie. I went over to Sandra's. I drove my car over their grass around the house to their backyard and parked it there so no one could see it from the road. Sandra, her partner, and I also closed all the blinds in her house so no one could view us through the windows. We then frantically tried to find a solution for this move. The couple who'd originally agreed to move me a week later had gone away for the holiday weekend so I couldn't reach them. Finally, Pam said she would round up her teenage son and bring her pickup truck to move me. It would take an hour for her to get everything together and drive from Portland to Vancouver. She told us to sit tight.

Meanwhile, the Guru kept incessantly calling my cell phone. I knew better than to answer it. We all stayed cloistered in my supervisor's house peering out through the curtains trying to make sure the members of the group patrolling up and down the streets calling out my name could not see we were in the house. Finally, Pam and her son arrived with the truck. Sandra and her teenage son also helped. Upon walking out of their front door, one of my closest friends in the group immediately accosted me, asking me what I was doing.

"I'm leaving," I replied.

Knowing it was best not to get into a discussion with anyone or say any more, I got into my car. They drove the truck over to the house I had been living in for the past couple of years. We all went into the house down the stairs to my bedroom where I still had some clothes and belongings. We started taking armfuls of my belongings to the truck.

The Guru continued calling me and several other people in the group about every ten seconds, barking orders. Finally, I answered her phone call.

All I would say in response to her barrage of questions was, "I'm leaving."

She tried engaging me from many angles to get me to talk, asking me where I planned to go, even expressing her concern for my safety, which I knew was baloney. I wasn't having any of it. I knew it was best to not engage in any conversation with her other than to say I was leaving, like a broken record. After all, she was a master manipulator who would hook me in if I'd said anything more.

After the first trip down the stairs to retrieve my possessions, we were all barred from going back into the house again. The reason given was that Pam and the teenage boys were not part of the group, insinuating they would corrupt the sacred energy of the house if they were to go back in. I had to rely on my housemates to get the rest of my things from downstairs. Pam, who weighed about three hundred and fifty pounds, stood at the bottom of the back stairs to the house holding up her cell phone, threatening to call 9-1-1 if there was any trouble.

Chapter 17: Freedom

We then went over to Lotus House to get the things I had already started moving there. Again, barred from entering that house, it was so hard for me to endure my roommates' reactions, as these housemates had become like family. It was hard to look at anyone's face while they were bringing my possessions up from the basement because I knew if I did, I would break down in tears.

I had to be strong and unflinching at that moment. I could only do this by pretending I was a horse with blinders on so I wouldn't get distracted by what was happening, or by those around me. I had meticulously planned my escape for early June, so it would be a quiet affair during a weekday with no possibility of confrontation, as I'd never handled confrontation well. Yet here I was, unexpectedly thrust into the middle of a huge public confrontation with half of the group. However, I surprised myself at how well I stood my ground and didn't cave even when I didn't get back a lot of my more valued possessions, including an expensive Le Creuset cookware set and a Hepa filter.

When we finished loading the truck we drove to Pam's house in Portland. Kay was there to help us unload the truck. As we were unloading, I found all kinds of crap loaded onto the truck which wasn't even mine, along with the painful realization of how much of my stuff wasn't there which I could never retrieve. Talk about having to let go of attachment to material things!

That evening, Kay and I went out to celebrate. After years of not being allowed to go out after dark without male accompaniment, we walked down North Lombard Street in a sketchy north Portland neighborhood after dark. The first thing we did was to find a bar-restaurant where we ordered a glass of wine as we'd also been forbidden to drink alcohol in the cult unless it was ceremonial mead provided by the Guru. Now we were out after dark, drinking alcohol, and celebrating our freedom–no more rules or taboos!

Now that I was finally out of the cult, I was so glad that I'd had the foresight to let the money the Guru confiscated from me dwindle down over the years by using it to pay my rent. I believe when I left the group, there was only about $600 of that money left instead of almost $6000. Even though I'd lost that money along with all of my Ramtha and Mafu tapes and some other possessions, I'd successfully escaped with my sanity, my dignity, my freedom, and my spirit still intact. It could have been much worse.

Kay became exceedingly resentful about the cult to where six years after she left the cult, she succumbed to colon cancer in late 2001. One day in 2003, I felt her presence strongly around me. I decided to try and see if I could get any channeled information from her. In retrieving this message, I received from her so long ago, it absolutely blew me away, first, that it was unmistakably her. During her life, her pet phrase, which she used all the time, was about flotsam and jetsam. Flotsam and jetsam are debris found in the water either intentionally or unintentionally placed there. I have never heard anyone else use those words other than Kay.

The second thing which I found even more remarkable was the information she relayed about dismantling the power and force of the dark side. In 2003, all I could relate it to was the cult we were in. However, rereading this message now, I realize how profound it was in foreshadowing the current global state of the world almost twenty years after receiving this message.

Kay's Message to Me in August 2003

Yes, I am here. Don't be alarmed by this process. It is more natural than you can ever imagine. It is quite fun, actually. It is like going underwater for the first time and realizing you can see and swim under there even though the medium feels foreign to you at first. It is easy, easy, easy! I want you to know that I love you and want to help you since you did so much for me before I left your plane.

My view is much expanded now. The vistas are quite breathtaking. In fact, I am to help you with a broader vista now in your life. I remember how hard it was—the struggle. It can be easier—much easier than you can imagine even right now. I see you strive and that you have been working hard, but it is like unclasping the harness to allow yourself to float. Float above the morass, the flotsam and jetsam. I have an expanded view now. I know more and I can see more. And more is coming to you—oh so much more.

I watched you go to Rosemere (the neighborhood where the cult was located). You have been working very hard these last years and also before with the cult. I can help you with all that. Padma (the cult leader), it is important to write about it (the cult) and her. Padma, for she is a little weasel—a predator. The time of the predators is up and you can help by dissolving the behavior and the manipulation. You hold that protection in your belly. Padma and the group, that is the manipulation, the dark side that is losing power, momentum and force. It has become a farce. We all chose to be a part of that to diffuse and diminish the power of what once were powerful ruling forces throughout history on and off your planet.

What is happening now is individuals like us are choosing completion of these experiences carried in the soul in order to, in physical life, break the spells and dismantle the codes and the control. That can only happen through participation on a human level when we individually make a choice to transcend and go beyond as you, I, and others have done.

We are the code breakers that are dismantling the grids of evil manipulation and control. It is powerful work. And we need to do it by living it and rising beyond the intimidation, control and fear.

As for my experience, I was so wounded and bitter that the wounding and bitterness became my physical demise. The wounding was my self-wounding at not thinking and feeling better of myself and allowing that kind of abuse to occur. They will be stopped. In fact, much diminishing of the force and manipulative intent and meddling they've been doing has already occurred. However, I have something important to speak to you about.

It is now time for the undecided to become decided about their path, their place, and their focus in the universe. You have been in limbo in your vacillation about bringing the word forth for too long now. It is now the time to rally and to give forth the best of you, for you have it in yourself to give. It is part of your soul contract and will affect and influence the soul contracts of many, many other beings. They are waiting for your call, for your presence, for your light. Do not hesitate out of fear, my dear one, as there are many gathered here together in oneness. I know you can do it. Try a little muster and the path will fly open for you.

Do all you can to conquer the inertia, the fear and the undeserving attitude. Many will stay in the state of unserving if they stay in the state of undeserving. Contemplate that one! Now is the time to focus within, like using a figure 8 and then express that wisdom, light and energy without to all you come in contact with. It is now time to demand and command a new way of interacting and being, to insist upon communication on a higher level, for you are creating your own world, your own hologram, as well as the collective hologram by what you take in and by what you give out.

It is now upon you the shift of the ages, as you know. It is what you all individually and collectively have planned for eons. Do you think for one moment that you would want to miss the fireworks? It is a grand adventure, a grand undertaking, and a grand achievement, for it signifies humans have come of age. It is the collective humanity shedding the garment of density and reclaiming their innate, natural, God-given garments of exquisite light, of exquisite presence, of great gifts, of great expression and great deliverance.

Rereading this message gave me insight and understanding as to why I agreed to be part of the cult in the first place even though it was beyond comprehension to my friends and family that I would become embroiled in something like this. It also helped me to clarify why I stayed in the cult for eight years instead of leaving at the first signs of abuse or control. This would have

Chapter 17: Freedom

been the logical thing to do. Unbeknownst to my conscious awareness, I had a soul contract which I was honoring to energetically help dismantle the evil found there. This is the path of the Magdalene, also unknown to me at that time.

In retrospect, I also realized that this was first-hand personal training in understanding manipulation, control and levels of frequency. The more Guru Padma kept us in confusion and low frequency through the instilling of fear, retribution, and knowing there would be consequences, the more we became malleable to what she wanted. Everything was always was about the Guru's agenda. It was never about supporting us in what we wanted or what was good for us, although we were repeatedly told otherwise.

We are all now being asked to do our part in dismantling the evil forces of control and manipulation which are now coming to light everywhere in our current world. We can do this by becoming more consciously aware of what is happening to us, and around us, by viewing it through an energetic frequency lens. What is the frequency level of the information, person, event or circumstance that is affecting you? Is it based in truth or lies? What can you do about it? How would you like it to be different? How can you shift your thinking, your emotional state, use tools, transmute your fear or negativity to raise your frequency and create space within you so the positive state you desire can show up?

Chapter 18: It's All Inward from Here

It wasn't until much later that I understood how leaving the cult was such a major turning point in my life and in my awakening. This wasn't only from having the courage finally to stand up for myself, saying no to the abuse, but the realization that the experiences I had in the cult helped lay the foundation for everything yet to come in my life. After enduring eight years of feeling victimized, I'd finally developed enough self-confidence and trust in myself to access my own answers within. Then I no longer always had to run to someone else to give me information, confirmation, or permission for what I perceived, wanted, or chose.

I realized being commanded to do months of "remote viewing," and having to report the results to the Guru was only one way I proved that ability to myself. Even though I'd been through years of teachings from Ramtha, Mafu and even Z about how to love ourselves, take our power back, and be our own "master," mentally I'd heard the teachings but deep down I never really assimilated them.

Because of my subconscious programming I never felt I was good enough or worthy enough to get my own answers, to trust those answers, and have what I wanted. It had taken me eight years of increasing restriction and abuse in the cult for me to "get it" and finally start trusting and living from my own innate wisdom. I'd changed from being someone intimidated by people in authority, to finding and recognizing my own 'inner authority'. Even though it felt like I'd paid a great price for it, it was worth it.

Raising My Frequency

Immensely grateful, it also helped me to understand and accept information from a "download" I received before getting involved with the cult. In 1988, most of my close friends were also Ramtha students on a spiritual path. I often wondered why I and all of my friends engaged in a spiritual journey suffered some type of abuse. Every single one of my close friends was dealing with repercussions of abuse; either physical abuse, sexual abuse, bullying, or mental or emotional/psychological abuse as had happened with me. It didn't make sense to me that we were all on a spiritual path of ascension, yet we all suffered. I meditated on this. I asked my guides to give me an answer about why this was so. The answer came about three weeks later in a "download" from my Councils of Light.

"You are not a victim. You are a volunteer. It is because of your spiritual fortitude and strength that you have willingly volunteered to take on the experience of abuse. You have volunteered to experience dysfunction and the depths of darkness so you could change it within yourself, thus holographically affecting the whole."

This helped me to view my many challenges in life from a different lens. It helped me shift my identity from that of a victim to that of a warrior of light. A warrior of light went into these situations because of their spiritual strength and fortitude and the light they could bring to others and the situation at hand. It provided a whole different personal frame of reference for me. Choosing to see myself as a warrior of light rather than a victim raised my whole frequency and the "story" around my life's struggles. The abuse I suffered in the cult ferreted out most of any remaining hidden pockets of victimization energy within me. However, there were a few barnacles of victimization yet for me to uncover at a later time. This gift of this realization was that it helped me move more into a state of empowerment rather than victimization.

Early on, the cult leader had given us synosin names, spiritual names that we were to use with each other instead of our given names. Our synosin names also represented a goal for us to live up to. My name was Rayaha Na Yo Yuccatti, which I was told meant "wealth of a thousand-fold which never vanishes."

Yeah, right!

That's a tall order, as I was always on the edge financially. I certainly didn't perceive myself as wealthy. After leaving the group, it occurred to me that wealth might not be referring to material or financial wealth, but the inner wealth of the soul and realization of one's being. In that regard, I saw that I have been in the process of living up to my name. This was the beginning of several clues in what I call the treasure map of the soul, the journey of why I was here and what my soul's purpose was. The understanding of this, however, would not completely unfold for another few years.

Since I'd left the cult and was no longer actively taking part in the teaching of Ramtha, Mafu, or Z, I was having to figure things out for myself.

Was this the reason having a teacher or guru seemed to make life so difficult?

Were their behavior and actions to get us to do it for ourselves?

What would I do if I were an Ascended Master?

What would I do if I tried inspiring my students to be all they could be, but they refused to apply the wisdom to their own lives?

How does one rectify this?

It seems students often can't get beyond idolizing or worshiping the guru or teacher. It is hard to shift that adoration from the outside authority figure to oneself.

I saw how using only a gentle, loving approach with students who insisted on continuing with their hero worship only strengthened that idolization and tendency to worship another. I also understood that using more harsh measures could cause the teacher to fall off the pedestal in the student's eyes. I reasoned one way to stop hero-worship is to get the student so pissed off, or so disillusioned with you, that they finally turn within to the innate wisdom within themselves. The crux of true spiritual teachings was always about this, for us to turn inward and become the Master ourselves instead of worshiping the guru or teacher.

Eight years it had taken me to get it. It's not about aggrandizing or worshiping these teachers, but applying the wisdom taught, so we could step into our unique path of mastery and spread our wings. However, I was still reeling from the experience of all those years in the cult, so I sought help. I went to a counselor for about six weeks who specialized in deprogramming people who had been in cults. I also reported them to the organization that keeps tabs on all the cults in the USA. Now I had to learn to sink or swim on my own. I was ready to do this, but I didn't exactly know how. It took a few years, but the next clue helping me to move forward fortunately presented itself.

I had been reading a book on shadow work called *Dark Side of the Light Chasers* by Debbie Ford. Somehow while reading Debbie's book, I'd found out she had just started a yearlong certification course called Integrative Coaching. In this course she was training people to become personal coaches specializing in shadow work. This was way before there was a proliferation of coaching training programs being offered everywhere. Even though the course had already started, my guides prompted me to sign up for this course. I was able to get myself admitted into the training program about a week after it had begun. The course took place mostly through teleconference calls, with two four-day, in-person retreats over the course of a year at the Chopra Center in San Diego. Personal coaching and mentoring sessions with the staff took place throughout the course.

I was finally being taught how to go within, how to navigate with a variety of tools, and how to address the shadow parts of myself. The shadow parts are all those disowned parts of ourselves, the internalized negative belief systems we've adopted, and made "real." It is all the hurt, blame, self-sabotage, low self-esteem, low self-worth, and victimization which influences how our external world shows up for us.

Debbie taught us sub-personality processes of how to have a dialogue with these disowned, judged parts of ourselves which most of us have pushed under the rug our whole lives. These behaviors and less than glowing parts of ourselves are what we've refused to look at or acknowledge were there. The usual pattern of the ego is to project these disowned aspects of ourselves onto others as blame and judgment, making it the fault of someone else. In reality, what we blame or judge in others is just mirroring back to us our own dysfunction or shadow part.

She taught us how to address a particular shadow aspect, give it a name, and find out what its gift was to us and how it served us. Once understood, we could then integrate it back into our consciousness. I recorded many of my sub-personality sessions during my training. Common threads which arose in my personal sessions were "beating myself up" and "not have adequate boundaries." Who or what turned up in these sessions as a sub-personality was often a total surprise.

When I first entered my internal space to meet with a sub-personality, the image of a fat, dirty, smelly, matronly homeless woman I'd actually seen on the New York City subway years before showed up. The person on the subway I'd seen was a bag lady who wore plastic bags and newspapers tied to her diseased swollen feet, which she was using instead of shoes. Shuffling through the subway car lugging various plastic bags, she would pull a sandwich and an orange out of one of them, which she then lay upon a sleeping drunk's stomach and walked away. I was so moved by that action of seeing this homeless person obviously in need of herself, showing such love and compassion, I never forgot it.

This homeless woman showed up as my first sub-personality. Even though she looked like the actual homeless woman I'd seen on the subway years before, this sub-personality woman had the most amazing eyes, eyes like those of the Virgin Mary. By her example, this sub-personality taught me about the infinite sea of love and compassion which existed within her. She showed how she could love every dirty, smelly, vile, diseased thing. She showed love and compassion for everything I judged to be horrible. I knew her gift to me was to help me find the gifts in all aspects of life, no matter how ugly they were.

In this inner experience she then took out an orange and a sandwich which she gently placed in my hand letting me know I was also worth receiving this sea of love, compassion, and nourishment. In the session, I was in tears that she offered this to me. When I asked for a name I heard, "This is Mary, mother of compassion." Every time I realized the gift of a shadow aspect, a new integration happened in the parts of my body which housed that shadow. Releasing in this way, I became freer and lighter. Divine energy then effortlessly floated in. Mary represented the gift of the dark shadow; the hidden, the Dark Mother, the yin female aspect.

I expected the light shadow would show up as the bum I'd met in Boston. I had to tell my mind to surrender to whoever wanted to come forward. In the visual that formed, I realized I was on a bus. A striking man in a white robe with gold trim, long brown hair and a beard stepped forward. It was Jesus. He ushered me off the bus. We sat on a park bench, then he crouched down in front of me to kiss my feet, saying how happy he was that I was becoming who I AM by integrating all these aspects of myself. He was most thrilled and excited that I was finally getting this. Even though he knew all, and was all, it was still lonely for him.

He said, "Because so few can mirror back to me my highest vision of myself, I am thrilled you can now mirror back the highest vision."

His gift to me was in integrating him within me. He could now serve me like an armature, a frame, like a coat hanger which would support me. I could surrender my pain to him and he would help me stand. I realized Jesus represented the light shadow of me in the yang or male aspect. Now, these sub-personalities of Mother Mary and Jesus sure surprised me, as I had ditched Catholicism when I went to college. I didn't particularly identify with Christianity or follow any religion espousing the need for Jesus to save us by embracing him as our lord and savior. Yet here they were within me, letting me know that surrendering myself to them in the way most religions teach was not the way. Showing up as sub-personalities within me, they amplified and showed me how their gifts were already qualities existing within me, helping me to hone, expand, and express those qualities in my life as I moved forward.

The coaching training program with Debbie Ford lasted for well over a year from September 2000 through the end of 2001, as we had to reschedule our in-person training in San Diego for December because of 9-11. One person in our coaching training program was flying out to our originally planned September event in San Diego. She was on the plane out of Boston which hit the twin towers. It was very sad for all of us mourning her loss.

On January 9th, 2001, I awoke from a dream. I rarely remember any of my dreams, so this was unusual for me. In the dream, I went to the doctor only to be told I had stomach cancer which was so far advanced they could do nothing for me. I felt very fearful and upset in the dream. What was most interesting to me about this dream, in retrospect, is that at the time I had the dream, I was a participant in Debbie's Integrative Coaching Training Program.

Chapter 18: It's All Inward from Here

Debbie Ford's biggest personal shadow piece, which she lied about to herself and the world for years, was that she had stomach cancer. She finally confessed this to Oprah Winfrey on February 21, 2012, in an episode of Oprah's Soul Sunday saying she'd had this cancer for probably eleven years. After her initial surgery to remove her stomach cancer tumor, she thought it was cured. This would mean her cancer was first diagnosed in 2001 about the time I had the dream. It may be just a coincidence, but I wonder if I'd tuned into the quantum field where there was a vibration of stomach cancer in Debbie's field which I'd somehow picked up on. I now know scientists are talking about how we are all intimately connected through a web of consciousness, as they call it. We are more profoundly affected by, and influenced by, this web of connection between all of life than we've been aware of previously. Debbie died from stomach cancer a year later, on February 13, 2013.

The only person in the Integrative Coaching Program from Oregon other than me, was a woman named Selina. When I went to visit her, there was a short flight of stairs leading up to her apartment where on a small landing was a spotlight shining on a framed picture of some wild-looking Master.

"Who is that in the picture on your landing?" I asked.

"St. Germain", Selina replied.

My entire story about interacting with the bum in Boston who I discovered was St. Germain tumbled out. She then shared the incredible story of how the lithograph came into her possession.

She shared how she was in one of the metaphysical bookstores in Portland one day when the clerk climbed up the ladder and removed a lithograph from the wall. He climbed down off the ladder with the lithograph.

Turning to Selina he said to her, "I know this is yours."

He just gave it to her without charging her anything for it. Now how many times does a clerk in a store do that? Selina had it framed. She said she always knew she was just care-taking it until the right person came along. She gave it to me as a present for my 50th birthday, saying, "I know this is yours. It belongs to you."

The St. Germain saga and mystery just kept growing and deepening.

Raising My Frequency

I entered another relationship in 1999 hoping it would develop into the intimacy and love for which I'd been searching my entire life. It didn't. Rich was someone I met through an expensive dating service before the days of online dating. Since I wasn't getting anywhere in the dating scene on my own, I swallowed hard, forked out the money, and hoped for the best. The first two people they matched me with were terrible. Rich was the third. A total computer geek who worked for Intel, at first, I wondered if I could even get through a 30-minute coffee meeting with this guy. Somehow, we managed.

A few weeks before, I'd taken this dating workshop. The presenter at this workshop suggested we meet with a person three times before writing them off. So, I tried this out with Rich. At the time we met I was house-sitting for a couple who I knew from the Argentine Tango community in Portland.

I agreed to take care of their senior cat while they were on a year-long bicycle trip, touring all over the world. The deal for cat sitting would be that I could live in their house rent-free for a year. They also told me I could use their computer but the hard drive was almost full. On my second meeting with Rich, I asked him what having a full hard drive meant. Personal computers were still a relatively rare thing in 1999 so Rich explained to me what having a full hard drive meant.

Following the protocol from the dating workshop, I had one more meeting with Rich before I would say yay or nay to him. On our third date, he arrived with a brand-new desktop computer which he'd assembled himself. He just gave it to me. You don't just ditch someone after the third meeting when they've arrived and given you a computer even more advanced than the one which I had at work. I couldn't say nay at that point so we continued to date. I kept thinking he was just shy and reserved and was not into doing things because he didn't get out enough. I thought that eventually, as we did more things, that would change.

After dating for a while, there came a point where he kept saying he should look for a house to buy as he had no tax shelter. Putting my mind to the task, I thought it would be fun to look for a house. I found the perfect house, still under construction, on a cul-de-sac with a strip of land behind the house. It was a perfect location, private and peaceful. The loose verbal agreement

Chapter 18: It's All Inward from Here

between Rich and me was that if he found a house to buy, I would move in with him. It wasn't so much a deliberate decision to do this, but more of a happenstance especially since my friends had come back from their bicycle trip early and I needed to find a place to live, anyway.

Rich purchased the house. At first, it was great. I knew Rich collected lots of cast-off computer parts from Intel, so I negotiated with my carpenter brother to build ceiling-to-floor bookshelves on three walls of the garage for Rich's computer parts. In exchange, Rich would build my brother and his wife a new computer. The deal was on.

As the months went by, what I didn't understand was that Rich had already attained his social limit. What I thought was a good starting point for expanding our activities and social life was really his breaking point. Also, he was much more of a hoarder than I realized. Within six months of living in the new house, he'd filled up all the shelves in the garage, then he started filling up the center of our two-car garage so there was never any room to park our cars.

When the garage and his office were overflowing with computer stuff, he then started filling up the living room until there was only a pathway from the front door to the kitchen. I think my 50th birthday party was the last time I saw the living room floor or my kitchen table as he'd put towels on it and had partially built computers on it from then on. Even though we were together for six years, we lived like roommates. I moved out of the master bedroom pretty early on because he insisted on feeding the two geriatric cats in our bed. I'd wake up in the middle of the night to a cat chomping dry cat food in front of my face. I couldn't take it anymore, so I started sleeping on the futon in my office from then on for the next several years.

It was obvious my relationship with Rich was never about a romantic connection. It was more that we had a soul "contract" before coming into this life for my technology training. That was what Rich could offer me and the reason we came together. I learned a lot about computers, technology, networking computers together, and web design. For this education, I was immensely grateful, but still disappointed with the lack of emotional bonding between us or any kind of bonding at all. He would leave for work about 3 AM every morning in order to get most of his workday in before anyone else showed up in his department at Intel. He would have to go to bed every night between 6 and 8 PM in order to get up that early. He'd go to bed and I would go out to dance Argentine Tango. Such was our life with virtually no common shared interests.

Even though he had a good heart, he knew I was unhappy. He wanted me to be happy but didn't understand how to fix it. I didn't know how to fix it either. Spending hours one afternoon on our bed crying my eyes out, as I felt so alone and desolate, I had another one of those experiences when the veils parted briefly. As I was sobbing, feeling so alone and bereft, I suddenly felt angels and beings pressed up against every space, nook, and cranny of my body. Behind the layer of angels pressing up against my body were more and more layers of angels and beings, not only filling the bedroom but extending way out beyond it. I felt so hemmed in by all these beings; it was way too claustrophobic!

I started hysterically laughing, asking, "Can't you back off a little so I can breathe? Can't I get a break here?"

I had suddenly gone from feeling utterly alone to claustrophobia in the presence of so many beings pressing in upon me. It shifted my entire state of being. As I was feeling sorry for myself when this experience happened, I realized I definitely wasn't alone, nor was I probably ever alone.

While I was with Rich, I continued pursuing my spiritual and self-help avenues. After receiving my certification in Integrative Coaching with Debbie Ford in 2001, I attended one of the channel Geoffrey Hoppe's Crimson Circle events in 2003. The woman sitting next to me at that event was all excited because she had just completed her QHHT (Quantum Healing Hypnosis Technique) in past-life regression with author and pioneer, Dolores Cannon. This woman told me all about the training with Dolores but mentioned it was only for certified hypnotherapists, which I was not. My guides again created a sensation of me having a volcano under my rear, just like they did when they wanted me to get up and speak to Shirley MacLaine years earlier.

Totally out of character for me, I followed their prompting to call Dolores Canon's office in Arkansas. I said I'd heard about the QHHT training and wanted to do it, but I wasn't a certified hypnotherapist. I explained that two years before, I had become a certified personal coach with Debbie Ford through her Integrative Coaching Program. I went on to say that almost all the training being done was through different induction techniques. Dolores Cannon's staff decided I met the qualifications, so they admitted me into her next training class in Arkansas. I flew to Arkansas. At Dolores's training, I met a woman from New York who trained and certified people in Transpersonal Hypnotherapy. After I received my past-life regression training and certification with Dolores Cannon, I then attended Joan Leone's intensive course in Scottsdale, AZ, becoming a Certified Transpersonal Hypnotherapist. Joan and I became friends.

Training in shadow work with Debbie Ford and becoming certified in hypnotherapy gave me tools to address shadow aspects and dysfunctional patterns within myself and with clients. In facilitating sessions, I viewed these dysfunctional shadow pieces like they were a polluted pond which could be cleansed using the tools and processes I'd learned. Through these processes, the negative impact, or low-frequency energy, shifted to something positive, which raised one's frequency opening the doors to insight, healing, and an elevation of consciousness. This is what I had been seeking to understand about *energy* from the beginning of my questioning and awakening at age fourteen.

Being certified as a hypnotherapist specializing in past life regression, I facilitated the recall of many past lives both in myself and with clients. Finding out about past lives may be a curiosity for some people, but the insights which come forth help us unravel and move through the healing our souls are asking us to do. Awareness of other lives can help us recognize and come to terms with underlying belief systems, attitudes, and similar challenges which have perhaps occurred in other lives. Accessing our unconscious may also get us in touch with more of who we are as great cosmic beings of light, with energy, ability, knowledge, and wisdom beyond what is normally available to us through our human brain and psyche.

This is all an integral part of the awakening process. If you view lifetimes from the perspective of your soul, it acts like an orchestra conductor coordinating all the different instruments so they blend into a harmonious journey of sound. Your soul similarly conducts, or coordinates, the journeys, the lessons, and the challenges for you to garner the wisdom from each lifetime which happens perhaps through hundreds or thousands of lives which you, as a soul stream, live. I believe during this span of lives inevitably there comes a point when your human aspect asks why, and how, you fit into a larger picture which is the catalyst for awakening.

As a hypnotherapist, I have seen certain behavioral patterns and dysfunctions which span several lifetimes. We come back into different lifetimes repeatedly to learn the lessons presented, so we can choose differently the next time around. Eastern religions call this karma. This is the refining process of the evolution of our soul. Believing we only have one life to live doesn't allow for soul growth or evolution. This all helped me understand how I might be of service and offer my skills and awareness of how we develop as souls. The specific way this was to come about was still in the ethers, however.

Chapter 19: Opening to New Directions

During our course with Debbie Ford in the Shadow work we kept journals of our experiences throughout the training. As I wrote my experiences down in my journal, sometimes it was just complaining, sometimes just writing down what occurred, and at other times I received a download from the other side. On Thursday, October 24, 2002, I received a download.

I went and sat on the couch by St. Germain's picture, the one I had gotten from Selina for my birthday. An energetic presence enveloped me. I sensed this was St. Germain. It felt like he was working with my energy. I then sensed this fast moving energy like dimensions were whirling through me, coming into me and moving out through me. I gave permission for St. Germain's energy to merge more fully with mine. I sensed it would, little-by-little, as I could accept more and more of his energy. I asked him for help in removing my perceptual blocks as I always felt so limited in what I could perceive or know for sure. I knew something started happening in my third eye. I realized I could only accommodate a small percentage of his energy. I had a "knowing" that this would increase with practice and trust. On the etheric plane, he started talking to me. This is what I 'heard' in my head.

"You have not been delinquent. The timing is nearing now. You have been preparing, my beloved lady. Watch for the signs and signals. You have already been aware of some of them."

A golden light being also came into my awareness. Jeheshua? That was the thought that came to me. Vaguely aware that this was another name for Jesus, I hadn't any idea how to spell it or how, or when, to use it. Eventually I would discover I was spelling it wrong.

Jeheshua took over the conversation. "*I want you to know about alchemy—not only the mental concept of alchemy, but actually becoming alchemy. You need to give your permission for this alchemical change to take place. It is truly the metamorphosis. You are being given the keys, the understanding, the concepts. Do not judge, do not doubt. All will be given freely in due time.*"

I sensed them joking around—due time, referring to labor and birth.

St. Germain then continued, "*You are due. Your due date is near. Know that we are with you always. Call upon us. You have listened well, but your listening will become more intense as it should be. Your life will not even resemble what it is now. You have needed this time to prepare. Go in peace.*"

They signed off as St. Germain and Jeheshua.

I hadn't any idea what they were talking about.

What birth?

What alchemy?

What metamorphosis?

As with all the downloads I receive, I am not entirely sure that I am not just making it up. Again, it is to surrender and release the doubt. These were hints; clues given on my timeline of things yet to come of which I knew nothing at this point.

The next year, in 2003, several pieces of the cosmic puzzle came together. That was the year I first met Cynthia Slon; the psychic who initially helped me understand I was living a blueprint that wasn't mine.

Cynthia also told me I was a member of the council that created Mother Earth. Even though that seemed really unlikely and far out on the one hand, I'd heard references to this twice before from other readings.

Having this knowledge wasn't for me to think I was superior or any different from anyone around me, but to instill confidence and greater trust in myself. In moving into greater trust, I would have the courage to do what I came here to do.

My tendency often was to shy away from things which seemed too grand, too improbable, and might require too much of me when I felt I didn't know what I was doing. However, my greatest desire beyond walking a spiritual path of mastery in this lifetime has always been to accomplish my mission. The year 2003 was also the year that catapulted me into full realization and awakening that I was a lightworker. In readings, Cynthia shared that Mother Earth and I exchanged DNA during her formation so that some of the chronic pain I would feel in my body was the reflection of pain and disturbance within Mother Earth's body and fields.

Whenever I have pain; she suggested I go into a meditation process to wherever the pain was in my body. I was then to ask how this pain is directing me to help heal Mother Earth. I wasn't sure if there was truth to this information or not, but I committed to doing this process. I diligently carried this out for about six months until I got distracted by other things in life.

I'd lay on my bed and allow myself to drift into a vision quest type of state. After completing the inner journey, I would then get up and write what I experienced without bias, judgment, or any idea if there was truth to it or not. Much of what I perceived was like watching Sci-Fi. Someday I plan to expand these eighty pages of notes from these visualizations into a book. Here is an excerpt from some of these notes.

Grid Work Excerpt

I woke up this morning with tightness and pain across my back. Tuning into how this tightness and pain connected to the Earth in my meditation, I sensed there was work to do in Antarctica. Focusing my awareness there, it seemed like there must have been some nuclear detonation or other weapons experimentation, as the grids there looked like black fused glass covering a very large geographical area. It seemed I couldn't work on them directly, so I asked for help from the galactic brothers and their ships to infuse the area with pink light from above and below, supporting and saturating the entire area with divine love and nurturing.

Surrounding this area of destruction, which was like a gigantic crater, there were a few intact bits of the light grid, truncated or frayed at the ends. The action I needed to take as impressed on me by my guides was to copy healthy viable sections of earth grids in the ocean, then paste the copy of healthy grid lines over the crater of the black-fused glass looking material in a circular pattern filling in the crater-like skin grafting.

After I did this, I asked for help to align and weld the connection points of the grid. When completed, I saw that 'pins of light' had been placed in a circular pattern around the Inner Earth's South Pole opening. These 'pins of light' looked like pink and purple faceted cut diamonds with their points extending deep into the Earth. It seemed we, the galactic beings and I, worked on placing these so when they connected with each other, the coding within these faceted points calibrated the sound and light frequencies, setting mathematically engineered principles into motion.

I also sensed this was going to be important in Mother Earth's upcoming ascension, as a series of rings placed throughout the circumference of the planet would assist her. As I watched what was unfolding further, it became clear these jewel-looking devices laid down like tiles would conduct the universal language of light throughout the grid lines of the planet, helping to create a new matrix.

Mother ships worked with me in placing these pins and grid points around the Earth. I wondered if some of the chronic extreme tension in my physical body could be related to these grids being out of alignment and inactive. Even though I saw the vision of what eventually was to be, it didn't seem appropriate that day to go any farther than working with this first ring. I set an intention that the blueprint for the rest of the work would come into my consciousness when the timing was right.

Besides doing "inner work" my inner guidance also prompted me to take part in several other "out- of-the-box" adventures. Earlier in the year (2003), I was pet sitting in Hood River, Oregon, for my brother and sister-in-law. They were on a mini-vacation before the birth of their first child. Even though it was a cold, blustery, drizzly day, my guides led me to drive over to the Stonehenge Monument in Goldendale, Washington, a replica "to scale" of England's Stonehenge, perched on a point of land overlooking the Columbia River. The stones here are all full sized, as they would have been in England before falling into ruins. I'd been there many times before when I was part of the cult.

There by myself in the cold, wet, and nasty weather, my guides instructed me to stand before each one of the inner altar stones and connect with them. As I did, all kinds of unusual verbal sounds and chanting came forth out of my mouth, something that had never happened before. The sounds and/or language which came forth were different for each stone. As I was vocalizing or "singing" to each of the inner altar stones, I received the impression each stone was a beacon which connected to a different galactic civilization.

I intuitively knew chanting the unique tones and sounds back to the altar stones was activating connections with their home worlds. At least, this was what I sensed. Three years later, I would co-author a book which contained a chapter about an Essene-Druid ritual at England's Stonehenge two thousand years ago where they would "sing the stones" of Stonehenge, causing the stones "to spin" becoming inter-dimensional portals. I guess this toning at the Goldendale Stonehenge was part of my soul memory, preparing me to be part of what was to come through later down the line.

Another adventure my guides precipitated took place in November 2003 between two total eclipses. Guided to do inner work with each of the elements, my guides had me take a print-out of the periodic table of elements to bed with me so I could work with eight to ten elements each night, many of which I'd never even heard of before. After quieting my mind, I went inside to a quiet space asking how I was to work with these elements. I was to connect with the essence of each element, then use the Violet Flame to transmute any mishandling or misuse of that element in our current reality or from past eras, or alternate, or parallel realities.

Intuitively, I knew each element had a specific tone and sacred geometry pattern associated with it which maintained its coherence and stability. As the Christ matrix became activated in each of the elements, the blending of the tones, light, and sacred geometry seemed to create a tapestry of sound and light in which each element rose to its cosmic higher ideal and purpose which would serve the highest good for all. After asking for help in releasing any negativity within each element, I then asked that each element vibrate at its highest capacity until the Christ grid matrix of each element vibrated with, and linked back up to, the Christ grid of the planet, thus preparing the way for planetary ascension.

Until now, I haven't spoken about these adventures my guides would send me on, as my family already thought I was a bit of a space cadet. Many of these things to them would be really far-fetched. Afraid my family and friends would think I'd turned into a total fruit loop, I've kept it to myself all these years. All I knew was that my guidance of what to do wasn't coming from my conscious mind or awareness, but a cosmic level of being, that multidimensional part which we all have, but aren't usually clued into. This also became a major step and responsibility in the awakening process.

In 2003, I also took part in author Neale Donald Walsch's first Humanities Team Conference. Neale Donald Walsch wrote the *Conversations with God* book series. About 1000 people attended the conference from all over the globe. Throughout the weekend, Neale kept hammering the point that we never know if something we'd do or say was going to be the 100th monkey, the tipping point when all of humanity awakens. After the conference was over, I was exiting a row of seats in the auditorium when I overheard two women talking in front of me.

I remember thinking they only believed what he was saying about five percent. At that moment, suddenly I felt paralyzed. I couldn't move or even take another step. Caught in a tractor beam like from Star Trek, I was in a moment of absolute immobilization. During that immobilization, I had a download that I was going to write a book.

Write a book?
What?

Chapter 19: Opening to New Directions

Who me?

I wasn't a writer. Writing had never occurred to me, or so I thought. I was a dancer and performer, not a writer. It somehow had slipped my mind that in 2000, after I quit my job at Portland Community College, my friend Greg Hutchins hired me to assist him in writing a book. He worked as a Quality Engineer. The book he asked me to help him compile and write was to detail perks that various Fortune 500 companies offered prospective employees to lure them to come work for them.

My job was to research the policies and hiring incentives of these companies, then write up my findings. What I was doing I didn't even think about as writing. That job soon dried up when the market did a complete about-face and companies no longer needed to go the extra mile to lure potential employees with lucrative perks. The focus shifted to the employers now having all the power. The book never got published. Greg was the first person to recognize my writing abilities.

He said to me one day, "I don't know how you do it. You can take the most boring, technical stuff, or corporate structured material, and talk about it in a way that is entertaining to read."

He had recognized a talent and ability in me I didn't even know I possessed. Remembering this comment from Greg helped me have the confidence down the line to take on writing projects and not feel that I would be a total failure at it.

So, after receiving the download about writing a book, I sat and tuned in with my guides asking them, "*What should I write?*"

The answer came back. "*Write what you know.*"

I replied, "*Well what do I know?*"

They wouldn't answer me. I had to figure it out on my own. As I kept pestering my guides, eventually I received information that I was going to be *Healing the Hologram*.

What the hell did that mean?

Couldn't they have given me something I even knew what it was?

I was still on my own. Finally, to make a start somewhere, I opened a Word document on my computer and started throwing sentences in there about what I was contemplating at the moment, starting with gratitude.

There was no plan, no outline, and no idea even what the book was to be about. But because I persevered in this haphazard writing, it organically unfolded over the next eleven years until finally, in 2014, these writings developed into the book *Soulweaving, Return to the Heart of the Mother*. This book includes spiritual teachings, channeled material, personal stories, a template for shifting from the old paradigm to the New Earth, and exercises to do at the end of certain chapters. I was amazed at how it had come forth when initially I hadn't any idea what I was trying to do.

Even though I'd experimented with automatic writing for a long time, in 2000 I put out the intention to become a clear channel. Repeatedly over the years, I realized how pretty tuned-in I was. Although I'd brought through some amazing messages, I was always way too self-critical of what came through, as I still wrestled with whether the information was truly coming from a higher source or something I was just making up.

To get over my overly-critical self, I posted to the Internet a channeled message from St. Germain that I received in 2004. I finally couldn't deny that the tone, the feeling, and the words expressed in the message differed significantly from how I usually expressed myself. I then realized without a doubt I was in touch with a being, a reality, and information beyond my personal human self. This, my first publicly released message, still feels timeless and appropriate for now.

St. Germain and the Hosts of Heaven Message

"We wish to come to you today, me and my council, to wish you Godspeed and an easy transition into your new life, which you are all creating collectively here upon your beloved Mother Earth. It is a great time upon your planet and a great time for all who are waking up and choosing consciously to develop in their understanding of light and of living a soul-centered God-given life. It is a time for self-

reflection and for giving yourself permission to view consciously what has gone on before in your world, as you've become aware that you have not only the chance and the opportunity to change it, but the God-given right to do so.

This is not from someone in a position of authority and power outside of yourself to do this, but from your divinity, your conscious choice to do so. It is not only a privilege, but a right given to you from the higher realms that you in this age have worked for lifetimes to create this opportunity to step forth and do. Now's the time! The moment of transformation is upon you and well underway. It is a time for the re-emergence of the spirit and of fulfilling the sweet tender longing that has been deep within your beings for a very long time.

That tenderness that has had to be hidden, so protected, lest it be vanquished, now will find its voice, its place. It is its day. Believe me when I say that you all are Gods, for surely this is so. It is now time for the blinders to come off and for the eyes to see. For the sights to come forth are magnificent, indeed. You must allow yourself and align yourself for the eyes to see, however, as you are the bridges of consciousness, the rainbow bridges of consciousness that are pulling up the vibration of the human consciousness upon this planet. You're the ones acting as transformers and translators of energy, and you are doing a magnificent job.

The human DNA is changing to that of the crystalline, or Christ, consciousness. A crystalline matrix holds the vibration of inter-dimensionality and the coding or records of consciousness or the Akashic records. As the crystalline nature of the inter-dimensional DNA now coming online becomes activated, it will allow the Akashic records to be more fully accessible, for they are part of your physical-etheric-interdimensional beingness that is all merging into the "ONE."

Hear me when I say this, you are the Gods and Angels of the universe once in full connection, full awareness, and full alignment who have volunteered to fall into the densest of worlds so that by one's individual choice, reunion or RE-UNI-ON can occur. It is to move beyond the negating of oneness, the separation of consciousness, back to the re-establishment of the "I" and the "One" both being the same, the unity consciousness.

It is time now for all beings to realize the acceleration of consciousness is occurring like a giant snowball picking up speed. How easy or difficult this transformation comes about in your life, for it will, depends on your willingness to take part consciously in this transformational process. This participation is through intent and desire to do so. It is through aligning yourself with your soul and your soul's purpose, and aligning yourself with Divine Will as this one who is writing has done, for she has felt stuck and stagnant for some time.

It is a blessing to be the conduit for higher consciousness to enter the lower realms and transmute it. All will benefit this way. It is a great service not only to humanity but to divinity itself. You are all honored, loved, cherished, and supported more than you can ever know. The time is now. The moment is now. For only "the now" exists.

I and my brothers of the light are part of you. We are part of the fabric of your crystalline DNA consciousness. Call upon us. Use us. Allow us to be your foundation and your inspiration, which assists you in accessing the temple of your soul. Your role is more profound than you think, not in the complexity of life, but in the simplicity of being truly who you are in love, in compassion, in honor and integrity.

So how do you know you are these things? By the shift that happens when you consciously intend to align with the temple of your soul in each moment. To consciously align in all that you do with Divine Will, With Divine Purpose and Divine Love. For then you will feel energy, lightness, peace, an upliftment, and perhaps insight or inspiration, for that is the God within the tenderest of places shining forth and speaking with you.

It is with joy, compassion, humor, humility, and love that we come to you, for this is our reflection of you, back to yourselves, that you've called forth. It is who you are at the core, in those deep tender places. We are here to assist you in reflecting that to each other and back to us, for in doing so we all return to unity, for there is no separation. So be it and so it is."

Namaste,

~ St. Germain and the Hosts of Heaven

The profundity of this message helped me feel more confident in my ability to access information from beyond the veil. Putting this message forth was the beginning of my life moving in a whole new direction.

Chapter 20: The Larger Plan Unfolds

I continued training in different healing modalities, including the Possibilities DNA School, learning how to work energetically with DNA. This training included activating the twelve strand DNA along with processes to determine where the communications breakdown happened on a DNA level related to traumas, issues, and diseases. I attended their advanced course in Coeur D'Alene, Idaho in the spring of 2004.

On the last training day, Margaret Ruby, the head of the school, stood up and announced she just finished the best book she'd read in years called *Anna, Grandmother of Jesus* by Claire Heartsong. She'd mentioned no books before, nor had I ever seen her be so passionate about something. By the title, I assumed it would be a typical Christian based book. However, I soon discovered it was far from the usual Christian view. It was way more metaphysical than anything I'd encountered. Something about Margaret's passion about it, along with my guide's strong nudges, made me decide I'd better go buy a copy even though I didn't believe it was my thing.

To say it blew my socks off was putting it mildly! It was the first thing I'd ever read about Jesus, the Holy Family and the Christ drama, which felt true to me. What really blew me away however was in the last chapter of the book, "Afterword from Claire." Claire talked about a 1987 life-transforming physical encounter with the Ascended Master St. Germain in the Grand Tetons. This was the first time I'd ever heard of anyone else recounting a meeting with St. Germain in a physical body like I'd had with him when he appeared as the bum in Boston in 1982. My guides strongly impressed upon me to contact her. I am usually shy. Reluctant to put myself out there particularly to well-known celebrities or authors, after receiving continual but gentle prompting from my guides, I surrendered. I finally emailed Claire and introduced myself. I let her know that I too had had a physical encounter with St. Germain. I asked her if she'd be willing to share more details of her encounter with him. I hoped it would shed additional light on my encounter with him and why it had happened for both of us. I didn't get a response from her, which wasn't surprising.

Who was I anyway?

I was just an anonymous person who'd bought the *Anna, Grandmother of Jesus* book and contacted her like I figured many people do.

Also in 2004, I assisted at the Wesak Festival in Mt. Shasta, California. A panel of channels including Philip Burley who channeled St. Germain, were presenters at this conference. After the conference, I put my name down on a long waiting list to get a private reading from him and St. Germain.

When I finally had the reading with Philip Burley, the very first thing he said to me was that I was like a long, cool, glass of water. Then he informed me that Master Jesus walked up to me and said hello in a very human friendly way. He then shared that Jesus had penetrating rays of light streaming from his eyes into mine which he said was *love incarnate*. Philip said that in all his years of channeling he'd never seen Jesus do this before.

Okay.

I am not sure what this all means.

When Philip channeled St. Germain, St. Germain greeted me by saying, "God bless you. We meet again."

"Were you the bum that day in Boston in 1982?" I asked.

"Most certainly! And that is why I say we meet again."

I finally had confirmation that it was St. Germain on the park bench in Boston that day. We discussed many other things in the reading, including how other beings such as Archangel Michael and Buddha also worked with me, among others. They, along with St. Germain, helped me with my writing and healing abilities. Then he told me of a very brilliant blue-white light, cosmic in

Chapter 20: The Larger Plan Unfolds

its nature, an entity who came from way beyond the beyond who also worked with me. He described it as a "great force."

"This being is gigantic," Philip said, almost like a superhero-representing a group soul. "This being connects with you particularly in your heart and throat chakras as you sit and write at the computer."

Philip continued on, "It is a rare moment when we have this kind of reality come into the consciousness of an earthling. Count yourself very fortunate."

I had barely started what I'd considered real writing at this point. I didn't know what to make of this reading except I remembered Bill Nakagawa in Hawaii being so amazed by this huge being of light which always seemed to be with me.

Was this the same being?

I seemed to collect a lot of puzzle pieces, but I still hadn't any idea what anything meant, or what I was supposed to do.

In the reading, St Germain said, "You see, the privilege of having a reading like this is very rare. My only concern for you is not myself that you even know me, but that you love yourself enough to do all the things that you need to do to become totally liberated from this earth plane, to be whole and spiritually healthy, and to be exceedingly happy!"

Well, okay...

I must work towards that.

I continued to take part in events which deepened my quest to understand *energy*, how to manage it, and how to use it to raise my frequency. I went to an Illumination Intensive in southern California, a three-day event where prior to the event we had to hand over our cell phones, watches, computers, iPads, or anything which would connect us with the outside world or even give us the time of day. The staff would get us up often in the dark to start the day as we hadn't any idea what time it was. There were a lot of interactions and exercises we did in the workshop, including an hour-long walking meditation outside each day. Freezing cold and windy on the second day, we were outside doing the walking meditation, but I found it hard to relax into a meditative state when I was so cold.

Fortunately, I found a temporary solution. I stuck the upper half of my body from the waist up deep into a bush for warmth and refuge from the relentless, frigid wind. I stayed there for the remaining fifty minutes of the meditation. The harsh wind had mitigated into a gentle cold breeze among the leaves. As I settled into just being in "presence" with myself and the bush, I marveled at how several of the leaves kept gently caressing my face as they wafted on the breeze. The rustling became a welcomed sound, deepening my meditation. Throughout the entire experience, I felt exquisitely touched, caressed, and loved, experiencing a profound deep connection to Source through this bush.

During that meditation, I also noticed the birds chattering away. As I got carried into their song, they showed me how they unwound low frequency energy out of people's auric fields through their sounds and songs, showing me an image of a large ball of yarn being unknotted and unwound. This was an analogy of how much tangled lower frequency *energy* people carry around in their fields. I did not know if this was true or not, but it felt true for me. I had never stopped long enough to be fully present with nature quite this way before.

If only I could feel this loved and exquisitely caressed like this by a man. I thought, that's all I wanted.

However, I realized this exchange with the leaves of the bush had given me a much broader experience of what love truly was. I was grateful it was so cold outside and that we had to wait for the full hour before we could go back inside, otherwise I would not have opened up to a deeper level of love I never knew was possible.

By the third and last day of the workshop, I finally understood what was going on around me. Several people were having spontaneous Kundalini experiences. What people were experiencing in that intensive were many ways they could activate the Kundalini and raise their consciousness. All this kept adding to my repertoire of exercises, processes, and insights into understanding more about *energy* and the awakening process.

About this time, my friend Sharon sold her house in Portland and decided to travel overseas for a while, spending some of that time in India to do Deeksha Training. For years, she ran a monthly meditation group and potluck

Chapter 20: The Larger Plan Unfolds

in Portland, which my friend Charlotte and I took over when she left Portland to travel.

After giving up any expectations of receiving a response to the initial email I sent months before to Claire Heartsong, in the beginning of 2005, out of the blue I received an email from her. It took me a minute to even place the name and remember who she was as the author of *Anna, Grandmother of Jesus*. In her email, she mentioned she had a cancellation for a reading on March 8th with Anna, the Virgin Mary's mother and Jesus's grandmother whom she channeled. She wanted to know if I wanted to take that spot. I didn't even know she channeled Anna for private readings. I didn't know what I wanted to do. Pretty much all of my questions had been answered in the reading I'd had with Philip Burley and St. Germain. Also, money was tight. I had just paid for the reading with Philip Burley a short while before. I didn't intend to ignore Claire and not respond to her request, but I honestly forgot about it.

About three weeks after receiving the email from Claire when I didn't respond, I then received a phone call from her confirming my appointment for March 8th.

I responded, "What appointment? I'm the one who wanted to know about your meeting with St. Germain in the Grand Tetons!"

She said, "I remember that now."

I told her I wasn't even aware she channeled Anna for readings for people. I reminded her I was the one who'd also met St. Germain in a physical body in 1982. Claire said she then remembered my email. Suddenly, she became very emotional. Even though I couldn't see her as we were on the phone, I could hear the emotion in her voice.

She said, "I think Anna really wants to speak to you."

Something in her voice got to me. I decided I'd better keep this reading, so I purchased the session. Later, I found out Claire had a year and a half long waiting list of people wanting to get in and have readings with Anna. Yet here she and Anna were trying to convince me to take that slot for the reading. Something was up! It wasn't like Claire needed to get me to commit to having a session with her trying to drum up business. When I had the reading, Anna told me she was one of my guides, the one who nudges me and helps me with my writing. She also said we were teachers together at Mt. Carmel (now Haifa, Israel). Anna also shared how she and I had been in every kind of relationship humans could be with one another throughout our lifetimes together.

Then she asked, "Do you know you are a character in the *Anna, Grandmother of Jesus* book?"

"Uh, no." I muttered.

She continued on, "Who do you think you were in the book?"

I hadn't any idea, especially since I'd read the book over seven months earlier. She told me which character I was since she didn't want to put me on the spot. In the reading, Anna also talked about how we were building the "New Mt. Carmel." I didn't know what that meant either or what I should do regarding any of the information from this reading, as it was all a little overwhelming. I just let it sit on the back burner for the time being and went on with my increasingly unhappy life.

My relationship with Rich had continued to deteriorate over the past four years. Even though I'd moved out of sharing the bedroom with him, Rich was totally content with the arrangement. As long as he had his computers, his cats and his projects and a warm body to talk to occasionally (me), he was happy as a clam. I, however, was miserable. At the tail end of an astrology reading, I had with someone in Portland, I mentioned the difficulty I was having with Rich. This astrologer glanced at our two charts.

He turned to me and said, "This relationship works one hundred percent for him and zero for you."

Yup, he was right! I'd known for a while I needed to leave the relationship. Besides being unhappy, I also wanted to move to open myself up for the possibility of meeting someone new who was a better fit for me romantically and emotionally. I knew I could not draw this person into my life if I still was with Rich.

Figuring where to go and financially how to make a move in which I could sustain myself was the big question. When I first knew leaving was in the cards and was inevitable, it took almost two years for me to move out. I found a roommate situation with someone who at one time was in the cult with me. Although she'd left a year or two before I left the group, we were happy to reconnect. Even though I loved the house Rich and I lived in, it would have been much more difficult to leave this wonderful house if it hadn't turned into a hoarder's nest. I was there for five years, the longest time I'd lived in any place in my adult life. I was in a relationship with Rich for six years. Leaving was bittersweet.

After splitting with Rich, it was even more financially challenging trying to make ends meet. I was trying to get a new business started, still worked with occasional clients, and I taught water aerobics. Nothing was working well for me to create financial stability. I intuitively knew I needed to have a reading with both Cynthia Slon and my friend Susanne Rollow, another psychic, a tarot reader I'd been going to for years in Portland.

I needed to get some perspective on why everything was so challenging for me at the moment and why nothing I did seemed to work. Around Labor Day, I'd tried getting these readings scheduled, but things would come up. Both of them postponed the date for a reading many times. I was desperate for guidance and information which could help me know what to do, as I was struggling financially and emotionally. Occasionally I had hypnotherapy clients who came to me for past-life regression sessions, but most of my consistent income came from teaching water aerobics at different fitness clubs and a retirement village in Portland.

When I thought it couldn't get any worse, it did. Early in December, I slipped and fell on the pool deck while teaching water aerobics and tore a ligament in my knee. All of my income streams had dwindled down to where teaching Water Aerobics was my only remaining consistent source of income. Now I wouldn't even have that source of income until my knee recovered which would be at least a few months down the line.

An opportunity presented itself which would provide me with most of my needed rent money for January, however it was the last thing I could ever have imagined doing. Rich, my ex-partner, whom I left the previous July, had tried online dating unsuccessfully with American women. Not willing to give up online dating, he started carrying on with two women from Russia. This online dating became serious with one woman as they started the paperwork for her to come to the states to marry Rich.

When I lived with Rich, he never wanted to go out or do anything beyond a three-mile radius of the house. He called me up and asked if I would come back to cat sit at the house. For three weeks over the Christmas holiday, he was going to Siberia (Ukraine) to meet his soon-to-be wife. He asked if I would stay at the house and give Feathers the cat insulin shots twice a day and take the other cat to the vet twice a week for IVs, the kitty version of dialysis, offering to pay me a small amount of money to do this.

So desperate for money to pay my upcoming rent, I told him, "Yes, I'll do it."

Meanwhile, I was still struggling with getting around as I was on crutches this whole time. While cat sitting, I finally had the first reading with Suzanne Rollow on December 29th, 2005 which I'd been trying to schedule since the beginning of September.

This was such a pivotal reading for me I've included a condensed excerpt below. Some language in the reading was very crude and the images unsettling, but this was necessary to portray accurately the *energetic* state I was immersed in. It started with communication from my guides, most of whom, Susanne said, were from the galactic realms.

This E.T. (extraterrestrial) group of guides said, "It does not appear you are going to suffer, suffer, and die in misery." (I felt that way at this point.)

Susanne continued, "As I looked at it, you are sitting in this chair trying to get up. There are these octopus' tentacle types of arms around you; around your waist and around your breasts. I couldn't tell if it was one creature or many creatures, but in trying to get up, every single part of your body was physically struggling against the imprisoned state you are in on that chair. It was scary to look at because something about that darkness was so intense it made me pull back and contract."

The guides all looked at you and said, "No need to fear."

Then you said, "I can't do it."

Your weight fell fully back into the chair. Their tentacles tightened further around you. You had an awareness somewhere deep within you that, yeah, the body could die in this. You knew you couldn't just stay in this heightened state of fear and struggle much longer.

Chapter 20: The Larger Plan Unfolds

Then you said, "Oh fuck it all. I don't give a shit."

When you said that, this solid ball of energy, which looked like a little duck-pin bowling ball, popped out of your heart into your lap.

"What was that?" Susie asked.

You said, "Oh that's the grief, it's so much, so compacted, it's a solid ball."

"That's not all of it."

Susie continued, "So, know there's nothing you can do to repair any of it or to make anything better? You're sitting in this incredibly helpless space calling out for help. You see beloveds walking by you, hearing your call, but they don't even turn their heads to look at you, which evoked old trauma within your soul memory of feeling like a leper."

Susie continued on. Jesus's energy just walked in the door.

He looked at you and said, "I understand. You know how close you and I are. Part of what you came here to do this lifetime is to continue the ray of energy I was working with. How can you embrace that ray fully without embracing the persecution and the betrayal by loved ones? That's part of it. Now I know it even feels like on the spirit level there is nobody walking with you. Obviously, to me spiritually, you keep incredibly good company out there, but what good does that do? It doesn't do any good, nor does it make anything better. It doesn't protect you at all."

Jesus continued with what he could offer, "Let's embrace each other. Come wail on my shoulder."

Susie continued. "I just feel like the biggest challenge; the hardest thing right now for you are the loved ones walking by and not caring."

Susie looked at Jesus. He's giving me this look which says obviously, he could love fully all those who betrayed him. He didn't blame them for his suffering. He used all of that pain and suffering to transcend.

"It doesn't feel like you're supposed to sit with yourself trying to work through it either on a spiritual or therapeutic (level) or any of that. I feel like what's really being asked is for you to continue to grieve about this. Every which way you've turned, you could get knocked down, be dying, call out for help and people still wouldn't respond. I wanted to say after everything you have done for everybody else, why are those scales so out of balance?"

Jesus says, "Don't try to figure it out. Trying to figure it out will only cause more pain."

Susie continued with the reading.

"It's like you are Mother Earth. You are every being on her. You are experiencing all the challenges. Part of it is your commitment to doing whatever you can during this time of significant change to assist the earth and humanity. Feeling all the injustices on all levels in your denser human body is one of those tentacles which represents all the people who walk right on by."

"You can't separate yourself from any of the pain, upset, challenges, or other hideous stuff which is happening on this planet right now. Jesus says he just wants fully to be with you while you bear the pain."

Jesus continues, "So, in the alchemy pot right now there's all this poison, but all the ingredients haven't gone into the pot yet. There are two other ingredients to this alchemy. When all three ingredients combine, the poison, along with these other two ingredients, becomes something incredibly healing and rejuvenation occurs. The poison is a necessary ingredient needed to make the new elixir. That ingredient, however, on its own can kill. But blend it with these two other ingredients, then alchemy happens. It's transformed."

I asked for more clarity on these other two ingredients.

Susie responded, "One of these other ingredients has a lot to do with something you are going to be receiving in your personal life."

In saying that, the beaten-down part of you responded, "I will not knock on anybody's door anymore. I not even going there. If there is something for me to receive, it is going to have to find its way to me."

Susie continued, "There was absolutely no appeal in knocking on the door, and seeing all of these little faces part the curtains to look out at you and then closing the curtains and walking away."

Jesus says, "This is not personal. It is not about your actions and energies or how people are responding to you. You'll have more understanding after the other ingredients mix in. But until it's transformed into whatever the new potion is, you can't drink it in the form it is in because it will kill you."

I'm confused.

What a paradox!

Chapter 20: The Larger Plan Unfolds

How was I to understand this?

Jesus went on, "You are supposed to feel the feelings and emotions coming up, which are all personal. There are a few relatives and other people who sort of want to help you, but what they offer you hurts even more."

Susie continued to explain. "They imply that obviously you aren't good enough the way you are. In order to be good enough, you are going to have to change."

Then this beautiful spirit which you are said, "But wait a second, this is what I always was."

And they would say, "Nope, nope, you wouldn't be in this miserable predicament then. You are in this predicament because either you haven't paid attention or blah, blah, blah or done blah, blah, blah."

Susie commented, "I just keep coming back to how much you are releasing and discharging on behalf of the bigger collective through what you are going through. But what do you do?"

He (Jesus) says, "Don't even look for moments of peace of mind or whatever. Just don't even look for it. Do nothing. Again, it could all change tomorrow."

Susie reiterated, "Right now you're not supposed to figure anything out. It's like everything is forcing you to lie down now. Here's this stinky betrayal pile of shit you have to lie down in. I don't feel there is any other choice or any other option as you've exhausted every other choice and every other option."

Susie went on sharing the next image she received.

"I am standing beside you next to a graveyard plot containing a coffin filled up with shit."

You look at me and say, "Well here I go."

"I watched as you fell head-first into it as it kind of oozed up over you."

Then this feminine being walked in carrying a lot of Mother Mary's *energy*, saying, "Just call me Mother."

She stood beside me saying, "That baby's mine. That baby is mine (meaning me)."

Susie went on, "She has a kind of shawl over her face and a gold headband around her 3rd eye. She picks up the hem of her white inner robes under outer blue robes and gracefully steps into that cesspool."

"I just watch her sinking, sinking down deeper into the mess until she's fully disappeared into it, yet there was still movement. Now her head started coming up out of it, covered with shit. Yet she opens her eyes and looks at me. Her beautiful eyes are alive and sparkly. She has you in her arms almost exactly in the same pose as the Pieta statue by Michelangelo where Mary is holding Jesus stretched out on her lap after the crucifixion. Here was this mature woman's body of yours being brought up and out. It didn't even look like you were breathing."

"Mary carried you to this really low, long body of water like an infinity swimming pool with a very gentle waterfall and some sacred pools. She laid you directly beneath the waterfall so the water hit you right down in the center of your body. It's like the water was clearing your spine from the front side. Then she put you completely in it, head first, so the *energy* started building in the head first."

"When the water started cascading over your body, clearing you off, there was still shit on each side. Then this beautiful, healthy pink skin where the water washed the shit away from you emerged from your center."

Mary said, "From the place of being in that grave, buried in that shit, you cannot get out of it on your own, as other people were encouraging you to do. You're not supposed to. It was all about me coming for you."

Susie described what she was being shown. She needs you to know that she's lifting her skirts now, coming for you in a very real, human way.

"I see you. I know where you are. I can't lose you." Mary says as she comes and scoops you up. Everything about this situation was that you're not supposed to be doing anything. I know you feel you can't take it anymore. It's almost like you wish an accident would take you out of your body because it is so intense. That could be a pretty darn good relief right now. But that is a "doing" thing. You're not supposed to *do*. I asked, "Will I clearly know when it shifts?"

Susanne said, "5-6 weeks into the New Year I would see it shift. There would not be the panic or pain anymore. December has just been the worst of the worst of the worst. I don't think there's been a worse time in your life. You've tried it all, tried everything, and you've tried from all different levels so valiantly. So, allow her (Mary) to come for you, to wash you clean. She says she's dumbed herself down to talk to me in this way. In February, you will be off and moving in a new direction and you will not be living in your present housing situation much longer. You are not to be concerned how it comes about."

"She's kind of shutting down all the light around bank accounts and dollars and cents, to not even let any of the minuses be visible. She says there is a home space that is coming for you. That is all yours. It doesn't feel huge, it's supposed to be smaller to nurture you. Also, it doesn't feel like the second I turn around, I bounce into walls. It's a place where you'll transform. This beautiful little home space is where the artist, the visionary, the Aquarian little being you are can come to life fully."

"Even though everything in your greater being says surrender to the dying of it, let go of it, and let them come for you; everything in your body says it's proven to me time and time again, that nobody comes for me."

Talk about needing to have ultimate trust!

Susie continued on, "Mary looks at me and says she knows the shit image bothers me. Everything that she tastes in you (Catherine Ann) is pure sweetness. You aren't allowed to take yourself down. There is no energy for it, anyway."

Mary continued addressing you, "My beloved sister, daughter, and mother, this is grace. It's like everything has turned upside down and inside out. It is like it's the opposite. In the middle of February, things could speed up."

For many months I had really been struggling with the feeling I couldn't even trust my own intuition anymore because it didn't seem to work. In order to prevent myself from being overwhelmed by the drama of earthly activities, I had to surrender to a particular place of awakened consciousness and aliveness. Then Susie asked me if I knew of Adyashanti, a spiritual teacher in the San Francisco Bay Area. I'd heard of him but had never personally experienced his teachings. She said his energy was coming in now.

He looks at you and asks, "How does it feel to be awake now?"

Susie and I both laughed and responded, "Like Shit!"

He continued, "What you are experiencing is part of waking up. The waking up process while you are still in a body, on this plane, is so intense it can make people go crazy, literally go crazy. Here you are in emptiness, nobody, a no-thing. It's one thing to know that, but we're meant to call out the demons within, meet them and love them; it's a whole other ballgame to experience that fully. I bow down to you for your courage to experience it. That takes tremendous courage."

Susie continued, "Well he just wanted you to know this from the humble place he sits. You are doing very well with it. It won't make you crazy if you keep on doing nothing. He thinks it's quite beautiful you are in that place where there's nothing to grab onto, that you don't even want to knock on a door anymore."

He says, "That is the beginning of the sweet surrender piece, finally the surrender piece. So, you'll be feeling more sweetness around you."

Jesus popped back in and said, "Then you let go of the personal attachment, the personal whining, and the shame of you, and all that kind of stuff. There is nothing personal about it. It's all been an incredible vehicle to support you in your waking up process. That's why awakened ones never encourage others. All of your experiences have brought you to that horrible place. So, you get to be, as usual, one of the truth tellers. There are people who want the same thing you want more than the pretty picture of what the "new agers" or "spiritual" people think it should look like. There are a few people who are ready."

The information from this reading was so profound not only in describing this initiation of sorts but also showing me that when we do the deep inner dive addressing the darkness or shadow within us, not only does the inner state shift, but the external shifts as well. The guides were right. In less than four months after this reading, my entire life shifted in unfathomable ways to an entirely distinct reality, a different timeline than the one I'd been living. I'd been receiving clues all along.

So here again, Jesus and Mother Mary showed up not only as sub-personalities within me, but in the reading with Philip Burley and this reading with Susie Rollow.

But why me?

Honored that they showed up, it didn't make logical sense. I'd ditched Catholicism long ago at age eighteen. I hadn't been interested in pursuing anything remotely Christian. I never prayed to them nor deliberately held them in my consciousness once I left the Catholic Church. As I recount this experience, I'm finally unpacking the profound wisdom this experience offered me and how pivotal it was for everything yet to come.

This reading revealed the deep spiritual initiatory process of completely surrendering to the darkness before the dawn could take place. I remembered teachings I'd received years before that the straight up path to ascension came about through embracing the dark and the light equally with no duality. This reading and experience helped me understand what that meant. To embrace the dark meant not trying to sweep it under the rug, escape it, fix it, or change it. It was to surrender to the alchemical nature of the divinity within it by being fully present with it in non-resistance. Then magic could happen. I was reminded that I'd experienced another profound initiation somewhat similar in its nature to this over twenty years before. Then I'd also entered a complete state of non-resistance, which caused my entire life to shift dramatically during that next thirty-six-hour period without me doing one external thing.

Out of the wisdom gained through this and other similar experiences, I eventually would start conducting workshops. I would teach how every day we live crucifixion, resurrection and ascension. Every time we judge, blame, or condemn something, someone else, or ourselves, we crucify that which is around us. Every time we take responsibility for our part in things, for our actions, and we're able to surrender to being totally present to what is in the space, we are enacting resurrection. Through resurrection, the frequency of the situation is naturally raised to a higher frequency, which is ascension. It is all about *energy* and raising one's frequency yet again!

In this experience of sinking into all that shit, this was crucifixion to the max. It was only when I was so tightly bound, could not even struggle, could not change it, could do nothing but let go and surrender, it changed. I had to stop struggling against the darkness (shit) thinking in any way I could change it or heal it. I had to stop thinking from my human level, thinking if I could only stop judging it, blaming it, thinking I was a victim, or resisting it because it felt like it would overwhelm me and smother me; things would change. It didn't. It was only when I fully let go of trying to do anything, or make it different, that the alchemy occurred.

By letting go and sinking into it completely, I "died" to it. I was fully present with it. In that deep depth of darkness, at the bottom of the cesspool, there was no separation, no judgment of myself, or it. There was only being with it, fully in oneness. It was being in unconditional love with it, just like when the sidewalk rushed up to meet and greet my foot.

When I surrendered to that place of no separation, I became the "whole," the yin/yang. I became the darkness and the light equally. It was only when this place of no separation, of no longer being in polarity, that the higher divine light aspect became accessible. It was as much an inherent part of me as was the darkness. I could achieve full sweet surrender to the inherent divinity within as this resurrection occurred only if I did nothing. This is what Mary showed me. This Divine Mother aspect, along with my willingness to surrender fully, were the two other ingredients to the alchemical elixir. The darkness-evil was the "poison."

I came into this life fully immersed in the poison. This wasn't only in the victimization and abuse I suffered in the early years of my life and later with various betrayals, but also in the in-utero toxic environment of my early gestation. My soul really set up the scene this time around for me to get this lesson without sidestepping it. I understood what a vital part of the awakening process this experience was. I also finally understood, for myself, what I believe Jesus was showing us on the cross. He literally and figuratively died to the lower nature of his humanness, to the polarity. When he became "as one" within himself, "one with the father" meaning the light aspect of divinity, he became the unified heaven and earth, male and female, darkness and light.

The greater aspects of divinity and darkness were no longer being separated through thought or emotion into opposing forces. It was only natural that resurrection and eventually ascension would occur through realization of unity. In this, the frequency kept rising. It was also crystal clear to me I needed

Chapter 20: The Larger Plan Unfolds

to experience and move through this deep initiatory process personally to gain the wisdom, understanding and frequency change.

No one else could do it for me, not even Jesus. He let me know he was there for emotional support and to give a shoulder to cry on but it was my journey, just as it is the journey of self-mastery each one of us does individually to become the Christ inherent in all of us. Going through this initiation was only mine to do without someone to step in to help, support or prop me up.

After having the first reading, which I knew I needed to have with Suzanne, the second reading I knew I needed took place with Cynthia Slon in mid-February 2006. The first part of the reading with Cynthia was what she shared with me about living the blueprint which wasn't mine as I shared earlier in this book. The second half of the reading shifted into a whole different topic when Cynthia paused for a minute as she communicated with my guides. They told her that there was a possibility I could connect with someone very close in my soul group and move out of Oregon to another state.

Yeah, right, "nothing I've done seems to work," was my thought regarding this remark.

I was skeptical, but the sequence of events bringing this about had already been set into motion. I just didn't know it.

During our January potluck and meditation group, which my friend Charlotte and I facilitated, someone who had borrowed my copy of *Anna, Grandmother of Jesus*, returned it to me. Charlotte asked what it was, so I showed her. She then asked if she could borrow it.

I said, "Sure," and gave it to her.

Shortly after she started reading the *Anna, Grandmother of Jesus* book, on the night of February 14th Yeshua (Jesus) came to Charlotte and whispered a message to her. He told to go to her computer to Claire Heartsong's website. Now Charlotte almost never surfed the Internet unless she had to do something for her work. So, she obediently went to the computer and brought up Claire Heartsong's web page. Buried deep in the text was one sentence in which Claire had put out an appeal for a business and spiritual partner. Charlotte sent Claire an email introducing herself, asking Claire if she would ask Anna (Jesus's grandmother) if there was anything she could do. Then she went to bed. In the

Raising My Frequency

middle of the night, Charlotte got up to use the bathroom. On her way back to bed, she said she heard a loud booming male voice in her head.

This booming voice said, "That's Catherine Ann's job!"

Charlotte's initial reaction was, "Catherine Ann? Well, what about me?"

The following morning, she'd gotten over her feeling of being overlooked. She was so excited to call me and tell me about this experience. She tried all morning to reach me but each time she tried to call, she'd get a strong feeling of, "No, wait!" Finally on her tenth try she gets the go ahead from her guides to call. However, when she received the go-ahead to call, she got my voicemail!

Frustrated, she complained to her guides. How could they give her the go-ahead to call when she only got my voicemail? Of course, I knew nothing of this until I checked the voicemail message after my phone reading with Cynthia. I also didn't know that Yeshua occasionally gave messages to Charlotte. When Charlotte and I finally talked, she was so excited. She exclaimed, "I know that is your job!"

Of course, I wasn't convinced, as nothing I had tried doing for so long had worked out. I wasn't even sure if Claire remembered who I was. Charlotte had already scheduled an interview with Claire, so she suggested I call and also schedule an interview with her. When I called to see about setting up the interview, Claire said she remembered me very well. She also remembered I'd had the reading with her the year before.

After our initial individual interviews with Claire, Charlotte and I also had a series of joint interviews with her. We all concluded that both of us were to go assist Claire. Charlotte didn't need the salary as she and her ex-husband had residual income from being founding members of a large, multi-level marketing company. Also, she didn't have the business and web design experience required for the position. I ended up being hired as Claire's business and spiritual partner while Charlotte went along as Claire's unpaid personal assistant. We made a plan to visit Claire in Springdale, Utah, for five days to see if we all were in agreement with this plan.

A few weeks later, Charlotte and I bought a plane ticket to Las Vegas. We rented a car and drove to Springdale at the entrance to Zion National Park where Claire lived. The drive from Vegas took a little under three hours. After going through St. George and La Verkin, there was a right turn where you started climbing up the hills into the desert. Soon all the street lights disappeared and there were no longer any houses. It was dusk and would soon be dark. I felt like we were driving into the void. I started getting nervous about what we might get ourselves into, especially after having been lured into a cult for eight years. When I expressed my concern to Charlotte, we just started uncontrollably laughing until tears ran down our faces. We were laughing so much it was hard not to pee my pants.

About fifteen minutes later we finally arrived at Claire's beautiful home. We went up on her porch to ring the doorbell. Valiantly, we tried to control our laughter as it hadn't yet totally subsided. The door opened. Claire caught us completely off guard. It was like being greeted by a munchkin from the Wizard of Oz as Claire is only four feet six inches tall, not at all what we expected. This only further caused us to burst out with a new wave of peals of laughter. My cheeks and ears turned bright red, burning with embarrassment at our behavior. Nevertheless, Claire invited us in.

Her first words to us were, "The Hathors must have gotten hold of you."

Hathors are ancient ascended masters of sound and light who often instigate laughter and bring joy. Thus began our interaction and relationship with Claire.

During the five-day visit, we got to know each other. We felt into the possibilities of this collaboration and came to the unanimous decision to move forward with the plan. What also helped with the decision was the assurance we also had places to live. An adjoining neighbor of Claire's had two cabins on his property, which he said he would fix up and rent out to us. Charlotte would move into one, and I'd move into the other. In our five days together, Claire also brought up the possibility that she was looking for land to purchase for a retreat center. I wondered if this was for the New Mt. Carmel which Anna had mentioned in my reading the year before. This visit was not all about work however, we also had some fun.

On St. Patrick's Day, we attended the parade and festivities in Springdale. One of these was the annual green Jell-O Contest. Participants submitted dioramas of whatever scene they wanted to depict. The only rule was that they had to make at least 50% of the diorama with lime green Jell-O. The one that caught my attention the most, which I couldn't believe was on public display, was the green Jell-O king size bed with seven pregnant Barbie dolls on it representing the seven sister wives. Although Springdale was probably the most liberal town in southern Utah, it was still a heavily Mormon area with polygamist colonies not too far away. There was a lot I was to learn.

Six weeks after our visit to Springdale, Charlotte and I rented a U-Haul truck and drove to Utah. The truck was mostly for my things as I was moving everything I owned—furniture, upright piano, and all my belongings—while Charlotte, who still owned a house in Portland, only took what she would temporarily need. We arrived and unloaded the truck, initially putting everything in the driveway so we could return the truck and not owe any more money. The neighbor who owned the cabins hadn't yet finished fixing them up, but we started moving things in anyway. I was carrying in a two-shelf press-board bookcase, which I usually used in my closet to hold shoes. When the owner saw me moving the bookcase into the cabin, he had a fit. He was irate that I'd move a piece of press-board furniture into one of his cabins. He had such a complete meltdown over this, he changed his mind about renting us the cabins and told us we couldn't move into them after all.

You've got to be kidding me?

It wasn't even like we were moving into a palace but simple, funky cabins.

What was the big deal, anyway?

I guess it was an easy out for him. Here we were with all our possessions in the middle of the driveway, having to come up with Plan B. Since Charlotte only had a few things for a temporary stay, we decided she would move into the second bedroom in Claire's house. Finding lodging for me was a different matter altogether. Springdale was small and housing was scarce. By a stroke of luck, and I am sure a bit of shuffling things around from the other side of the veil, a vacant apartment which someone had been holding on to for about ten months suddenly became available.

It was an upstairs apartment in a small two-story apartment building in Springdale. The rent was way more than I could afford, so Claire co-signed the lease agreement with me, promising to pay the difference. To all of our relief, I

Chapter 20: The Larger Plan Unfolds

now had a two-bedroom place of my own to live in. It wasn't until later that I reflected on the readings I'd had in January and February that predicted this. Had I known I was going to have to move a piano up and down the stairs, I might not have opted to bring it along.

Finally, we started getting Claire's business all set up. I networked all the computers together and did all my geeky stuff to get ready to help Claire. Claire always knew there was to be a sequel to her first channeled book. Years before, she apparently had a stern talk with the Councils of Light saying she didn't want to have to sequester herself away like a little monk working on the sequel like she'd done when she wrote the first book, *Anna, Grandmother of Jesus*. She wanted the Councils of Light to bring her a support team.

Charlotte and I turned out to be that support team that the Councils of Light promised to Claire. How on earth, of all the people Claire knew, did Charlotte and I end up in this position? It was a mystery to me. Just a few months before, I felt so challenged. I was like a bug who'd flown into a sliding glass door, smashed itself to a pulp and was sliding down the glass. I wondered how the Councils of Light decided Charlotte and I were the ones they were looking for and waiting for. Eventually I found out.

Then I realized this collaboration we were about to embark upon was probably the birth, the alchemy, and the metamorphosis that St. Germain and Jeheshua (my then spelling of his name) were referring to in their download to me four years earlier. What that would look like I did not know. I just knew I had to commit fully to the process whatever that entailed.

Chapter 21: Finding My Soul's Purpose

Finally, we were all set up and ready to begin. Claire went into her bedroom to channel the sequel. Charlotte and I were in the living room holding the space as her support team. In the middle of the third day, after writing only two chapters, Claire came out of the room dejected and confused, saying the *energy* was really "flat."

It wasn't the same heightened *energy* she experienced when channeling the first book. In writing the first book, Anna's energy had so encompassed her and raised her frequency in order for her to bring through the information that now she wondered what was wrong. She asked Anna what the problem was.

Anna replied, "Go ask Catherine Ann for a past life regression session."

Apparently, the Councils of Light had a whole different plan and execution of that plan in mind, which would take the triune energy of the three of us to pull it off. I got a tape recorder and found a microphone. Claire lay down on the couch as I got the equipment set up. We put an eye pillow over her eyes and covered her with a blanket. Theo, Claire's cat, always would show up for the sessions, lying either across her legs or on her chest area. We were ready to begin.

The Councils of Light came through first and greeted us. They gave us a specific protocol to use each time to prepare ourselves for the session, then the sessions started. We did sessions once or twice a day for the rest of the summer of 2006. I would facilitate the sessions by asking the questions and operating the recording equipment. Sometimes Charlotte was present for a session, but most of the time she was busy transcribing previous sessions. I would also help with transcribing sessions when I could.

Anna had already told me in a past life I was this specific character, Lizbett, who was the daughter of Yeshua (Jesus) and Mary of Bethany. Knowing this, I suggested to Claire that she try regressing me to see what would happen. I showed Claire how to facilitate the session although occasionally some of her questions were somewhat leading rather than being opened ended. But hey, this was her first time conducting a session. I brought through information from Lizbett. In being guided into this altered state, it was like an inner movie playing in my head, not unlike some previous inner movie experiences I'd had. This inner movie was just longer, with a lot more detail.

During this summer of 2006, we were pretty sequestered. It was like we were in our own little reality bubble. Mostly, the only times we went to town were when we went to eat buffalo burgers at this one restaurant in Springdale. We found we needed to eat red meat every once in a while, to keep ourselves grounded. Our energy would get pretty high doing these sessions so we needed some way to assist us in getting grounded back to our normal state. During the summer we also hosted some potlucks and gatherings at Claire's home. At these events, Claire would channel Anna for the group and answer questions. Claire's home in Springdale was the perfect place to do it, as we were within the energetic field of the Great White Throne. The Great White Throne is a monument in Zion National Park only a couple of miles away. Anna talked about the Great White Throne at different times sharing that it is a 12th dimensional portal. I am sure it had a bearing not only on the potlucks but also on the work we were doing with Anna on the sequel.

During that summer nineteen unique characters came through in the sessions with profound and even sometimes shocking information. In facilitating the sessions, I often had to ask some mundane types of questions to establish the identity of the individual as I hadn't any idea who would show up. I had to come up with questions to find out if they were an adult or a child. Were they male or female? Where were they? What were they doing? And what was the information they specifically came forward to share?

The sessions were more than just a download of information. Claire's body would sometimes take on sensations or feelings which the character was experiencing. When the character Nathaniel came through, Claire's body began noticeably to twitch and thrash around. Her face became distorted as if in discomfort. Nathaniel relayed an account of being tortured.

The most frightening moment for me came when Myriam of Tyana was in the body, initiating what the Egyptian alchemists called *The Opening of the Mouth*. I thought the session had come to a close and had prompted Claire to return to her normal consciousness. From a position lying down, suddenly Claire's body shot bolt upright with a piercing, blood-curdling scream. Myriam of Tyana, who I didn't realize was still in the body, was addressing the universal collective wound of suppression and repression of the Divine Feminine, for all of us not being heard. After that session Claire experienced excruciating neck pain only to find out many months later that she'd torn ligament in her neck from that occurrence.

Because most of the characters coming through had taken vows of secrecy and silence to protect the teachings, it was difficult for them to be forthcoming with what they had to share. I worked with the characters on a couple of different occasions helping them to release these vows of secrecy and silence so they felt safe enough to speak. Assuring them that what they were sharing would be for a different time and place in the distant future, I honored and thanked each of these characters for their courage to share what they'd long held and cherished in secrecy so it could now come out publicly.

Besides doing these sessions, Anna kept talking about how people who came to her audiences were Magdalenes. She shared with us that Magdalene was not just an individual, Mary Magdalene, but an order of consciousness to which both women and men throughout the ages have belonged. This Order has been present in all cultures known by different names throughout earth's history. All the Essenes and Holy Family members with Jesus 2000 years ago were Magdalenes, as are many of us today. Anna said we are the future selves of those Essenes and Holy Family members who seeded the light, along with Yeshua, thousands of years ago. We have incarnated now to bring those seeds planted two thousand years ago to fruition.

Most people, however, do not understand who they are and that they are Magdalenes. The mission of the Magdalenes is to seed the light and go into the darkness where no one else will go. They are the lighthouses, the light workers, the ones who just by their very presence, keep the light from being snuffed out in all kinds of situations of abuse and corruption whether it be in families, companies, churches, institutions, governments, organizations or whatever. Magdalenes are not a religion, they are a frequency in consciousness. I realized that the download I received in the late 1980s about being a volunteer, not a victim, was the definition of a Magdalene.

There is a chapter in the first *Anna, Grandmother of Jesus* book where all those working closely with Jesus before the crucifixion went to the Great Pyramid on the Giza plateau in Egypt to prepare for the coming ordeal. Everyone had a part to play. Even the healing and miracles Jesus performed throughout his life weren't done solely on his own.

He was part of a group consciousness both in the seen and unseen worlds which worked collectively with him and through him. Everyone, called to train in the zero-point field of the King's Chamber in the Great Pyramid, was there to rehearse their parts for the upcoming Christ drama. This way they would all know what they had to do. Also, it would help them cope better with the drama and trauma that would assault them as they witnessed this event.

One day Anna, through Claire, addressed the three of us. She said we'd all been rehearsing on the inner planes for eons for the roles we are stepping into today. Also, it was never about the Christ drama being the epitome of what was important as religion has made it.

Anna said, "The Christ drama was only the "dress rehearsal" for us for today."

She wasn't meaning only the three of us, but all the Magdalenes and lightworkers who are awakening.

All I could say was, "Holy Crap!" That's a tall order to live up to!

It made sense to me. We are the ones now to take the consciousness seeded thousands of years ago in the elements and in the genetic lines of humanity into full fruition through our insights and creations. We are being asked to reclaim our divine connection, so now we can do our part in bringing forth the New Earth through the present shift of consciousness. The New Earth is what Yeshua, the Holy Family, and the Essenes were seeding all those thousands of years ago. We are the ones trained for eons on the inner planes and in our sleep state to bring this about. I realized that was my purpose. That is what this awakening journey has been about.

The sessions continued throughout most of the summer, then out of nowhere, they abruptly stopped, even though I didn't really feel we had finished yet. I suppose it was because Claire was getting involved in a new relationship with someone in northern California and Charlotte was often off doing things with her ex-husband.

Right before the sessions abruptly ended, the three of us signed up for a tour of the south of France with Claire's friend Finbarr Ross. Finbarr owned a tour company Celtic Mystical Journeys, now called Sacred Mystical Journeys. Charlotte and Claire had also signed up to go on his England tour taking place before the France tour, but I couldn't afford to do that. Besides working with Claire, I'd also started working part-time for Finbarr as his office person registering people for the tours. In addition, Finbarr also hosted two Divine Feminine Conferences each year, one in the US, and one in Europe. He asked me to come help with the Divine Feminine Conference being held in Reading, England, at the tail end of the England tour. So, before the France trip started, I first went to England to assist with this conference.

Weeks before the scheduled Divine Feminine Conference in England, both Claire and Charlotte had left Springdale. Claire first went to visit her new love in California before going on to England. Charlotte, who'd met some man through an online dating site, agreed to meet up with him in England to tour the crop circles before Finbarr's England tour began. So here I was, yet again, alone, feeling left behind and confused why others around me seemed to always have people interested in them and would go off on romantic adventures, yet that didn't seem to happen to me. Left at home in Springdale caring for Claire's cat Theo, all of my emotional wounding came up again, plummeting me into yet another "dark night of the soul" period, as this familiar pattern of staying behind now to care for Claire's cat instead of the Guru's dogs repeated itself.

All of my self-doubt about being worthy or being lovable along with all the other negative thoughts I'd had about myself overtook me like a tidal wave. This was the next deeper level of these issues. I didn't know if it was the right thing to do or not, but I no longer had the strength, or will, to work through it or push it away. I just surrendered to the pit of darkness with full on wailing and feeling sorry for myself for weeks. It was like I was trying to purge all the rejection, invisibility, betrayal, disrespect, dishonoring, and lack of self-worth out of my system.

Even though it appeared it came from other people, I knew I was really doing these things to myself, so I persevered through the agony finally coming out the other end. It was also time for me to pull it together and pack to get ready to leave for England. Fortunately, traveling to Europe also helped me to shift out of these depths of despair.

After the England tour finished, we all went on Finbarr's South of France tour. We had a great time. This was only my second time going across "the pond." In 1998, I attended a ten-day Argentine Tango workshop in Berlin, Germany, which only came about because the tuition for the workshop was really reasonable and I lucked out purchasing airfare for a ridiculously low price. I just happened upon a mistake on their website, which the airline had to honor.

Now here I was in the south of France which was stunningly beautiful. The group got along well except that Claire was suffering a lot of pain. Besides having pain in her hip, she also experienced a lot of pain in her neck. This was from the injury she sustained while we were doing the sessions in which different characters in the sequel came forth. (See the "Opening of the Mouth" section in *Anna, the Voice of the Magdalenes*). Claire would often stay behind in the hotel rather than going hiking or on certain excursions with us. If you remember, it was only later on that she found out that she'd torn a ligament in her neck. Also, she eventually had a hip replacement done.

Margaret Starbird, the pioneering author of the book about Mary Magdalene, *The Woman with the Alabaster Jar* about Mary Magdalene, was also on the trip with us. Margaret was very Catholic and married to someone in the military. I felt like we (Charlotte, Finbarr and I) rattled her good Catholic schoolgirl, strait-laced perimeters a bit because we three were such the antithesis of that. But she was a good sport. One thing that touched me the most about this trip, however, was the relationship with our bus driver Karim. There were only twelve of us on the trip, so we didn't need a big bus. None of the smaller buses was available, so we ended up with this huge tour bus much larger than what we needed.

The driver, Karim, from Marseille, France, confided in Finbarr, who was Irish, how terrified he was to meet Americans. He feared we would hate him because he was Muslim. Our trip to France took place only five years after 9-11. This couldn't have been farther from the truth. I knew right away he was a Magdalene. In fact, as the tour went along, I became convinced he was a soul-stream aspect of the character Nathaniel in the Anna books. He always watched over us, keeping pace with us as we explored the different sites. Walking along the upper rim, keeping watch on us while we were down at the Cathar sites, he dedicated and committed himself to our welfare and well-being, yet he never interfered with what we were doing.

Once we were driving uphill on this winding small French countryside road on our way to Mt. Bugarach which is talked about in the Anna books. We came to a small bridge with concrete rails on either side. It was clear it was too narrow for the huge bus to navigate. Karim had us all exit the bus. In an amazing feat of skill, luck, and a miracle from above, he managed to back up this huge bus, eventually getting it turned around. Rarely have I met someone in the travel industry with such a large heart, dedication, and sense of integrity. I felt such a soul connection with him. I literally cried for two hours the day he left us, as we no longer needed the use of the bus. So much for him, fearing we were going to hate him.

As we drove up to Mt. Bugarach, I experienced an intense emotional reaction of deep soul resonance. Lizbett's parents conceived her in a cave at Mt. Bugarach. She spent her first years of life growing up in the Essene community there. Lizbett was the character in the *Anna, the Voice of the Magdalenes* book whom Anna said I had been. As tears welled up in my eyes and spilled down my cheeks, my body was having its own intensified remembrance of the soul's memory of this place.

Another profound experience for me was our visit to Aigne, the snail village. To get into this village, you had to follow the spiral path leading to the center of the village where the small chapel stood. We all streamed into the tiny chapel. It was so small; it took only a few minutes to view everything in it. I was the first to sit down in a pew to meditate. Although I had my eyes closed, I sensed that one by one, the others also found spots and sat down to meditate, a totally spontaneous occurrence.

Suddenly, in my inner vision I saw and felt a divine presence standing before me extending their forearms and hands outstretched towards me with their palms up. I knew I was to place my forearms and hands energetically on top of theirs like some kind of initiate's form of a greeting. As I did this, I became aware the presence before me was Mother Mary.

Holy crap!

Now Mother Mary was standing before me telepathically asking my permission to come around behind me and step into my body. Questions and concerns arose in me. I was definitely hesitant at first.

Could I really trust my intuition?

Was this truly Mother Mary?

What if letting someone step into my body harmed me or possessed me?

After a couple of minutes entertaining these kinds of thoughts, I had a little pep talk reasoning with my ego self who was definitely fearful of this prospect.

How often does Mother Mary come to you and ask something like this of you?

Well, never...

Get over yourself!

Just do it.

I eventually consented. Next, I knew Mother Mary had come around behind me and stepped into my body. I could feel a merging somehow. For about ten minutes, I felt her mucking around in there. It was sort of like when you know someone is up in your attic moving around but you can't hear them clearly or really know what they are doing. That was how I felt.

Finally, she was finished with whatever it was she had been doing. I felt her leave as she backed out of my body, leaving something behind. Suddenly I felt lit up like a Christmas tree. It was the first time I realized some sort of activation had taken place within me, which I came to call the personal Magdalene grid. It was like activating a secondary higher dimensional meridian system beyond the physical meridian system in the human body which Chinese Medicine recognizes. I realized having this activation could help me access, anchor and expand a greater volume and frequency of light, sort of similar to switching over from the United States 110-volt electricity to the European 220 volts. It was definitely an upgrade in my energetic capacity. Before this experience, I never knew something like this even existed.

Towards the end of our south of France trip, we went to Lourdes. I expected with all the information I'd heard about Lourdes that this might be a highlight of the trip. For me, it wasn't. Lourdes was like little Mexico. There were rows of booths selling mostly tacky religious souvenirs. I stood in line to experience the Grotto and yes, there was some *energy* there. However, I didn't believe this was only from Mother Mary having appeared to someone there in the 1800s. Clearly, I felt it was as much the *energy* of all the worship and adoration projected onto this site by the masses of people visiting daily, along with the original *energy* imprint from Mother Mary.

It had become very clear by this point in my life that most people haven't any idea who they are. They repeatedly project their power, their gifts, their wisdom and their spirituality onto the Saints and the Holy Family members, onto gurus, teachers, clergy and whoever they think will be their savior. My experience at Lourdes showed me that. In Lourdes, there were these long outdoor rows of sinks and faucets. Later, when looking at the pictures which we took there, there was one picture with all kinds of mysterious looking mist or fog floating around these sinks, which I believe were beings from the other side as it only showed up in this one particular photo.

After visiting the Grotto, a couple of us went upstairs to tour the Cathedral of Our Lady of Lourdes. When we walked around behind the altar during the tour, there was a series of half-sized doors about waist high, which they opened or closed to regulate the flow of people entering the altar area. The doors were all open when we first started entering the area. After we'd gone through a few of these half size doors at the back of the altar, someone, whom we didn't see, came in and locked all the doors preventing us from being able to get out.

Apparently, priests were arriving on the altar for an unscheduled mass. Trapped, not wishing to be "onstage" in the middle of the mass, our only choice was to walk straight forward towards the front of the altar. We had to do this right in front of the congregation where we could then descend the side stairs at the front of the altar. There was no way to be inconspicuous or to hide. I just kept my eyes straight ahead as I was afraid to look at anyone. I knew the entire congregation gathering for the mass was looking at us and our little escapade.

Okay, you just have to be bold and go where no layman has gone before, borrowing and tweaking the words from the Star Trek tagline.

At least I could amuse myself during the height of embarrassment!

From Lourdes we took a train to Paris, spending one night there before returning to the States. I remember we went to a typical Parisian restaurant where most entrees were different organ meats. I believe they also had a fish offering on the menu. Our group, being almost all Americans, ordered all of the fish dishes on the menu completely depleting their supply. I guess none of us could handle ordering organ meats.

Upon returning to Springdale after the France trip, everything changed quickly. All three of us got popped out of living in Springdale. Claire moved up to northern California to be with her new beloved. Charlotte went to live in a house co-owned with her ex-husband in Southern Oregon. So yet again, I faced the dilemma and the decision of figuring out where to go next.

Chapter 22: Coming Full Circle

Charlotte invited me to come live with her in her large Gold Hill home outside of Medford as a roommate. I rented part of the downstairs area, which I turned into a studio apartment of sorts minus a kitchen. It was great at first. As the crow flies, the property was within the field of the Oregon Vortex and not all that far from Crater Lake. We were out in the country where deer would congregate, lying all over the lawn. A few weeks a year, a large territorial peacock would annually take up residence on the wrap-around front porch, fiercely claiming and defending it as his domain. It was hard to even get in the front door without that peacock coming after you. I was glad when he finally flew away.

While living in Gold Hill, I was busy working for Finbarr remotely. He had a problem with his PayPal account, so he had to find a different merchant payment gateway which we couldn't get to work properly as the money never would transfer into the bank account. I was under a lot of pressure to get this payment gateway to work as not only did Finbarr have tours coming up, but he also had the upcoming Divine Feminine Conference in England, which people were trying to pay for online.

While still trying to figure out this merchant account problem, Charlotte and I signed up for the sound healer, Tom Kenyon's workshop in Seattle. Our friend Alan who was on Finbarr's South of France tour also came to the workshop with us. At every break during the Tom Kenyon workshop, I had to occupy myself with sorting out the problem of Finbarr's non-working merchant account.

Meanwhile, a whole drama was unfolding with Charlotte, Alan and me, which I had no clue about. When we got back to Gold Hill, Alan called me up to fill me in on what was going on and encouraged me to call him if Charlotte got out of control. He felt she had become quite unstable.

The next day, after returning from the workshop in Seattle, all hell broke loose. Charlotte was angry with me because of the negative energy she felt I was spewing everywhere. I'd been very careful not to complain or carry on about my difficulties, unless asked. However, I was still stressed, having not yet found a solution to the payment problem when the Divine Feminine Conference was scheduled in a matter of weeks. We still had no way in which people could pay for it. I was trying to calm down and not feel so desperate.

We were in the kitchen where Charlotte was ripping me a new one about all of this. She couldn't understand why I couldn't just be "happy." Like that was going to solve the technology issue. I just took it all in like a doormat, as I still didn't deal with confrontation well.

Finally, the only thing I asked her was, "What is it that is making you so triggered and upset?"

She totally lost it, hurling a 20-ounce full glass of water across the kitchen at me, just missing my head. I skidded on the spilled water and fell, hurting my knee. This was definitely out-of-control behavior.

With the help of my former partner Rich's computer knowledge and my brother's web design knowledge, we finally figured out the problem with the merchant account. A short bit of code needed rewriting to make it all work which I would never have been able to figure out on my own. Nobody in tech support for the Merchant Gateway software or the bank could figure this out, as they kept insisting it worked fine when it didn't. Thankfully, it all got sorted out in the nick of time. I could finally let myself relax a little.

Now that this big problem had been solved, I could start doing my inner work around the situation with Charlotte. I was heartbroken our relationship had come to this, as we'd been good, tight friends for a few years. I had never seen her display behavior like this before. When I went inside to my inner space and started looking at the situation, I realized she was having a lot of difficulties with her ex-husband, who was still the hand that fed her. Her anger was really towards him, but she didn't want to upset the apple cart, so she diverted her anger towards me instead because in her mind, I was expendable. I asked to understand the "gift" in this situation.

I would often forget about the amount of *energy* I carry and how it affects everyone and everything around me. Immersed in the energy of disharmony, chaos and anxiety when stressed, I didn't realize this compromised *energy* blasted out all over the place, affecting everyone and everything in my surroundings. Even though I wasn't particularly carrying on with a lot of drama or complaints about my situation, part of the mastery being asked of me now was for me to realize when I was in a state like this. When in an anxious state, I needed to use certain energetic shields, tools and visualization practices to keep this *energy* in check and contained so it didn't affect everything around me. It wasn't at all that I shouldn't allow myself to feel the emotions and frustration that came up, but just to be aware of the need to manage the *energy* component of it. This was a great lesson for which I was grateful to Charlotte.

I have also come to understand that the issue with someone is not always just about that person or situation. Sometimes we need to be popped out of a situation to move us along our timeline so we will be ready for what needs to unfold next. Also, sometimes people's frequencies become so different and incompatible that it's almost impossible to stay in that relationship. I stayed living in the house with Charlotte a few months longer, but issues continued to crop up to where she demanded that I move out by the end of the month. I told her I'd leave in a couple of weeks when she got back from her next business trip. This wasn't the first-time issues escalated to such a degree that I got popped out of the situation. I'd experienced enough by this point to not put the blame on Charlotte for this turn of events even though I felt hurt. It was Spirit's way of popping me out because it was time for the next adventure to unfold right on schedule in my soul's plan.

In Newport, Rhode Island, where my mother and bi-polar brother lived, my mother's rental apartment on the first floor of her house had been vacant for fifteen months, so she had invited me to come and live there. I went not only because I needed a place to go but also because of concern that my brother might inadvertently harm my mother as for years he'd refused to take some of his medications. This resulted in all kinds of aberrant behavior repeatedly landing him in trouble. So, I gave away all of my things, had another brother take my piano to his house in Hood River, Oregon, and I sold my car. Then I flew to Rhode Island with a couple of suitcases.

While in Newport, I got a job teaching water aerobics for the YMCA there and also started teaching Argentine Tango classes at a local ballroom dance studio. I continued to work part-time remotely for Finbarr as his office person and for Claire managing the sales of her *Anna, Grandmother of Jesus* book.

One day after mailing out copies of *Anna, Grandmother of Jesus* at the Newport post office, heading back to my mother's car, which I'd been driving for nearly two years, I finally saw it! *I'll be damned! There it was, my mother's lime-green Volkswagen bug!* Now this wasn't the way I usually spoke or thought, I was just so surprised.

VW beetles would never have been my first choice of a car if I were buying one. It was now twenty-five years after my encounter with St. Germain in the Boston Common in 1982, when suddenly I realized every single crazy thing, he said to me during that encounter showed up as events on my timeline over this twenty-five-year period.

He'd said to me all I needed was a bug, a sleeping bag, and to travel light. Here, I'd been driving my mother's Volkswagen beetle car (little bug) for almost two years and never realized this. Also, after leaving New York, I'd moved to the Pacific Northwest, often camping at Lake Cushman on the Olympic Peninsula; I'd worked up at Mt. Rainier; and finally, the beer bottle the bum had been holding had been bottled in a plant in Rhode Island. Now here I was, living in Rhode Island, not a place I'd ever thought I'd be. Dozens of moves later, hence the suggestion to travel light, I was back with my family of origin. St. Germain had engineered the whole thing decades before, including being the catalyst for Claire and me getting together for the work we were to bring forth. That chapter wasn't over yet, however.

After a couple of years, I was getting restless in Newport. I knew my life would just stagnate if I were to stay there much longer. I began feeling like a fly

Chapter 22: Coming Full Circle

stuck on flypaper, knowing if I didn't do something different soon, I'd never be able to move on. Meanwhile, my mother was so happy to have me "home" in Rhode Island. Coming back to the family dynamic was an initiation. I, like most of us, differed completely from the person I was when I first left my family and went out on my own. In returning to the fold, your family often relates to you like you are still the child, or person, you were when you left, which isn't the truth anymore.

The challenge is to be who you are and not lose yourself to others' views, assertions and opinions without burning bridges. I felt I had navigated this, so now it was time to come up with a plan for leaving Rhode Island, which wasn't so easy.

My mother had the fantasy that out of her five children, she would leave her house to me and my youngest bi-polar brother. This way, as we were the only two unmarried children, I would then take care of my mentally ill brother for the rest of my life.

Not that I didn't feel for her, but all of me was screaming, "No, *I don't think so!*"

I intuitively knew I had other things to do, even if I didn't know what they were. I only knew I couldn't stay stuck in Newport anymore.

I had become close friends with a fellow tango dancer, Alison, whom I knew from the Providence Argentine Tango community. She'd moved back to Massachusetts after living in the Middle East for over thirty years and was divorcing her Iranian husband. After he received a terminal cancer diagnosis, she returned to Kuwait to care for him during the last year of his life. Alison had taught ESL (English as a Second Language) in Kuwait for decades.

I also had another friend who'd recently completed a certification course, TEFL (Teaching English as a Foreign Language), in Egypt. Between the two of them, they convinced me I should look into teaching ESL. It could be a new career direction for me and a plausible reason for me to leave Newport. Alison and I talked about me applying for ESL jobs in the Kuwait universities, which paid well in Kuwait once I got certified. We also had a dream of opening an Argentine Tango center and school together in Kuwait. This was the plan at least.

In 2008, I applied to the TEFL certification training in Buenos Aires, Argentina, mostly because it would be a way for me also to experience Argentine Tango there. I flew to Buenos Aires and found a cute little studio apartment in the Recoleta area of Buenos Aires, which was walking distance from the school where my course was being taught.

The course was intense! I was fifty-five years old in a class where most people were in their twenties, having just come out of college. There was one thirty-year-old guy who'd recently gotten out of the British military, and one mother in her early forties there with her husband and child. The other students barely had any interaction with me, as they didn't know how to relate to me. I was like a grandma to them. Rarely do I think of people in terms of age, so I didn't expect this reaction. I had no friends or even acquaintances while I was there.

Also, the course work was very challenging. I hadn't been in school like this since graduate school thirty years before. Things were being taught about grammar and the English language I'd never even known before. During the third day of the course, right away, we started student teaching local Argentinians. Nothing like going from the frying pan into the fire! Holy smokes! I persevered and graduated a month later with my TEFL Certification.

Meanwhile, on the weekends and some evenings, during my time off from class, I tried to attend as many tango events as I could. Challenging as I don't speak Spanish, before going to Buenos Aires, several people assured me, this would not be a problem as many people spoke English there. Yes, however, the people who spoke English were the educated ones, the professionals; not the doormen, the store clerks, bus and taxi drivers, or those that served the public. Challenged by the language, particularly in the grocery stores and on public transportation, I couldn't read the labels or the street signs. In looking for half and half which I don't think they have in Argentina, I ended up buying all kinds of strange things to see if it was half and half ending up with an assortment of yogurt, buttermilk, Kefir, and many other unknown questionable things because I didn't know what the labels said. Daily life in Argentina was pretty well accomplished only by trial and error.

Chapter 22: Coming Full Circle

Finding my way around mostly on public buses to get me to the different Milongas (tango dances) around the city was also really challenging, and using cabs all the time was too expensive. Sometimes tempted to just hibernate in my little apartment watching great Spanish pet commercials on TV, even though I didn't understand the language, I'd have to remind myself I was there for tango. So, I had to give myself little pep talks to force myself to go out. Again, I was doing all of this on my own. I went to some more well-known traditional Milongas, which usually didn't even start until almost midnight and would go till dawn. Going to these Milongas was a total bust as most locals would not ask you to dance, especially if you were an older, single, foreign woman. At these Milongas, I had to settle for just watching.

Fortunately, I found out about Tango Queer, which was great even though I am not gay! I started going to classes there regularly because I've danced both the woman's and the man's part for years, partly to develop my skill in dancing both roles so I could become a better tango teacher. There were fabulous instructors there. At Tango Queer, people learned both roles practicing being the lead, then switching to practicing follower's part before moving on to the next partner. I also found dancing there to be refreshing. People were more accepting of you, unlike the stuffy atmosphere, old etiquette, and rules in most of the traditional tango salons.

The other place I would sometimes go was the afternoon Milonga at Glorieta, the outdoor gazebo in the Barrancas de Belgrano Park. Here is where the old-time Milongueros would go dance. They often had only a small repertoire of steps and figures which they led, but many of them had been dancing these same figures for forty to fifty years or more, so they were exquisite leads. I discovered you had to show up a few times before someone would venture forth and ask you to dance. Finally, after going and watching the first couple of times, I got asked to dance and then asked to dance again the following week.

In the traditional Milonga venues, women would lead other women in a class, but it was strictly taboo to lead another woman at a Milonga dance. I was in a class, as a lead, in one of the traditional salons before the Milonga one day when I realized the woman I was partnering was chattering away. It took me about a minute to realize she was speaking English. *English!!!* I asked her all kinds of questions, finding out she was there on a tango tour with a group from Philadelphia. She invited me to tag along to a few Milongas with them over the next week.

At least I got to dance with men from her group, so I felt a little less dejected. I was fortunate to be in Buenos Aires during one of the big annual Tango Festivals held in an abandoned department store building where we could watch free tango performances, competitions, and dance at public Milongas. I even ran into a woman there whom I had known from the tango community in Ashland, Oregon, which I was part of when I lived in Gold Hill.

At one of the Milongas, it surprised me when this middle-aged man asked me to dance. He was an absolutely fabulous lead, but a lecher. Part way through dancing, he shoved his tongue in my ear. Hundreds of people were watching, so I didn't want to make a scene. A few hours later, at another Milonga, he singled me out and asked for a dance again. I am a good and experienced dancer, but it is hard to find good leads who challenge you in a way that you can step up your level of dancing, interaction and creativity.

Dancing tango is basically an improvised conversation between the two partners. Torn because this guy was a fabulous lead, however, the price I had to pay was putting up with sexual harassment. However, I decided having a dance with a good dance partner was worth it. Of course, I spoke no Spanish, and he spoke no English. After the dance, he kept motioning to me. He wanted me to go home with him, but I kept shaking my head. *No, no way.* Finally, he gave up and shrugged his shoulders with a little laugh. I knew he was telling me in his macho Latin way he had to try at least.

Coming home back to Rhode Island after Buenos Aires was a challenge. My intended plan to find work teaching ESL in Kuwait now that I had my certification went up in smoke as the economy totally shifted in 2008. Nobody was hiring, including universities and schools in Kuwait. My only available options then to teach English were in Thailand and places like India, where the pay was maybe $12 an hour. That wouldn't get me anywhere. I also never thought about how the United States has age discrimination laws, but many other countries had an age ceiling of thirty-five years old for hiring people to teach English. I did not know about any of this when I took the course at age fifty-five, as it never occurred to me it would be an issue.

What I clearly learned about myself, however, through this crazy experience, was how courageous I was, and that I had the chutzpah and drive to persevere through anything that was daunting, without giving up. I hadn't really recognized this in myself before. My time in Buenos Aires was a training ground for what was coming up next in my life, which I had no awareness of yet.

Chapter 23: Back on Track Again

After returning from Buenos Aires, I was at a loss about what to do next. I had let go of my work for Finbarr, as I couldn't maintain that while I was in Argentina. I also let go of my water aerobics teaching job at the YMCA. So, what was next? Out of the blue, I received a call from Claire Heartsong. We hadn't really communicated much during the previous three years when all of us got popped out of living in Springdale, in October 2006.

When we left Springdale, we didn't know if any of the information we'd gathered in the sessions we did when the 19 characters were brought through from 2000 years ago would ever be published. Anna had let us know the Councils of Light felt the information was way too controversial for the level of humanity's consciousness and wasn't appropriate to release to the public when we concluded the sessions in 2006. Claire was now calling me to say she finally received the go-ahead from the Councils of Light for us to compile the information we'd gathered into a sequel to her first book, *Anna, Grandmother of Jesus*. Claire asked me if I would come to California. Of course, I would!

I was fortunate that one of my brothers who lived in Bellevue, Washington, had bought a new car so he offered to give me his old BMW which had electrical problems. Gratefully, I accepted his offer even though I'd have to deal with the dashboard problems. Hey, it was free at least! I was excited to be off the flypaper of being stuck in Newport. Finally, I had a reason now to return to the West Coast. My mother, who was still holding onto the fantasy that I'd stay in Rhode Island to care for my youngest brother, thought I was crazy to leave, however, I told her there was no way I was going to retrieve my brother's defective car from Bellevue, Washington, and drive it all the way across the country to Rhode Island. I was going to stay on the west coast. That was that.

I flew to Washington State, stayed in Bellevue for a few weeks, got the car and then drove to Claire's house in northern California. She and I started brainstorming how, and what, to do with all the information we'd collected through the regression sessions we'd done. It was like an octopus as the input from the nineteen characters took place all over the map geographically from the north of England, Scotland and the Himalayas, to Palestine. The information also shared by the characters spanned multiple timelines from Yeshua's (Jesus's) early lifetime to the life of a monk, one of Anna's descendants, who lived a century after most of the Holy Family members had died. It was hard to figure out what the overall context or theme of the book was to be and how to organize it. As Claire and I were on a long walk trying to brainstorm and figure this out, we talked about what the differences were between the Magdalenes of 2000 years ago and the Magdalenes of today.

In tuning into it, we realized the Magdalenes, those Essenes and Holy Family members of 2000 years ago, were merely a tiny band of people who would forever change life on planet earth. How were they to do this? Certain members went through rigorous initiations to develop supernatural abilities. In order to preserve and communicate these teachings, what we now call psychic or paranormal abilities were required. Some developed telepathy to communicate with other members over long distances. Some could bi-locate (the ability to be in multiple places at a time or transfer your body from one location to another almost instantly) as it would often take months, even years of walking or traveling by caravan to get somewhere.

More advanced initiates, such as Jesus and Mary Magdalene, Yeshua's twin flame aspect, could materialize and de-materialize at will. Others, like Anna, learned the ancient Egyptian Rites of the Sepulcher, which would maintain physical immortality in the body as long as the initiates consistently practiced them. Anna, who lived to be over seven hundred years old, practiced these rites.

Chapter 23: Back on Track Again

Shown why this small band of people needed to develop extraordinary skills to maintain and preserve the longevity and integrity of their teachings in their day, many of the abilities they needed are already inherent in our technology and culture today. Today we have instant communication, global travel, computers, technology and science to record and distribute information. What's important for the Magdalenes to focus on today is spreading the light and finally sharing the wisdom they've protected and overseen for eons. As Anna reminded us many times, we are the future selves of those beings in the time of Jesus 2000 years ago. Tuning into all of this, Claire was remarkable at channeling the details. I was much more attuned to the bigger picture. As we were brainstorming, I had a big ah-ha moment which gave me the overall context for the book.

It's briefly mentioned twice in the *Anna, the Voice of the Magdalenes* book, that at the time Yeshua lived on the planet, there were eleven additional Avatars and their consorts (twin flame partners) also alive on the planet. These Avatars probably lived in the Himalayas and in the Andes Mountains. These fully enlightened, fully realized Christ-Magdalene beings would naturally produce offspring who would also be born at a higher frequency level as Anna's, Yeshua's and Mary Magdalene's descendants were. The major mission of the Magdalenes 2000 years ago was to seed the light into the consciousness, into the elements and into the genetic lines. In the *Anna, the Voice of the Magdalenes* book we share all the descendant charts of Anna's children, Yeshua's children, and the lineages they seeded throughout different areas of the world.

If there were twelve pairs of fully realized Christed-Magdalene beings on the planet then, I could see that it would take approximately 2000 years of crossbreeding between all the descendants lines stretching across the planet so that today we would have the awakening of the Christ consciousness, not only in our consciousness, but dormant in the physical genetics contained within the DNA of most of the humans on Earth. Therefore, we can have the second coming of Christ in all of humanity today because it's not only in our consciousness but seeded in our literal genetics.

To me, even though not explicitly stated, this was the organizing principle of the book. We named the book *Anna, the Voice of the Magdalenes* because the narrative voice wasn't the singular voice of Anna, as it was in the first book, but a narrative from nineteen different *Magdalenes* who each had a voice and their own stories and wisdom to share. Claire and I spent the next year working on expanding the narrative, organizing it into comprehensible chapters that somewhat made sense chronologically, and worked out the charts of all the descendant lines. While working on the book, Claire didn't want anyone else to see it before it went to print, so Claire and I elected to edit it ourselves, passing it back and forth to each other to accomplish this.

Knowing absolutely nothing about publishing or print set up, by trial and error, I had to figure out how to set up the interior layout of the book with the chapter headings, chapters, footnotes, charts, photographs and all the other information included in it so it would be ready to send to the printer.

A couple of weeks before we sent the manuscript off to the printer, Claire sent a copy of the manuscript to Ariane Publishing, the French Publishing Company out of Montreal, Canada, who had translated and published the first Anna book in French. This way they could get started on translating the sequel.

Charlotte, who was part of the team bringing forth this information years before, had gone back to her Mormon husband. She desired no longer to have her name associated with the Anna books. Virginia's company, S.E.E. Publishing published the first *Anna, Grandmother of Jesus* book. I considered taking over SEE Publishing from Virginia Essene after she retired, but a lawyer cautioned me against this because I'd be liable for any issues which arose with previous books or authors associated with S.E.E Publishing. I consequently created a publishing company of my own, LightRiver Media through which we published *Anna, the Voice of the Magdalenes*.

Guided by the Councils of Light, Claire and I had shown up, taken on this task, and now it was time to let it go where it may.

Chapter 24: On the Move Again

Now that Claire and I had hatched a plan, it was time for me once again to figure out where I was going to land. I'd signed up for a weekend marketing workshop in Los Angeles, so I knew at least I was going to drive down to southern California. After the workshop, I contacted my friend Vickie, whom I originally met through Claire, about going for a quick visit. She and her husband own an 850-acre ranch in Virgin, Utah, up on the Kolob Plateau on the back side of Zion National Park. So, when the workshop was over, I drove to Utah to stay with Vickie for a few days.

In the marketing workshop, one of the presenters shared a template for streamlining the writing of nonfiction books. I suggested to Vickie we try using this template to see if we could jointly write a book about relationships. Vickie was also a published author under the pen name of Angelina Heart and an expert on twin flames. To accomplish this, I initially stayed in a beautiful log home on their property which previously had been Vickie's mom's residence before she passed away.

One morning, I was by myself cooking bacon and eggs for breakfast. I sat down to eat, offering a perfunctory blessing of my food while my mind was elsewhere. Suddenly into my awareness came the pig who had given up his life to become my breakfast, another one of those thirty-second parting of the veil moments. The pig communicated to me first how honored he was to communicate with me this way. Then he impressed upon me how he'd lived and died for this very moment of the exchange of love, of the nurturing and sustenance he could provide me by being of service to me. This service, I realized, was far more than just being the physical vehicle providing me bacon that morning. Tears ran down my face, dripping into my eggs. This experience brought me to a new level of gratitude and appreciation for the divinity and life force within the food we ingest. Even if you eat something which once had a face, it didn't matter. There was no judgment in that regard. There was only the acknowledgment of love being exchanged and the soul being fed. I felt honored by that little pig. These experiences would periodically crop up to keep me engaged and prompting me to go deeper in my quest.

In order to continue on with my collaboration with Vickie, I found a roommate situation in St. George, Utah. Vickie and I would meet a few times a week to write, so the rest of the time I tried to entertain myself as Vickie was busy with their ranch. There was not a lot to do in St. George especially if you were an older, single, non-Mormon woman. I think in those six weeks I went to more movies than I'd seen in the previous three years. I needed to be in a community in which I could be more active, so after about six weeks I moved to Las Vegas as it was a good in-between place to either work with Vickie in Utah, or northern California for collaboration with Claire.

The deciding factor was the Argentine Tango and the ballroom dance community in Las Vegas. At least there was an opportunity to do what I loved there. I rented a cheap funky apartment, more like a dorm room than an apartment, as there was a shared bathroom for the three apartments in this building. It was reminiscent of my Perry Street, 5th floor walk-up days in New York City almost forty years earlier.

In the mid-90s, while still working at Portland Community College, I'd had this inner movie scene play out in my head. It showed me speaking onstage to an audience of thousands. I couldn't for the life of me imagine what would have led me to that point, or what I'd speak about. Around the time this inner movie happened, I'd attended a business workshop, *How to Handle Difficult People*, as I'd often have to deal with belligerent students who didn't want to cooperate or do GED Testing which the court system often mandated that they take the test.

Throughout the workshop, my attention gravitated to the woman teaching the class. Dressed professionally in her suit jacket, business skirt, and heels I kept thinking to myself, I could do that.
I think I'd like to do something like that.
Now that the *Anna, the Voice of the Magdalenes* book was at the printers, I had heard about a heart-based yearlong marketing program in the San Francisco Bay Area. After attending a free weekend workshop with them, even though for me it was a lot of money, I joined the program. I knew nothing about marketing, but I also knew I would need to do some marketing for the *Anna, the Voice of the Magdalene* book now that it was being published.

Divided into three sections, the first section of this yearlong training was geared towards getting private clients. The second was geared towards doing online courses and the third focused on speaking and selling from the stage. Speaking from the stage was the part I was most interested in.

Prompted by this inner movie of my speaking on stage, I also joined Toastmasters to get over my fear of public speaking. The awareness of needing to be comfortable with public speaking was the primary motivation for me deciding to register for this year-long marketing program.

For the first few months of the marketing program training, I would either drive or fly to San Francisco one weekend a month. It was tiring and expensive. After a while, I realized nothing was holding me in Vegas, so I moved to the San Francisco Bay Area as my course was not quite half over at that point. First, I found a roommate situation in Newark, California, with a woman who was a senior flight attendant on American Airlines. After about a year she put her house up for sale so I couldn't stay living there. I found another roommate situation across the bay in San Mateo with a professional astrologer. We got along great! Even though I was just going along doing what I felt like I needed to do at the moment, it wasn't until I looked back in retrospect that I realized every decision and action I took was part of a larger plan guided by my Councils of Light from the other side.

Even though Claire had gone into retreat in 2006, she willingly spent a year working on the sequel with me. After the book went to the printer, Claire wanted to retire once and for all. I didn't want to step on Claire's toes, but I knew someone needed to shepherd these books out into the world. That someone would have to be me. Yikes!

I got over my apprehension and did my first public talk and half-day workshop at East West Books in Mountain View, California, in December 2010. Until this point, other than Toastmasters, I'd never spoken publicly except to give GED testing instruction or to teach dance or water aerobics. As much as I tried to push the feeling away, part of me still felt petrified to speak publicly. I calmed my nerves by asking the part of me who was Lizbett in a past life to stand squarely in the center of me. I visualized myself speaking from her place of knowledge, authority, and strength. It worked! I got great feedback that the workshop was outstanding, and even life-changing, for some people. My talks and workshops became more focused on understanding how we are Magdalenes and how that relates to our daily lives.

In Springdale, Utah, when we worked with Anna in bringing through all the characters for the sequel, she'd talked about various people who attended gatherings as being Magdalenes. This was the first I had heard of that concept. This understanding became the foundation for all of my work from then on. Basically, I had no coaching about the Magdalene understanding, was given very little information about it, and I realized I had to rely completely on my inner direction, intuitive knowing, and soul memory. There was no external person I could even ask if what I was sharing was true, pertinent, or would have relevance and meaning to people. Claire and Anna were unavailable.

Almost no one was talking about this back in 2006. I was on my own. I only had my inner Councils of Light to rely upon. As I started doing talks and workshops, it was only the response of my audiences that let me know how much impact and relevance they experienced from these teachings. When one is directed by their soul to share their piece meant for the whole, it is like standing on top of a mountain with no one else to rely upon except yourself, which is a profound initiation.

Over the next several months, I spoke at a couple of churches and did a few more fledgling workshops. I also engaged in a project for five months helping Virginia Essene, who'd been a pioneering spiritual author for decades to complete her last book.

Chapter 24: On the Move Again

She lived close by and wanted help to compile several years' worth of material she'd channeled into an eBook as her health was declining. She knew nothing about eBooks and enlisted my help. Once it was complete, I published her book, *What Every Human Must Know to Survive and Thrive on Planet Earth* both as an eBook and a print book under my company LightRiver Media. Virginia had been the person that had sent Claire back to square-one three times when writing *Anna, Grandmother of Jesus*. As the original publisher of *Anna, Grandmother of Jesus*, she had also written the foreword to that book.

Chapter 25: International Travel Begins

In the summer of 2011, my friend Evelyn, who'd also been on Finbarr's south of France tour in 2006, suggested we take a road trip to Utah to see Vickie, whom she also knew. I was always up for an adventure, so of course I was in. After arriving at Vickie's later that afternoon, Vickie offered to drive us around the Smith Mesa, a large area of mostly dirt roads way up the Kolob Plateau Road above where Vickie lived. It was wild, unspoiled country with some spectacular views overlooking Zion National Park.

We spent about two hours driving on the Mesa as the late afternoon erupted into the spectacular colors of sunset.

"What ever happened to Merlin?" Evelyn asked Vickie.

Apparently, Merlin was a real guy who owned property about five miles above Vickie's ranch which was already a good twenty miles up the Kolob Plateau Road turnoff from the road to Springdale. All the wayward Mormons who didn't want people to see them drinking would drive the twenty-five miles up the Kolob Road to go to Merlin's Pub.

Evelyn continued, "What happened to it?"

Vickie replied, "He sold it to a psychic."

I piped in, "Is she any good?"

"Yeah, she's great!" was the reply.

We went back to Vickie's house to make dinner and I forgot about it. Early the next morning we got a call from Vickie as we were again staying in the log house on her property. She said she'd talked to the psychic, Mariangela, about us. Mariangela apparently cleared her schedule so she could give readings to both of us that morning. This was a total surprise out of the blue!

When my turn came, I walked into the session room with the two Anna books in hand. Mariangela said she'd heard about these books but hadn't read them yet. This reading with Mariangela took place in mid-August 2011, a little over a year after the book *Anna, the Voice of the Magdalenes* had been published. I asked questions about how to move forward with the books and then asked another question that had been puzzling me. Another psychic friend had casually had mentioned to me that I needed to go back to France to do grid work there. Not understanding what that meant, I asked Mariangela.

She shared information about twelve locations on the Earth, dormant feminine points on the land, which were ready for reawakening and activation now. She gave me the locations for all of them but the first one, which I had to figure out by myself. The other locations given to me were St Marie La Mer, France (near Perpignan as there are two St Maries in France); Fortingall, Scotland; Isle of Man, British Isles; Crestone, Colorado, USA; Valley of the Queens, Egypt; Melbourne, Australia; Ephesus, Turkey; Maui, Hawaii, USA and four more. The preceding locations were the ones which I and participants accompanying me eventually physically visited, performing the Magdalene Grid Activation ritual in each location. I'd been told that all the activations were to take place between 11/11/11 to 12/12/14. The other locations included in the list which we weren't physically able to get to within that time frame were Chaco Canyon, New Mexico, USA; Banff, Alberta, Canada; Varanasi, India; and Abadiânia, Brazil, which was to be the last Grid Activation.

There had been a lot of channeled material around 2006-2007 which said a Christ Grid had been completed around the planet by the Archangels, Ascended Masters and the unseen realms. The information brought forth in the reading with Mariangela suggested there were also corresponding Magdalene Grids, or Divine Feminine Grids, within Mother Earth herself which needed activation. We could facilitate these activations through a process of planetary acupuncture to anchor energy now emerging through the shift of consciousness. I also received information that this time period of increasing chaos in individual's lives, along with extreme weather, earthquakes, hurricanes and fires upon the planet, was a "cracking" happening both in individual's lives and upon the Earth itself. It's a cracking of the old paradigm, the cracking of the ego, so a greater opening to spirit could anchor onto the planet. This would create the opening for the new templates, systems, products and information to take root in our world. I understood and agreed with this.

But who was I to be the one to spearhead this?

As I was wondering about this, my guides reminded me to look back at the clues throughout my life connecting me to the Holy Family. I'd received clues all along, even though I'd completely turned my back on anything remotely Christian when I went to college. I remember reading a book as a teenager about Jesus's life, which was the first inkling something more was there. This book evoked a lot of emotion in me, which I didn't understand since I didn't resonate with the teachings of the Church.

The next thread of awareness came when reading the *Life and Teachings of the Masters of the Far East* in 1984 when I was working up at Mt. Rainier. I had just finished reading about the banquet scene in which the Masters held out their hands and platters of food would then just appear in their hands. While reading this chapter, I fell asleep for about fifteen minutes before going to dinner one evening. I had a day-glow lucid dream in which I was there at the banquet along with these amazing spiritual beings like Jesus, Mother Mary, Buddha and many others. My first reaction was, *oh my God, these are my peeps! These are my best buddies!* I was not trying to conjure anything up. Even though there was no way I could explain it, I knew deep down they were my family, my very intimate, closely related real family. I woke up shocked and in disbelief that this could be at all true.

Who could I even tell this to anyway without sounding absolutely crazy?

The next thread showed up when I was in the cult. At some point, we studied the Knights of the Round Table and the whole Camelot era. Part of what we did in our studies was to figure out lineages of mythological beings and legendary entities. Everyone received past life identities connected with this research, that is everyone in the group, but me. I thought to myself maybe I didn't show up as any figure people would recognize in history because maybe I hadn't ever done anything of any significance. When I finally received an identity, it was Sir Galahad, the pure knight who is said to have achieved the vision of God through the Holy Grail.

Holy Grail!

Holy Crap!

That was a tall order to live up to.

The Magdalenes showed me that reincarnation doesn't happen only in one human body incarnation to another human body incarnation, but as incarnations more through a collective soul stream.

The Magdalenes gave me an image of a large oak tree. This oak tree represented the whole soul stream. Each branch and leaf in each season is an incarnation of that soul stream. So, there are many others who are also soul stream aspects of Galahad, or the Holy Family members, or any other of the well-known figures in history. In discovering past-life identities, what I want to know was:

What was their downfall?

Where did they fall short and not accomplish what they set out to do?

And on the flip side; *what were the talents, energies, wisdom and abilities they developed?*

How did these talents and abilities add to the soul stream?

How could I tap into and use these talents, abilities, and knowledge for what I am doing now?

Just being attached to a past life identity because someone was famous did little for me. I wanted to understand their inner workings, their pitfalls, and their achievements.

I believe people who get attached to past life identities think a past life identity will make them more important in the eyes of others than they currently feel about themselves. It is a total ego stroke. Knowing about past life identities only helped me to further access the wisdom and *energy* found there, nothing to go around and broadcast to anybody.

The most important thread here for me was the fact that Galahad's father was Lancelot. We learned in our studies that Lancelot was an incarnation of Jesus. When I was in the cult, I started consciously working with the idea that if I truly was an aspect of Galahad, and Lancelot was my father in that lifetime, then I could call upon this Lancelot-Jesus archetypal energy to help me heal. I could ask him to help me heal from the psychological-emotional abuse I'd suffered in this lifetime with my current father. I would do very deliberate inner healing work asking Lancelot-Jesus to stand in for my current father to help heal the dysfunctional distorted lower frequency *energy* within me. This all happened long before Claire had even written *Anna, Grandmother of Jesus*.

Later, when working with Claire, Anna told me I had an incarnation as the character Lizbett in the *Anna, the Voice of the Magdalenes* book. Lizbett was the daughter of Yeshua (Jesus) and Mary of Bethany. Here it was again. I realized I came in as part of the bigger plan as most of us have. I came in with certain knowledge, energies and abilities within my soul stream to be of service in these times. This awakening process has been showing me bit-by-bit who I am and why I am here.

I also intuitively realized it was important that my name be on the front cover of the *Anna, the Voice of the Magdalene* book and that Claire and I needed to share equally the copyright because it gave me the credibility and authority to be the one to shepherd this material out into the world. Claire had initially put this material out to the world, but had withdrawn. If it were to happen, it was up to me now. After the reading with Mariangela as all of this settled within me, I realized I had a choice whether to facilitate these Magdalene Grid Activations or not. But how could I "not" do these Magdalene Grid Activations set before me if they served a larger purpose? The decision was now clear. I was at peace.

Even though in my mind I wasn't feeling confident about it, my guides kept telling me all I had to do was to show up. The rest would take care of itself.

Talk about surrender and having faith!

The guides had me revisit the threads of connection to the Holy Family to help bolster my confidence. They wanted me to know I absolutely had the authority to facilitate these Magdalene Grid Activations.

After receiving the initial reading from Mariangela, I had to figure out where the location of the first grid activation on 11/11/11 was to be. The only information given was that it was on, or near, the Prime Meridian, the Greenwich Mean line passing through England at Longitude Zero. I somehow knew it wasn't Greenwich, England. Each planetary location given in the reading also was loosely analogous to a human body part. I knew the First Grid Activation was analogous to the heart, representing the pumping of blood and the beginning of circulation. It seemed fitting for the first one.

While my friend Evelyn and I were staying at Vickie's for a few days after having the reading, I received about six phone calls from a woman in France who coincidentally lived about forty-five minutes north of Lourdes. I started telling this woman, Loes, about the reading. When I looked up the Prime Meridian line to see what other cities or towns lay upon it or near it, the only other place other than Greenwich was Lourdes, France. I knew this was the answer and the confirmation of the location for the first Grid Activation.

Upon returning to my house in San Mateo, California, where I was living with my astrologer roommate, I was like a deer in the headlights. The thought of carrying out what the reading suggested was beyond daunting. I had absolutely no experience leading trips or tours as I'd barely even been on any in my life. I'd also only recently started conducting workshops and speaking publicly, so hardly anyone knew who I was. On top of all of that, I was seriously in debt. It was crazy. How could I pull this off as I didn't have any resources or knowledge of what to do at all? I was just barely getting by financially as it was. My guides clearly let me know it was okay if I said "no" with no repercussions if it felt like it was too much. There was no judgment. No one on the *other side* would think any less of me. Still, it was a hard decision to make. Paralyzed with indecision for about three weeks, I knew I needed to decide soon as it was only about eight weeks until November 11th, when I would have to be in France if I elected to do it.

I appealed to Anna and the Councils of Light, asking them if they really wanted me to do this, to get me there. If that happened, I would do it. I had no clue exactly what I was to do, or even consciously what a grid activation was, but I would show up. In the reading, I was also told before starting the Grid Activations, I needed to go to Chalice Well in Glastonbury, England, to get water from the White Springs to bring to each of the Grid Activations.

Anna and the Councils of Light granted my petition, guiding me to talk to my former flight attendant roommate about buying one of her D3 airline passes. Using her pass, I flew standby to London round-trip for about $550

Chapter 25: International Travel Begins

(taxes and fees) without having to select scheduled flights way ahead of time. I further lucked out by getting a seat in first class on the way to London, sitting next to the American tennis star Mardy Fish's' coach. He tutored me on how to work everything in the first-class console as it was all new to me.

When I finally said yes to this proposition, I emailed my mailing list announcing the launch of the Magdalene Grid Activations along with an appeal for someone in England to help me get to Chalice Well to get the sacred water from the White Springs. The only response I received was from this woman, Sheila, who was an artist. She lived an hour and a half drive from Glastonbury and said she would help me in any way she could. The problem, however, was she did not have a car, and she didn't drive. Since she was the only one who responded, I took her up on her offer. When I landed at Heathrow Airport, I rented a little car and drove the two-and-a-half-hour drive to Sheila's town. It was dusk. This was the first time I was driving on the opposite side of the road through more roundabouts than I'd ever seen in my entire life. I got there in one piece, found parking, and found her door even though it was well after dark. As soon as she opened the door to welcome me in, we instantly recognized each other on a soul level, even though this was the first time we met in this life. It was just like we were picking up where we left off in the last life. We recognized each other and were close friends.

The next day we drove to Glastonbury and went to Chalice Well to get the water. At Chalice Well there are two separate streams of water, the red stream full of iron which gives it its red color and the white stream. There is a small cave there which houses part of the White Spring. The cave was only open for a few hours a day on certain days of the week. Fortunately, it was open the day we were there. Upon entering, there are different areas where people have constructed altars. In one area, someone constructed a canopy archway of fronds above two rough-hewn wooden benches. At the far end of this canopy archway was an exquisite oil painting of a priestess or a Goddess. I sat down on one of the low wooden benches, closed my eyes and tuned in. Suddenly, I sensed a being standing directly in front of me.

In my inner hearing, loudly, in a commanding voice, I heard, *I am Mother Isis.*

My first thought was, *holy crap, you are real!*

I had never particularly thought about Isis as a real being beyond the ancient Egyptian myths. I also didn't know she'd refer to herself as "Mother."

After collecting the water from the White Springs and eating lunch in Glastonbury, we continued driving to Cornwall on the coast. The weather was nasty. Torrential rain came at us sideways as we drove towards the coast. Sheila, not feeling well, started puking out the car window. I couldn't pull over as there was no shoulder on the rural roads in England. When we got to our hotel, she went upstairs to have a bath and wash out her clothes. I took a towel and tried to wipe off everything which had blown back onto the side of the car door. When Sheila came down, she informed me she didn't get carsick. She said the only other times in her life when she'd experienced projectile vomiting were both about twenty minutes before she'd given birth to each of her two sons.

She exclaimed, "This is about birth!"

This was preparation for some kind of cosmic birth.

The next morning, we went to Tintagel on the Cornwall Coast. Legends say the remnants of the castle there were the birthplace of King Arthur. In the town there is also King Arthur's Hall, which is a combination of a museum and artwork collection related to the Arthurian period. Shelia and I went down to the beach below the ruins of Tintagel Castle, where we both received all kinds of "downloads." While meditating in Merlin's Cave, in my inner vision I sensed this gigantic crystal located somewhere beneath the cave. I don't know whether this was a third-dimensional crystal, or a crystal in a different frequency or dimension. As I was tuning into it, this crystal shot a beam of light to a corresponding crystal somewhere in the Andromeda Galaxy which returned a beam of light back to the one beneath Merlin's Cave. It was a trippy affair.

One thing about this process of "awakening" is that we are being opened up to more of who we are as multidimensional beings who have greater access to other dimensions besides our usual third-dimensional reality. There is currently no way to prove or confirm these experiences other than knowing it's true. It is the same with hypnotherapy sessions. The client just knows at some level what they are witnessing or experiencing is true, just like having a concrete memory from their childhood. Again, you can't make this stuff up. I would have no reason to make anything up or even particularly share it with anybody not similarly attuned, other than I am writing a book about my experiences of awakening. Each experience just gives more clues which unravel the mysteries of the universe and the process of soul evolution.

Sheila and I returned to Wiltshire, the town in which she lived. I needed to get ready to leave for France later that day. Driving through the narrow English streets in this cheap little rental car, I tried to get past this big utility truck parked on the side of the road. It was exactly like a fire engine in the United States, except it was a yellow utility truck, instead of a red fire engine. Something protruded out into the street from the back bumper of this large truck, which apparently caught the bumper of my rental car. The next thing I knew there was this loud grating noise.

In my rear-view mirror, I saw the whole back end of my little rental car sitting in the middle of the road behind me. The utility guys who witnessed this occurrence were gracious enough to help me out. They picked up the back end out of the street and then just snapped it back on the car.

Snap on?

Really?

I guess this wasn't the first time they'd seen something like this. When I got to the airport, I returned the rental car. Fortunately, I'd purchased the full insurance coverage, which I never do. Maybe it was because I was driving on the opposite side of the road for the first time in my life. The only lasting damage was a slight scratch on the passenger door. It took me so long to fill out the paperwork that I almost missed my flight to France. I went running like hell to the gate and just made it before they closed the doors.

In France, I first went to Mt. Bugarach and did a half-day workshop there. Hugo, this Belgian man who attended the workshop, came back to the Lourdes area with me. We found a bed-and-breakfast place to stay (not together, however) close to Loes' house. Loes was the French woman who had called me six times when I was in Virgin, Utah, while visiting Vickie. Loes offered her home for the preparatory workshop necessary to build a unified field among the participants in order to come together for the actual Grid Activation. I put out an email announcing that the First Magdalene Grid Activation was to take place in the Lourdes, France. I only charged a workshop fee for this four-day event, letting people know they would be responsible for their own lodging and food. Beside me and Loes, two other women signed up, one from Switzerland and one from Canada, and a French man, a friend of Loes', who was also going to come. The day before the event was to start, I received a frantic call at the bed-and-breakfast place Hugo and I were staying at.

It was Loes' husband hysterically crying into the phone, saying Loes was dying. Earlier that morning her foot got tangled in the cord for the blinds and she fell headlong into the sharp corner of the kitchen table. Hugo and I rushed over to their house to help Loes. Badly injured, in shock, with blood everywhere she refused to have an ambulance called. Loes was not at all a fan of allopathic medicine. When we got there, she was not in good shape at all. Her long hair was all matted with blood still oozing out of the wound in her head. I stationed myself at Loes' head while Hugo was at her feet.

Loes said to us, "I know you can heal me."

I was glad she had such confidence in us. I thought maybe in some other lifetime I might have been capable of this, but I certainly didn't feel capable of that kind of healing now. This was scary. Finally, Loes' husband called for an ambulance without letting Loes know as she was vehemently against it. I knew I had to talk Loes into changing her mind about going with the paramedics. I gently talked to her about how God's healing works in all kinds of ways, even though the allopathic medical staff in situations like this. Hugo, frustrated with Loes' reluctance turned to her demanding, "Do you want to live or die?"

It was a moment of reckoning. In facing that decision, Loes decided she really wanted to live, finally agreeing to go in the ambulance which arrived about ten minutes later. The ambulance took off. We went to follow in her husband's car but had trouble getting it started. Finally, the car started, and we set off for the hospital.

The rural country roads in this part of France were hilly and winding. The ambulance was going so slow that I saw several people pass it. It took no time at all for us to catch up with it. After about a twenty-minute drive, we all gathered in the waiting room of this small hospital for the better part of the day, waiting for word on Loes' condition. Meanwhile, her husband went back and forth to the small airport, picking up the two participants who were arriving for the Grid Activation. He brought them back to the emergency department's waiting room.

Here we all were, Hugo from Belgium, a woman from Canada, a woman from Switzerland, Loes' husband and me, all passing the time by talking about the Anna books while we waited in the waiting room of this small French rural hospital. There was only one other French couple in the waiting room besides us. They apparently understood English and overheard us talking. They approached us all excited as they'd overheard our conversation. They'd read the Anna books in French and couldn't believe they were meeting one of the authors of the book. Now what was the chance of that happening?

The hospital released Loes later that day. She'd also hurt her ankle, which she had X-rayed and bandaged. However, Loes refused to let them X-ray her head. Not being able to assess anything further without an x-ray, the doctors bandaged her up and sent her home. The next morning, we all congregated at Loes' house to start the workshop part of the Grid Activation. The French man who had signed up to attend the workshop didn't understand English well enough, so he bowed out. Loes was okay for the first hour but then quickly went south health-wise so fast she couldn't function. Even though I was very concerned about her, I couldn't abandon my small group of Grid Activation participants.

We had to regroup. We took our workshop outside to continue the event. We found outdoor fields and a stream with a small waterfall where we conducted some exercises to build our unified field. Because of Loes' injury and the man who bowed out because he didn't understand English, there ended up being only three of us at the first Magdalene Grid Activation.

Having to be outside in nature set a completely different precedent for all the rest of the Magdalene Grid Activations. Everything was originally planned around having an inside workshop type of experience which, because of Loes' accident now had to be revamped according to our new set of circumstances. We also had to find a ride to the location for the ritual part of the Magdalene Grid Activation.

Loes had previously scouted out Gazost for the first Grid Activation site. This was a gorgeous pristine alpine area close to Lourdes. Performing the first

Grid Activation at the end of a road next to an idyllic little stream with a white horse up on the ridge overlooking where we were was almost like a fairy tale. The horse seemed to serve as a Celestial guardian of the ceremony somehow.

The three of us carried out this first activation at 11 AM local France time on 11/11/11. We came together in one unified field acting like a human acupuncture needle for the earth through using meditations, visualizations, toning, elixirs and essential oils. I was so grateful to have this first location activated, as there had been so much unexplained interference in getting to this point. A few days after the completion of each Grid Activation, I would channel a message to the participants of each Grid Activation. Here is the message for this first Activation:

11/11/11 Lourdes, France Message

"You Magdalenes are the heart of my heart, as is all of humanity. You are my precious gems of mobile nature and infinite reach, conduits, and mirrors of the Great Source. Today my heart awakened anew in oneness reflecting the 1:1 oneness in the sacred three (11/11/11), polarity unified in the Beloved.

The heart activation surrounding Lourdes brings the energy of the Holy Mother, the Magdalene, to the hearts within all of mankind, all animals, all fish, all insects, all minerals, all plant life, all elements; all beings within and without–the grand mirrors of the ONE.

This is the ancient wave of divine expression and experience carried in all three time-space continuums, anchored, reawakened, and manifested once again. My deep gratitude to you, my Beloveds, for facilitating as the catalysts and awakeners for all of humanity. My heart is your heart. You have blessed my body and yours."

Adonai, Mother Earth, the Magdalenes and the Hosts of Heaven.

The second Magdalene Grid Activation happened four days later outside Perpignan, France, near the border of Spain. The number of participants doubled to six of us. Taking the different exercises out into nature to prepare us for coming together in a unified field, we visited St. Baume where Mary Magdalene was purported to have lived. It's now a Catholic chapel etched into the granite face of a mountain. This was one of the many locations of initiation caves which the Magdalene and Essene initiates used in Yeshua's time. The first time I visited St. Baume on the south of France tour was with Finbarr six years before. As I climbed the steps, I heard my guides say to me, "You are blessed among women."

As usual, I didn't really know how to receive or incorporate this information.

We continued on to Rennes Le Chateau where the staff at the local bookstore there were so excited to meet me that they had me autograph every copy of *Anna, the Voice of the Magdalenes*, which they had for sale in both English and French. Used to being more invisible than notorious, this was an interesting experience for me.

One of my favorite parts of this second Grid Activation was visiting this amazing cave which was closed to the public the day we were there. Someone in our group knew the owner, so she arranged for him to open it for us. We had a private entry and spent a long time in the cave by ourselves, where we carried out several of our exercises to prepare for this next Grid Activation.

Somewhere along the way, we also went to the lake on Mt. Bugarach. Hugo met us there. He'd stripped down to his birthday suit and dove in. It was mid-November in France, so it was freezing cold. He took on the role of John the Baptist as we all baptized each other into awakening to the Christ-Magdalene consciousness and the New Earth. The rest of us took part by wading into the water only up to our knees. The channeled message for this second activation helped us understand more of who we are and why we were here taking part in these Grid Activations.

11/15/11 St Marie la Mer Message

"Blessed are you Magdalenes who once again are awakening to your true nature and purpose. You carry deep within you the codes of awakening to everlasting life–divinity remembered. Your voices and your very presence weave the harmonies of the heavens with the melody of Mother Earth, so the song of Source emanating from within can be heard and recognized by all, once again.

You are keepers and conduits of this harmonic wave of response and remembrance. It is the pulse and the heartbeat of the Grail. Blessed are you, the Magdalene keepers of the Holy Grail, who elicit the song of Source once again so that all of this world and all within the universe may recognize and know themselves as ONE, yet again.

You are the catalysts, the awakeners, the harbingers. We honor you greatly for your dedicated souls, your pure hearts, and your perseverance in this mighty work.

Adonai,
Mother Earth, the Magdalenes and the Hosts of Heaven."

As I was willing, and took action, to step into facilitating the Grid Activations, more awareness and understanding kept opening up. I finally was getting my footing and felt less like a deer in the headlights. Besides facilitating the Magdalene Grid Activations, I started doing day-long workshops related to the Magdalenes under different titles. There was so much ground to cover, they quickly became full weekend two-day workshops. I would put out a request to my mailing list asking for people who were interested in hosting workshops in certain areas to contact me. This is how I facilitated these initial workshops in France just over the Swiss border, and in Belgium, which Hugo hosted. People who attended my events would graciously offer to let me stay with them, although there were some instances where I needed to get a hotel room.

My newfound friend, Helen from Switzerland, attended the first three Grid Activations. A healer, she said each time she attended an Activation her healing practice became tremendously amplified. She and her husband owned an Airbnb in southern France, not too far from Cannes. I was so fortunate to stay there with them for several days. I also stayed in Romainmôtier Switzerland for a while with someone else who had a bed-and-breakfast there who attended a Grid Activation.

Back in the states my sound healer friend, Gila Cadry, who does ancient Hebrew chants, contributed her live channeled Hebrew chants to my workshop. This was great in that it catalyzed a lot of soul memory for people. We started doing weekend workshops up and down the West Coast of the US together throughout 2012.

As I continued offering workshops and doing Grid Activations, it became more and more clear the Magdalenes (both women and men) were now being called forth to serve as the transmitters, especially as we came together in a unified field to serve as the acupuncture needles for the different global activation points. In this way, we, as Magdalenes, served as the midwives of the new consciousness being birthed. We also served as the link for connecting the awakening Magdalene grid of the planet with the newly completed Christ grid surrounding the planet. Through doing our small part in activating the macrocosmic interlocking frequencies of the twin-flame Christ-Magdalene planetary codes, we did our part in assisting the potential of all life on earth to awaken.

As this larger picture unfolded, it also became clear the Magdalene workshops were not only for gaining a greater understanding of the Magdalene Order, ourselves as Magdalenes, and for activating our personal Magdalene Grids, but also for receiving the preparation and fine-tuning needed to be the conduits for the planetary activation points. I was clearly informed people who wished to take part in the Grid Activations must take part in a preparation process (the workshop part included in the Magdalene Grid Activation tours) to attune, step-up their frequency and create a group field in order to fully and safely serve as the conduits for the different planetary activation points.

For the third and fourth Magdalene Grid Activations, I partnered with Ani Williams who is a sound healer, singer, harpist and creator of twenty-two

Magdalene music CDs. She'd led tours to France and England for years. We led the Grid Activations in Fortingall, Scotland, and Isle of Man together. Having her play her music and share her wisdom and experiences with us on these Grid Activations made them very special. In Scotland, one highlight was spending time at Rosslyn Chapel, which is talked about in the Da Vinci Code movie.

The actual Grid Activation in Scotland took place in a field just down the road from the ancient Yew tree in Fortingall. In our book, *Anna, the Voice of the Magdalene*, many years after his resurrection Yeshua (Jesus), in his more ethereal form, sent out an invitation to all the illumined beings on the planet to gather in Fortingall, Scotland, referred to as the *Great Gathering*. We believe the area in which we performed the Grid Activation could have been the site of the Great Gathering written about in the book. I had another profound experience of awakening while we were in Scotland.

We were in Edinburgh attending a midday choral concert at the Edinburgh Cathedral. I was sitting in a chair by myself in an area of the cathedral slightly off to the side. In my inner awareness, I saw St. Germain and Portia, his twin flame, flanking me on either side.

They asked, "Do you want to know what twin flame union feels like?"

"Yes," I bellowed back in my mind.

Then St. Germain and Portia slid across my body like sliding glass doors; one in front, one behind until their heart centers lined up with my heart center. Then Yeshua and his twin flame, Mary Magdalene, came and did the same thing, sliding across one in front, one in back but perpendicular to St. Germain and Portia. The four of them, all with their sacred heart centers aligned with mine, helped me recognize the divine portal within my heart center, which I recognized as the Holy Grail. My heart was the womb of this grail!

The next thing I was aware of, a white dove upside down, similar to the one seen in Christian literature, pierced my crown chakra, descending through my crown and third eye until it reached my heart where it ignited the Grail. I became very emotional as a monumental energetic shift occurred within me. Apparently two friends of Ani's whom I hadn't met yet were sitting behind me holding the space. Later, they told me they could see something was happening with me so they just continued holding the space for me.

After the concert, I found Ani. We all went to lunch in the cathedral cafe where I shared my experience with them. After lunch, Ani and I were on our way to an art museum. There was a midday downpour, so I grabbed my purse and other things close to my chest, trying to keep them from getting soaked. I was wearing a small little money pouch with multiple zippered pockets slung over my shoulder close to my body. Ani and I found refuge from the rain in the museum.

As we were walking around, I kept feeling something hitting the back of my leg. Looking down, I discovered it was my little shoulder pouch which was hanging by one strap. Someone had tried to cut it off my body. Twelve hundred British Pounds were missing out of one of the zippered pockets. This was the cash I was carrying for payment of the admissions fees into sites, local transportation, and other expenses for the group during this Activation. Amazed that they hadn't taken any of the Euros or my American money from the other zippered compartments, it was only the British Pounds they'd stolen. I felt totally violated.

I was at least grateful I hadn't lost my whole zippered pouch and all of my different currencies. We alerted the museum staff who called the police who came to investigate. After investigating for about forty-five minutes, they said I was the victim of a professional pickpocket ring and there was no hope of getting it back. Panicked, crushed, and embarrassed, I had to tell the group what happened. Several people offered to contribute some money to help me make up for the loss which occurred. I had to accept their offers, which was so hard for me to do so we could continue our trip.

This whole pickpocket scene happened less than an hour after having this incredibly high Holy Grail experience. I realized what was being played out was the extremes of polarity. Because my energy frequency became so elevated into the light, it quickly drew the exact opposite level of low frequency to me in this form of being robbed. It doesn't mean one should not raise themselves in the light. I believe it was such a sudden drastic change which I hadn't yet integrated within me, that drew this polar opposite *energy* immediately to me. It was quite a lesson about *energy* and consciousness.

Next, Ani and I led the Isle of Man Magdalene Grid Activation, unprepared for how stunningly beautiful the Isle of Man was. Here we rented two vehicles, a van and a car. Ani opted for driving the car. I ended up driving the nine-person van. Here again I was driving on the opposite side of the road, changing gears, using my left hand to operate the stick shift on the floor and trying not to look as uneasy as I felt. Talk about being all turned around! I just had to look at this as a new adventure.

Chapter 26: Amazing Occurrences

In stepping up to facilitate these Magdalene Grid Activations, I developed a basic format to prepare the group to build a unified field to carry out the activations. When the opportunity to lead these Magdalene Grid Activations was first presented to me, I hadn't any conscious idea even what a grid was, or what activating it, or awakening it, meant. Usually, our human self feels it needs to know everything about something in our rational conscious mind if we are going to write about something, facilitate something, or teach others about it.

I had none of this going on when I started facilitating these activations. Clearly, I was being guided, but the choice was entirely up to me. If I moved forward, all I was being asked to do was to *show up*, *pay attention* to my inner promptings and knowing, and *follow through* with the action my impulses or intuition were leading me to take. That's it. By my willingness to do this, the rest started falling into place.

As I went along, I realized I was receiving a massive education through input from the other side, which helped build my conscious understanding and awareness of what was taking place. I realized it was not my human self who was in charge, but my multidimensional Higher Self that was the absolute Master of this process with exacting precision. All I had to do was trust this larger part of myself to move into action as it presented each step, and have faith that everything was going to work out.

In retrospect, I can see how much courage, faith, and trust it took for me to say yes to all these adventures. Truly flying by the seat of my pants I'd never been to any of these places before, nor had I previously met the people who assisted me, housed me and came to my events. For everything I did—workshops, speaking engagements, Grid Activations, and tours—I either charged a fee or offered it for free committing myself to following through, no matter what, hoping for the best. It was sink or swim. I'd never entertained the thought I would sink, although there were many events in which I didn't break even financially.

Fortunately, other events along the way made up for it. All these years I've somehow scraped by, however, not yet to where I could build any kind of financial security. Money was never the motivating force. If it was, I would never have embarked on this path.

Looking back to 2006 when I first started working with Claire, I think overall I'd be lucky if I've even earned a nickel an hour for all the time and effort which has gone into what I've done. I've always focused way more on my passion for the awakening process, along with understanding and sharing the spiritual journey in a way that makes a difference, inspires or affects people, than making money. I've received feedback many times from people who've shared how much what I've facilitated or shared has affected them. People in Perth, Australia, after a weekend workshop even said what I'd done in that workshop had changed Australia. That was something you don't hear every day. I believe when people are affected profoundly, it is not by our human part, but it is when we can let our divine multidimensional-self take the lead and be in charge.

As I continued offering more and more events, I realized the divine multidimensional aspects of ourselves are knowledgeable and powerful. If we surrender to these higher aspects, and let our human self partially step to the side, relinquishing the tight reins of control, then miracles happen, synchronicity happens and living in a higher frequency or dimensional state happens, if only momentarily. This was what I believe took place during these Magdalene Grid Activations and at other events. Each Grid Activation had its own unique set of occurrences and experiences for each person involved.

During the Isle of Man Grid Activation, Ani Williams and I were looking for stone circles on the island where we could do some of our processes. This turned out to be much more of a challenge that we thought as many of them were on private land. Being lost, Ani turned into a driveway to ask for directions when a woman came out to talk to us. It turned out she was the President of the Tynwald Association, the Parliament of the Isle of Man. We told her what we were looking for, so she stopped what she was doing and offered to help us out. She led us to some stone circles on private property she owned on the Island where we could do our ceremonies. It was an amazing stroke of luck and synchronicity.

When it came time to do the actual Grid Activation on the Isle Man, the place we were guided to was an old small stone ring out in a field. I knew the activation ritual needed to take place inside the stone ring. However, it took a couple of days of toning and working with the *energy* before it felt like we received the go-ahead to climb over the ring of stones into the center. It seemed to be an ancient place; a portal guarded by a dragon. We disturbed this dragon, which was purposeful, not an accident. This dragon represented the steeped patriarchal culture. Duh! Of course! This was the Isle of *Man*. This grid activation was all about the masculine.

The dragon guarding the old patriarchal ways needed to go. I believe that things such as dragons, fairies, mermaids and other elementals really exist but live in different dimensions or parallel realities to ours. However, they can occasionally interact with our dimension.

A few months later, Gila, my sound healer, who does the ancient Hebrew chants, and I went to Australia. We traveled all over Australia doing full weekend workshops. Part of me felt like I'd come home when I arrived in Australia. It seemed I had a lot of soul memory of not only being there before, but identifying Australia as "home" in many of my lifetimes. As usual, I put out an appeal for people in Australia and New Zealand to get in contact with me if they were interested in us coming to their area and knew of someone who could host us. I set workshops up in Palm Beach, the Central Coast, Melbourne, Perth, and Mullumbimby, Australia.

Kaliana Rose, the person who offered to host my workshop in Mullumbimby, was an international workshop leader herself and rarely hosted other people's work. She told me she was in communication with an ascended Aboriginal woman whom she referred to as the Giantess. It was the Giantess apparently who'd invited me to come.

It seemed a lot of the Aborigine's culture based its practices on segregation between men and women. In some Aboriginal cultures, there was a distinct, but equal division, between "men's business" and "women's business" in terms of child rearing, training, and carrying out certain responsibilities. During the workshop, Kaliana came up to me announcing something remarkable had happened. Apparently, the Giantess known as AttaMaya, had so merged with her ascended male counterpart twin flame aspect, PayaMaya, they now individually wished to be called only by their conjoined name, AttaMaya-PayaMaya, as they no longer saw themselves as separate entities. I got the impression from Kaliana this was a big deal as it had never happened before. This theme would also carry forth into the Melbourne, Cairns and Uluru Grid Activation about a month later.

This theme of the masculine and feminine uniting also showed up with my friend Deb meeting her soulmate Michael in one of my workshops in Australia. They also came to the Australian Grid Activation. Participants in the Australian Grid Activation were a band of what I would call wild Aussies plus Gila and me, as we had such an outrageous time being with each other.

The Australian Magdalene Grid Activation took place in three different areas: the forest outside of Melbourne, the sea which took place on a piece of coral reef out on the Great Barrier Reef that Deb and I facilitated, and at Uluru, formerly known as Ayers Rock, the famous Australian desert monument. We had fabulous adventures along the Great Ocean Road and at Uluru. In each of these three places, we performed our unified field acupuncture needle ritual to activate the grid. At Uluru, when doing the Activation ritual at the well, a body of water visible a little way up a portion of the large rock monument, I sensed a circle of Aboriginal elders in their light bodies surrounding the well.

They've held the sacred knowledge from the stars since the beginning of time on Planet Earth. Each one now seemed to unite with their twin flame. When that happened, they went poof-back to Source. It seemed like they communicated to us that their job upon this planet was now nearing completion. It was being passed on to us, the light workers and the awakening ones of humanity. The torch was being passed to us to shepherd this knowledge. It was time for us to take responsibility, as we had now reached maturity as the ones who seeded the light long ago.

"*Wow*" was all I could say.

It felt like it was releasing the old templates so we could now set the new ones into place. I also heard that about five days after we'd left Uluru, that region had the largest earthquake they'd ever experienced. The old was being shaken up. A couple of weeks later Gila and I flew to New Zealand to continue doing weekend workshops there. While there, someone invited me to attend a channeling event of someone else.

I was sitting in the audience when I felt this very intense *energy*. I couldn't discern whether it was positive or negative *energy*. Someone told me it was the *energy* of the Maori warriors present in the etheric realms. Sitting there, I sensed Aboriginal elders also in the etheric. An aboriginal elder and his twin flame aspect stood behind the etheric presence of each of the Maori, activating them also to complete their template and return to Source. It was quite amazing to witness in my inner vision what was happening. As with other experiences, there is no way to confirm anything in a factual way. I felt like I was mostly just watching the show and being given the understanding.

In Auckland, New Zealand, while doing my workshop there, Judy Satori, who channels different star-being light-languages invited Gila and me to attend her Magdalene Manuscript four-day retreat in Coromandel, New Zealand, as her guests. I'd heard of Judy but knew little about her work. My schedule was full, but the universe miraculously created a circumstance whereby it rearranged our workshop schedule so we could take Judy up on her offer.

The retreat center at Coromandel was one of the most beautiful places I'd ever visited. The first thing I was acutely aware of was Saint Germain etherically glued to my side. I wondered what was up. That first evening of the workshop, I received a very clear, clairaudient message. Usually, I'd get more of a feeling-knowing sense, what I refer to as a "download" but this was like a person was standing next to me whispering loudly into my ear.

"*An angel will come to you. Soon thereafter, you will start your ministry just like Yeshua (Jesus) did.*"

Now this was totally unexpected!

The next morning, Judy channeled Mary Magdalene, Joseph of Arimathea, and an Archangel called Alariel. I had never heard of Alariel. She said Alariel was a very pure Archangel, an androgynous being, seated to the right of Mother-Father God. Alariel's task was to return the Divine Feminine to Planet Earth. Later in the afternoon, Judy asked if there were questions. I asked for more clarity of what I needed to know, or do, to move forward with my work. Judy said I would get many downloads throughout the retreat, and then she said I had a strong connection with Archangel Alariel. She said I was a major "ripple" on the planet and that I would take my work to Asia, the Middle East and South America. Now I know better than to assume any information from a channeled source or information in a reading is always true. I just hold myself open to the possibilities without expectation.

All I could think of was *Holy Crap*, my standard reaction! Meanwhile, I still strongly felt St. Germain's presence next to me in his light body. I felt like saying,

"*What's up? Why are you hanging around like this?*"

During every break, people were crowding around these jewelry cases which had exquisite, expensive vibrational lab-created jewelry in them. I didn't want to face any temptation, so I wasn't even going to look at them. That resolve didn't last long. By lunchtime on the second day, my resolve had dissolved. Completely drawn to this Alexandrite reddish-purple faceted pendant, supposedly connected with the consciousness of St. Germain along with assisting one to open up the Akashic records, this piece of jewelry wouldn't leave me alone. I eventually succumbed to this feeling and bought the thing. As soon as I'd purchased it, St. Germain disappeared from my side. He was there to make sure I bought it. I remember thinking, *great, thanks. Are you going to pay for it?* It was about $800 well beyond my $20 budget. After clearing it, the *energy* of it was so intense it took a couple of hours of wearing it to get in sync with it. Later in the afternoon, we hiked up to the Tara Sanctuary at the top of the hill. Here was the most spectacular view of the mountains and ocean. At the sanctuary we did a ritual where we received downloads, "energy packets" from Mary Magdalene.

During this process, I had a distinct feeling of being stamped, like being stamped with a rubber stamp.

I heard the words in my head, "*You've been imprinted. We are going to channel.*" I felt this was Alariel.

What did this mean?

Could I really do this?

Would I know how?

I just sat with this experience for a few days. Wearing the pendant amplified my field in such a way that this imprinting could take place. After the retreat was over, I mentioned this experience to Judy Satori and asked her about this. She tuned in, finally smiled and said to me, "If you were to take Alariel at the highest level and bring that *energy* down through all the dimensions until you reached the Earth plane dimension, she said it's you."

Me?

Are you kidding?

Now this was unexpected news. With this information, I realized I didn't need to be overly concerned about how to 'channel' Alariel. I finally understood if I am an aspect of this Archangel Soul stream, I have been being downloaded with that wisdom my entire life. I just didn't know it. I wondered if it was Alariel's presence which Bill Nakagawa in Hawaii first tuned into when he said there was a huge being of light with me, and later the bluish-white group soul presence that Philip Burley mentioned to me when I'd had the reading with him.

Two things happened after I returned to the United States from being in Australia and New Zealand. The first was staying with a friend whom I had not seen in 17 years since I left the cult. When you left the cult, you were dead to them. People still in the cult could no longer have any interaction or contact with you. Dyana had been one of my closest friends when I was in the cult.

When I was hiding from the group inside my boss's house the day I left the cult, Dyana had been the one walking up and down the street in front of the house, calling my name. She was one person I was heartbroken about having no contact with once I left.

With the dissolution of the cult after the Guru died, she moved to California where she got a job managing a Christian bookstore. One of her customers told her about the Anna books and loaned her the set. She told me they sat on her chair next to her bed for months before she finally picked one up to check it out. She saw my name on the front of the book. Incredulous that this might be the same person who was once in the cult with her, she rummaged through the book, looking for my picture. Yes, it was me! She contacted me right before I left for Australia.

On my way back from Australia three months later, I had to change planes in San Francisco to a connecting flight to Las Vegas where I lived then. I arranged for a stopover to see her and stay with her for three days upon my return. This was definitely another instance of synchronicity and the universe connecting us once again. We have stayed in touch and remained friends ever since. Also, when I got back home, I looked up the name Alariel on the Internet. The only credible references I could find were three books by Stuart Wilson and Joanna Prentis; *Power of the Magdalene*, *The Magdalene Version*, and *The Power of Conscious Co-Creation Beyond Limitations*.

In these books, the author, Stuart Wilson, went through a regression back to an Atlantean lifetime. His guide was the angel Alariel. Also, when I got back to the States, I had a reading with someone in which I asked about Alariel. The information which came through was that there are many huge cosmic beings-angels, archangels and Masters-incarnated here in human embodiment to assist with the shift of consciousness in these transitional times. As a Magdalene, I understood this mission.

Later in 2013, I facilitated the Crestone, Colorado, Magdalene Grid Activation. During this Activation, I coached each participant in freeing themselves from issues which held them back. One participant in this Grid Activation was Jean Trebek, wife of Jeopardy host, Alex Trebek. Jean had the inclination, borne out of love and patience, to focus on being the rock at home.

With so much focus on Alex in their life, I assume the question of her heart might have been–have I allowed myself to realize my full expression? This was understandable to me as anyone who was a partner to a mega-celebrity might feel that way.

What the Magdalenes kept showing me was something very expansive about Jean of which she was unaware. Jean was looking at this primarily from the human third-dimensional perspective, as we all do. In the multi-dimensionality aspect of who she is, they showed me she had a huge compassionate presence. I was shown that Alex's impact on so many people the world over wasn't solely because of his extraordinary talent, outreach and attention to the detail of his work. It was also because of the added dimension of Jean's innate Magdalene Divine Feminine presence, which worked unconsciously, and in synchronicity, with Alex's presence. They showed it to me like fiber optic cables going out to every TV around the world where people watched Jeopardy. The potent energy combination of Jean's Divine Feminine Magdalene energy field, along with Alex's masculine energy exemplifying his talent and mastery of his craft, opened hearts and minds, affecting all who watched him. The Magdalenes kept showing me Jean was an integral and important factor in Alex's success. It is the power again of the male/female union in cohesion rather than division, which was operating here.

Another pivotal experience for me happened during the actual ritual part of the Crestone Grid Activation. It was pouring rain outside, so we were all crammed into a little red tepee in the "I AM Harmony Garden" in Crestone, Colorado. I was facilitating the ritual when I had a sense of a being, or angel, behind one of the participants. This person, an extremely creative and gifted artist, was totally insecure with quite a negative self-image. Tuning in, I asked if what I was sensing was her guardian angel.

I received the reply, "No I am her!"

This woman's central core had become so narrow, it was like a thin piece of wire. Her being (etheric body) was to the back and side of her because her central core conduit was way too small. This part standing to the back of her was exquisite. I thought to myself if she could see herself and how beautiful she was, she would never have a limiting or judgmental thought about herself ever again. People need help to get over the "small versions" of themselves. Many people need to develop a much larger circumference and capacity of their central core in order for them to anchor and expand the amount of light needed for them to do what, on a soul level, they came here to do.

Seeing the situation with this woman brought into crystal clarity how I could further assist people with this. After the Crestone Grid Activation, I had the opportunity of staying at the Trebeks' home in Studio City, California for about a week while I finished writing my manuscript for my Soulweaving book. I spent that time staying in their son's room while he was away at college. Jean fed me and took care of things so I could just focus on my writing. I'd shared none of my writing before.

Years earlier, I'd only ever let my roommates hear a couple of sentences from the introduction up to this point. It's very hard to let others see our writings, or to have our voices heard, because so many of us experienced persecution or died in other lives for what we knew or might have shared in the past. So as Magdalenes and initiates, we've had lifetimes of taking vows of secrecy and silence.

It was hard to feel safe enough to share what was so close to my heart. I attached the completed manuscript to an email to Jean, took a deep breath, gulped and pressed send. My manuscript was now on its way to Jean's computer for her to read. I shouldn't have been concerned. Jean loved my book, *Soulweaving, Return to the Heart of the Mother*.

She wrote the endorsement on the back of the book saying in part it was one of the most significant publications she'd ever read, putting it right up there with the *Course in Miracles*. She ran study groups on *A Course in Miracles*, so she was very familiar with that material. Privately, she told me that my book was especially wonderful because it was so contemporary and relatable. Grateful to Jean for helping me feel so supported in releasing this material, it had all started with the "download" I received during the first Humanities Team event where I had an absolute "knowing"' I was going to write a book. Even though I had co-authored books with Claire Heartsong and Angelina Heart, I knew this was the book.

Chapter 26: Amazing Occurrences

The next Grid Activation was at the Valley of the Queens in Egypt. My friend Joanie, who had led tours to Egypt before, co-led this Activation with me. Because the airfares were going up around the holidays, we flew to Israel about a week before Thanksgiving, staying with a friend's mother in Jerusalem for about ten days. Then we went down to the Israeli resort town of Elat on the southernmost tip of Israel for a couple of days. From there, we crossed the Taba border on foot into Egypt. At the border crossing, the guards stopped Joanie as she had all kinds of over-the-counter medication in case anyone on the tour needed something.

We knew we couldn't say anything about running a tour or that we were doing anything other than being tourists. The border patrol let me through, but detained her. They went through all her suitcases and possessions multiple times as they continued to interrogate her. They were trying to figure out why she had so much over-the-counter medicine and what she was up to.

I walked a short way past the border to a little dirt road parking area on the Egyptian side. It was desolate, out in the middle of nowhere with nothing but sand and a small broken curb. Absolutely nothing was there. A few taxi drivers occasionally pulled up, asking if I wanted a ride, but I declined. I knew I just had to wait. Not knowing what was happening with Joanie, I didn't have any way to get in touch with her. I had no choice but to sit down on the broken cement curb and wait.

Also, I had no information on who the car and driver were who we were supposed to meet. I didn't have any idea what I would do if she didn't show up. Finally, about two hours later, she emerged from the border patrol detention area. We finally met up with the van and driver which she'd arranged who drove us all the way down the whole Sinai Peninsula, which was quite a trip!

One afternoon we stopped for lunch in an open-air restaurant, (they all were), next to the Gulf of Aqaba. Suddenly, Joanie heard her name being called. It was someone she'd known from years before who was in this tiny windsurfing town on the Sinai Peninsula. The synchronicity on this trip amazed me. Our driver took us to the airport in Sharm el-Sheikh, where we caught a flight to Cairo.

The night we arrived in Cairo we had dinner with friends of Joanie's. After dinner, we were heading back to our hotel when suddenly our eyes and faces started stinging and burning in unbelievable pain and discomfort. There had been a riot in the nearby square. Officials had released tear gas into the crowd which drifted down the side streets to where we were. Even if you put your scarf over your eyes and mouth trying to stop the onslaught of the tear gas, it was still horrible. Nothing like receiving a pleasant welcome to Cairo.

We met our small group of participants a couple of days later. Egypt had mixed energy. Some of it, positive, and much of it was very dark. A lot of stuff got stirred up there. None of the big boats was running on the Nile when we were there so we rented a small felucca boat, a traditional wooden sailing boat. We sailed for a couple of days on the Nile, and then we went to a section closer to the Aswan Dam, where the water was clean and we could swim in the Nile.

We visited many of the temples and performed the actual Magdalene Grid Activation in the Valley of the Queens, where we invited the somewhat toothless guard to take part in one of our group exercises with us. He led us around to a private area off the beaten path for doing the ritual. He declined at first, but after a bit of reticence he finally joined in. After having this experience, he let us go inside to see the colorful painted walls of Nefertiti's tomb as a private group. After completing the Grid Activation in the Valley of the Queens, we then went to the Great Pyramid on the Giza plateau.

The weather turned cold and blustery. A huge downpour flooded the streets. Cars, carts, and all the camels and donkeys struggled through almost a foot of rushing water. Everything was a mess, including us.

The upshot of all this was hardly any tourists were going into the pyramid. We could get into the pyramid and climb up inside to the King's Chamber, where we were by ourselves for an hour before anyone else came. We took turns lying down in the sarcophagus. I had quite an amazing inner visual experience, which I am sure was part of my soul's memory as I lay in the sarcophagus. When we entered the King's Chamber, it was much smaller than I'd expected. The next morning, we woke up to a blanket of snow covering everything. We were also freezing as none of the hotels in Cairo have heat, as it rarely gets cold like that there. So, within forty-eight hours of us doing the Grid Activation in Egypt,

Chapter 26: Amazing Occurrences

it snowed in Cairo for the first time in one hundred and twelve years. Now that was another synchronicity, beyond mere coincidence!

One of my favorite Magdalene Grid Activations was in Ephesus, Turkey. Ephesus is the ancient city name for what is now an archaeological site and museum. It is close to the present-day city of Izmir, Turkey. The original itinerary for the Ephesus Magdalene Grid Activation was to include the archaeological site, Göbekli Tepe, said to be the oldest temple on the planet, far older than Stonehenge or the Egyptian pyramids. However, skirmishes erupted on the Syrian border only twenty-five miles away, which didn't feel safe.

Three weeks before the trip was to start, I felt a need to revise the itinerary going to Konya where the Persian poet Rumi was interred, instead. When we went to Rumi's Shrine, one member of our group prostrated himself before Rumi's mausoleum as was the local custom. I sensed Rumi's presence with us. In my head I heard Rumi say, "What are you doing that for? I am right here." I knew he was etherically standing right there next to us.

We flew to Cappadocia, which was like a fantasy land with all its fairy chimneys and natural rock formations, some of which were carved out and made into dwellings. We also took a hot-air balloon ride over this enchanted landscape. There were dozens of balloons all in the air at once, a magnificent sight. Trying to keep costs low, my intention in Turkey was to rent a van and drive myself. It quickly became clear that plan wasn't going to work. Fortunately, there were a couple of people on the trip who chipped in to get a van and a driver. We needed to drive around the coast of almost half of Turkey to get to the site for the actual Grid Activation on our way back to Istanbul.

I originally planned to do the Grid Activation at the House of the Virgin Mary, but this location was way too crowded with too many tourists, and too heavily fenced-in and guarded. We performed the actual ceremony and ritual for the Grid Activation, about eight kilometers away on a beach of the Aegean Sea.

When we went to rent a van and driver, I asked for a driver who spoke English. Of course, the rental company assured me the driver spoke English. He did not. Even the driver of the van, who was Turkish, got lost a few times and had to ask for directions. I could see him watching us in the van's rear-view mirror sometimes. I guess we differed from other tourists he'd encountered. We had a mixture of nationalities in our group; however, most were British and American.

When we got to Pamukkale, one of the most magical places I've ever experienced, the van driver paid his own way to join us in the thermal pools. Pamukkale is an absolutely breathtaking series of travertine natural terraced pools with turquoise water in them cascading down a hillside. Besides the terraced pools, there was a thermal pool section, which had a separate entrance fee. This was a large hot spring pool of crystal-clear water in which you could clearly see all kinds of Greek columns and archaeological ruins way below the surface of the water where you were swimming. I'd hadn't experienced anything like it before. A few days later when it came time to do the actual Grid Activation on the beach of the Aegean Sea, the van driver gestured to us, asking if he could come along.

I said, "Yes." What was he going to do otherwise?

We did all of our Grid Activation preparation and ritual things including meditating, toning, ingesting elixirs, using essential oils, and doing certain movements and all kinds of what I would consider "woo-woo" stuff to those who wouldn't understand what was happening. Our driver just imitated what we were doing and followed along, although he couldn't understand a word we were saying. It amazed me how fully he took part in all of it.

When we got back to the hotel, the van driver put his arms around the shoulders of the two men on the trip in camaraderie. He asked the front desk person to translate from Turkish to English for him. First, he addressed the two men, saying, "These are my brothers. These are my brothers."

Then he asked, "What did you do to me? My heart will never be the same!"

Even though he didn't have a clue what we were talking about, or what we were doing, he totally got it. He felt the *energy* of the Grid Activation on some level. That was one highlight of all the Magdalene Grid Activations for me.

Ephesus Turkey, November 11, 2014
Magdalene Grid Activation Message

"Beloved strands of my heart, for that is what you are. You each have come here either in your light bodies, or your physical bodies, to my home in Ephesus, for I have invited you here. You are the ones who responded to the call even though more were called, but did not heed the signal.

This land of Turkey has seen much heartache, and the land has suffered through many years of the patriarchal system. You have reconnected the Magdalene Grid lines, allowing a deep, powerful, and beautiful release. I, Mother Mary, and the ancient ones from Turkey would like to express our eternal gratitude for the Activation of the Magdalene Grid here. The sweetness felt for this energy, reawakened, along with what it did for Mother Earth, can't accurately find expression through human words, only through light language.

You have walked upon the land that I called sacred, where I spent the last years of my life before my ascension. You came to pick up the codes and energy deeply embedded by me and my Magdalene brothers and sisters into the land here and the etheric planes both within and above the earth plane in this area now known to you as Turkey.

Your presence as Magdalenes, and as strands of my heart, has reawakened the energy of the Christ-Magdalene seeded in Ephesus so that all Magdalenes may once again bring forth the work of ushering in the New Earth which we, Magdalene-Essenes, seeded long ago. It is your turn now.

I, all the Magdalenes, the Councils of Light, and your own team of unseen help are with you every step of the way. We humbly are in gratitude to you for your willingness, your devotion, and your dedication to serve the Mother/Father God. I bless you in your lifetime and your journeys in this world. Go forth and be the inspiration to your upcoming generations, just as we've inspired generations for eons past.

What you will do will influence humanity, not only on this planet, but into the farthest reaches of the galaxy. And you'll be recognized in a far greater way than we've been known. Go in peace. Go in love. Go united in the one heart of God/Goddess, all that is. I look forward to greeting each one of you personally when you return home here to the 'other side' as you call it.

Namaste,
Mother Mary."

I kept trying to get the four remaining Magdalene Grid Activations to materialize, but postponements kept happening or we didn't have enough people to register for them. The last Grid Activation we physically carried out was the Maui Grid Activation in Hawaii in February 2015. This ended up being the last one because when it took place, it was already outside of the time frame given for these activations, which was to have been between 11/11/11/ and 12/12/14, but it took place three months later. When I was making no headway getting the remaining Grid Activations scheduled, I finally went and had a reading in which I asked why nothing was materializing.

I was told the window on the timing had closed. The remaining four locations we physically didn't need to facilitate because Mother Earth had completed them herself. There was no longer a need for us to go, which was why they weren't materializing. I did however lead two other tours, a second tour in England in March 2016 along with giving a two-day workshop at Chalice Well in Glastonbury, and an Israel tour in 2017. I knew I was to lead a tour in Israel, as *energy* work was needed there to help bring the masculine and feminine energies back into a more harmonious balance.

It amazed me when visiting sacred sites in Jerusalem that two or three different places all claimed to be the location of certain events in Jesus's life. Even though you could visit these places, no one knew for sure where things happened. Of course, this would be true. You can't get it externally. You'd have to turn within.

Personally, I found the energy in Old Jerusalem to be heavy and almost stifling. The most uplifting energy and rewarding experiences for me in Israel were at Elijah's cave in Haifa, when we were sailing on the Sea of Galilee, when we spent time in the forest opposite Mt. Tabor where the transfiguration of Jesus was said to have taken place, and also at the Dead Sea. Besides me and my sound healer, Gila, who spoke fluent Hebrew, there were six other participants on the Israel tour-two American women, two women from Finland and two women from Japan.

In Israel, I rented and drove another large nine-person van on this trip. I found driving in Jerusalem very challenging. Streets were often really narrow. People sometimes parked their cars with their back ends sticking out into the street making passing them difficult. Also, some roads which passed through outdoor malls didn't accommodate the passage of large vehicles easily. Rounding a huge cement pillar in a tight turn in one of these malls, we all heard the unmistakable sound of the van scraping the cement pillar.

Upon later inspection, there were only a few scratches on the door handle and the side of the van. The rental company takes pictures of the vehicle you rent before and after you rent it, comparing the images to see if you've incurred any damage. Obviously, they would charge for any damage you caused, but it was unlikely that they ever repaired the previous damage to the vehicle as the van was full of scratches, dings, and dents when we rented it. We set out to rectify any damage we incurred with touch-ups using a black magic marker and toothpaste. It worked! I didn't feel bad about doing this, as the van was pretty banged up when we initially got it.

At the Dead Sea, we had a flat tire. The company who rented us the van would not help us at all. After spending a couple of hours trying to figure out where the tool was located to get the spare tire put on the van, fortunately the hotel at the Dead Sea finally came up with an employee who knew what to do and could help us. I found out renting cars in other countries differs vastly from car rentals in the United States. I think I suffered PTSD from driving in Jerusalem. I found it very stressful driving in Israel, but I just had to persevere through it. There were many more adventures and challenges, of course, that took place on these tours and Grid Activations, which made them special for everyone. Everyone had their own unique challenges (initiations) and breakthroughs.

Chapter 27: Integration

In 2014, I entered into another relationship. This was the first relationship I'd had since I'd split with Rich almost ten years before. When Derrick and I first got to know each other, he told me he'd been the CEO of his family's very successful business. He could see how tired and overwhelmed I was, so he offered to help me with the business side of my work. He promised he would draw up a business plan for me. I'd been looking for this kind of reliable help for years. Even though I'd had several assistants for short intervals over the years, none had really worked out.

I'd been wearing a hundred hats doing everything myself including writing, print book setup, publishing, web design, marketing, the shopping cart, the back end of things, travel, planning tours and workshops, accounting, teaching, channeling, personal healing sessions, and many other things. So thankful finally to have this kind of help and partnership, we eventually became romantically involved. Also, in trying to be supportive of what Derrick wanted, we ended up moving to Austin, Texas, from Las Vegas as he always had wanted to go there.

As part of training him on all aspects of my business, and because I so desperately needed help with the business end of things, I paid his way to accompany me on the Ephesus and the Maui Magdalene Grid Activations with the intention that once trained, he would take some of the load off my shoulders. As we went along, I soon discovered he had talked a good game. He made it sound like he was helping and doing what you wanted, but in reality, there was very little follow-through. I realized it wasn't so much that he wanted to help me, he wanted to be me! He wanted what I had—to have recognition as a writer, teacher, and workshop leader. Of course, there were things which he contributed, but it was not at the commitment or responsibility level that he'd promised me. Months later, I was still waiting to get the business plan he promised me when we first met.

In Maui, I gave him his chance to lead a portion of the grid activation process. Exhausted and dragging at that point, I probably shouldn't have gone through with facilitating this Grid Activation trip because I was so tired. I gave Derrick an assignment to lead some of the processes I do with the group. These processes I assigned to him were to build the unified field so the participants would be ready to come together as the human acupuncture needle for the planetary activation. This way I could rest. I could also see how well he did with it. He pulled it off, proving he could rise to the occasion if he was pushed. Rather than feeling pleased about this, it just annoyed me more than ever that he wasn't showing up this way all along.

Finally, I literally ran out of money. I knew I couldn't afford to support both of us any longer, nor could we afford to stay in our condo in Austin. We had to break our lease. It had been hard enough trying to stay afloat financially myself, but now I was done with supporting him as well with very little contribution coming back. I told him the relationship was over. As psychic as he was, he didn't see this coming. I had no choice.

I stayed in Austin for another five months in a live-in pet sitting position. When that ended, again I faced the dilemma of where to go next. It's great to have opened-ended options, but not so easy to decide where to go when there is no tangible reason to move somewhere, like a job, a relationship, a community, a volunteer project, or whatever. I thought about returning to Portland, Oregon, but it was too far away from Texas. I wanted to go somewhere I could drive within two days so I could move all my stuff in two car trips.

I had been told in a couple of different readings I'd had over the years that Asheville, North Carolina, had a lot of spiritual stuff going on there. It might be a good place for me, and it was a two-day drive. I decided on Asheville sight unseen, packed up my car and moved there. Someone who had attended one of my Austin workshops also decided to move to Asheville, so we agreed to be roommates and rent a house together.

Around Christmas 2015, the idea of channeling Alariel started pulling on me, trying to get my attention. This had come forth a couple of years earlier in my experience with Judy Satori in New Zealand. I had put this whole notion on the back burner. Now it was clamoring to move onto the front burner of my life. I finally acquiesced. I invited a couple of people over, along with my roommate, just to see what would happen if I opened myself up to channel Alariel. I didn't know if anything would come forth. In the 80s I tried verbal channeling when I lived on Bainbridge Island, but my only models of channeling back then were full-trance channels who remembered nothing that transpired when the session was over. When I tried it, information came through, but I thought I was doing it wrong since I was still fully present and aware of everything that was said. I did however feel altered as if my head was wrapped in cotton candy. I stopped trying to channel because I was sure I wasn't doing it right.

Around the year 2000, I started writing my channeled messages. I rarely went back to look at them as I was always too self-critical. In getting ready to write this memoir, I looked through this material amazed at the wealth of channeled information I'd written over the years. Even though the thought of channeling verbally in person wasn't comfortable for me, I'd committed to moving forward with it. So, I got quiet, aligned myself with my center, Higher Self, and Alariel. I opened my mouth and hoped for the best.

Of course, the session went fine, as they all do despite my insecurities. The words just seemed to bypass my rational thinking mind and tumbled out of my mouth even in response to the questions asked. One person asked about a disturbing poltergeist occurrence at her brother's house. Upon hearing the question, I hadn't a clue! Suddenly, this little thread of awareness trickled down through me. The information given, in response to this woman's question, was that her brother in a previous life was a famous medium. He'd missed this aspect of himself and the notoriety.

Even though he had professional people come and close off the portals to this disturbing supernatural activity in his home—which stopped it—he had re-opened the portals to get in touch with this aspect of himself. The guides assured him there were other ways he could now get in touch with that aspect of himself without having to open portals to destructive forces. This wasn't something I would have ever have thought up by myself! I remember then saying to myself, "Okay, I can do this."

Committing to doing this channeling thing gave me an idea. I still intended to continue to share my teachings about the Magdalene Order and seeding the light. I changed the nature of my events, offering shorter three-to-four-hour events instead of full weekend affairs. These events would introduce people to the idea that they could be present-day Magdalenes, along with my stories of how this all came about working with Anna (the grandmother of Jesus) and Claire. Towards the end of each event, I would spend the last half hour or more channeling Alariel and the Hosts of Heaven for the group. Thus, *Seeding the Light* events were born. I first offered these events on a trip to California and Arizona. They seemed to be a success. They were much more affordable for people who knew nothing about what I did.

During this trip to California, I also went with some friends to the Whole Life Expo in Los Angeles. My friends let me have a corner of their vendor table to sell my books and the *Blessings from the Heart of the Rose* Oracle Card deck, which my artist friend Sheila created. Sheila was the English woman who came with me to get water from the White Springs at Chalice Well to bring to all the Grid Activations. As an exquisite artist and channel, she wanted to create a card deck. She had already designed 25 cards; however, I told her she needed a minimum of 44 cards to create the deck. Over the next year she came up with the additional cards and the accompanying booklet. I published this card deck through my company and had it manufactured in China. This was another huge learning curve as it was something I previously knew nothing about.

At this expo, I also met someone who worked for the Hollywood Foreign Press. I told him about the Anna books. Claire and I had a purchase option agreement in place for about three years with someone interested in turning the Anna books into a film or video streaming series. Unfortunately, after three years, they canceled the agreement. It would have to come about another way. I sent copies of the two Anna books to this person in the Hollywood Foreign

Press who liked the books, but he asked for the script. There was no script yet. This was the second time someone asked for the script. This was another project to come back to sometime later down the line.

Sheila, who lived in England, had been on a waiting list for about three years to conduct a workshop at Chalice Well in Glastonbury, Somerset, England. She had already postponed it once because of illness, then she decided she didn't want to take the slot at all. She begged me to take the slot in her place. Of course, this conversation took place only about six weeks before her scheduled weekend slot of March 12-13, 2016. It was very short notice for pulling things together. I didn't know how or when I'd ever have this kind of opportunity to do something at Chalice Well again. So, I finally agreed, sending up a brief prayer to all my guides to help me with this. If I was going to fly all the way "across the pond" to England, I felt I also needed to schedule other events there, too.

Even though I agreed to do this workshop on such short notice, I also decided to schedule a *Little England Tour* where participants would visit sacred sites in England along with attending the workshop at Chalice Well, which I included in the itinerary for the tour. People not signed up for the tour could also attend the workshop for a separate fee. Other synchronistic events miraculously fell into place. Simon, a participant in several Grid Activations, had purchased a home in Glastonbury which he'd turned into an Airbnb. His primary residence was in Australia, although he was English. I rented his Airbnb home in Glastonbury for a week for lodging for the tour participants.

After the tour, I started doing my *Seeding the Light* events throughout Europe. Through my mailing list, I put out for people to host these events, along with an appeal to find a traveling partner who would buy the Eurail Pass (unlimited train pass) to go on this adventure with me. Cynthia, a friend of mine from Sedona, took me up on this offer as she had never been to Europe before. She also came on the Little England Tour. Here we were, both senior citizens traveling around the British Isles and Europe on the trains like eighteen-year-old kids. But what an adventure! I started doing my *Seeding the Light* events first throughout Ireland, then throughout Europe.

In Enniscorthy, Ireland, there was an old mill which was being converted into a healing center. Even though it was not completely finished yet, my event was the first one that was held in this new center. The most amazing thing, however, was that the entire construction crew working on this remodel attended my event. This was by far the most men I've ever had attending one of my events, as I believe there were about ten to twelve of them. They loved it!

When we traveled up to Northern Ireland to do an event there, we had to find a place to be for a few days after the event as it was around Easter time and not a good time to travel. We found a wonderful bed-and-breakfast where we stayed for a few nights. We became friendly with the owners and their grown children. Initially, we paid them to take us to some sacred sites in the area, then eventually they just offered to be our tour guides, taking us to several other places.

They took us to the prehistoric monument, Newgrange, and Tara Hill. We stayed in touch with each other for several months after I returned to the states. Next, we went to France, even though no one there had responded to our request to host events. We rented a car for a couple of days so we could be tourists going to St. Baume, and Saints-Maries-de-la Mer, where they hold the gypsy festival each year. Then we got back on the train once again and headed to Italy.

In Italy an American woman, whom I had emailed back and forth with for about a year, responded that she wanted to host an event at her home in Bologna. She'd married an Italian and had lived in Italy for the past thirty-three years. We spent the entire four or five days we were in Italy staying at their house. Other than going out to eat ice cream once, which was scrumptious, we all had to make our own spaghetti or ravioli if we wanted to eat while staying at their house. Cathy's husband had a job as the pasta maker for a restaurant for several years when he was a teenager. He made theirs from scratch all the time.

Once he made the pasta and cut it into strips, it was our job to make it into raviolis by putting the filling in, then sealing it. I tried, but my ravioli-making skills were terrible. The filling always leaked out of my raviolis when they were being boiled, as I hadn't sealed them adequately. We were told if we wanted to eat, we had to make our own pasta. Such was the learning process. I was very grateful to get to know them better and stay there for a few days.

After a brief time in Italy, we went on to Bucharest in Romania. Bucharest was the most amazing response of any place during the whole European tour. There were so many people registering for the event that the host had to find larger venues several times. By the time we got there, ninety-one participants had signed up for the *Seeding the Light* workshop which meant with the staff, there were almost a hundred people at this event. The translator was so excited to attend the event, she offered her translation services for free.

I wondered if this overwhelming response may have been partly because this part of the world had been behind the iron curtain for so long that they yearned for spiritual input, teachings and guidance. I was so grateful not only for the response, but the money earned from this event helped offset the deficit incurred from many of the previous events. Previous to the Bucharest event, the largest number of people at an event was about twenty-five to thirty people in Dublin, Ireland.

After Romania, we took the overnight train to Budapest, Hungry. We had what people later called the "East European travel experience." I crawled up and hung out on the top bunk. We were on the train for the better part of two days. There was nowhere to go and sit outside of our sleeper car other than the chairs and tables in the dining car. Cautioned to always have one of us stay in our sleeper car at all times to guard our possessions, we couldn't both leave as apparently there was a lot of theft on the trains. Cynthia and I would take turns going to eat in the dining car.

It took some getting used to the motion of the train to fall asleep at night. Finally, late into the night I had just drifted off to sleep when suddenly there was a lot of banging and racket going on. The train had stopped at a border crossing. The border patrol noisily boarded the train, checking everyone's passport with their intimidating demeanor. This was unexpected and unsettling, to say the very least. Finally, we got to go back to bed about forty-five minutes later.

Just as I was falling asleep for the second time, the whole thing happened all over again, with yet another border crossing stop. Again, the border patrol boarded the train, woke everyone up, and checked our passports. Finally, we returned to bed but could only sleep for about three more hours as we had to get off in Budapest at 5 AM to change trains to go to Germany. I finally understood what people meant when they talked about having the East European train experience. We went on to Erfurt, Germany, a picturesque village not bombed during World War II, so its quaint historical architecture was still intact. We had a wonderful host there who put us up in her home, as people did in most other places. Again, I had to use a translator there and also later in Greece for my workshops.

After Germany, we continued on to The Hague in the Netherlands. Here my traveling buddy Cynthia and I parted ways as she flew back to the states. She told me she would never travel with me again. I just laughed. I agreed with her. I'm not sure if I would ever travel with me again either, at this hectic pace. Even though we had the Eurail pass, this trip wasn't like traveling in other circumstances where you could just take your time exploring places. I had a pretty tight schedule to keep, so we were on the go all the time. I was not at all offended by Cynthia saying this to me. She got to Europe and saw an awful lot, even if it was traveling through at break-neck speed. I continued on to facilitate a full weekend workshop in The Hague.

In the Netherlands, Irene, the woman hosting the workshop, had an unexpected visitor, her friend Nikki, who spontaneously arrived from Greece for a visit. Naturally, Irene brought her to my workshop, even though Nikki knew nothing about who I was or what I was doing. She was into it, though. The workshop was small, but very international, as there were people attending from the Netherlands, France, Greece, Poland, and Romania. Nikki extended an invitation for me to come and stay with her at some point. I asked her how she felt about me returning to Greece with her right away. Surprised at my request, she agreed. I had kind of hit the wall at this point and knew I needed to rest for a while. Able to buy a plane ticket for the same flight Nikki was on later that afternoon, I flew to Athens with her.

I was in Greece for about three weeks, staying in Nikki's apartment during the day while she worked at her office as a psychologist. On weekends, we went sightseeing. One weekend we took the ferry to Mykonos and from there, we went to Delos, a cool archaeological site associated with the myths of the Greek Gods. I loved that trip! I did two *Seeding the Light* events at different locations in Athens.

We were in Greece during the Greek Orthodox Easter time. Friends of Nikki's invited us to a retreat place up in the hillside country outside of Athens. Several families brought their children and food for a feast, along with their ancient Greek instruments. The host roasted a whole pig on the outdoor spit for the Easter meal. Everyone had a relaxed, fabulous time playing music, sharing stories and camaraderie. It was a very special event. I felt honored to attend. When we returned to Athens, even though I was trying to rest, I had a period where I had difficulty sleeping.

Often, I would wake up in the middle of the night around 4 AM. Unable to go back to sleep, I would get on Facebook. The morning of May 6, 2016, while I was staying at Nikki's apartment in Athens, I'd just read a wonderful article on Twin Flames followed by a post about Donald Trump titled "The Taco Bowl." Immediately catapulted from this very heart-centered expansive article on understanding the purpose and energetic dynamics of twin flame union to the insanity of Donald Trump, along with everyone's reactions and comments, I knew it was time to address this. I've dedicated my entire life's work to bringing back the balance of the Divine Feminine and the Divine Masculine, understanding what that is exactly, and how to bring it about.

Through my awakening journey, I have done deep inner work regarding twin flame union and healing the extremes of the issues it brings up. I have shared about this journey in many of my other books. As I've discussed in earlier chapters, through the shadow work with Debbie Ford, and later through many other healing modalities, I've learned that everything exists and can be shifted within ourselves. In my *Soulweaving* book, I talk about this as weeding and cultivating your inner garden. I had been asking to understand more fully exactly how to unite the masculine and feminine. I started asking myself, within, "Where is the masculine and feminine out of balance?"

Reacting to the post about Donald Trump, I had to own that he scared me. From how the media portrayed him, he represented to me the extremely out-of-balance patriarchal figure based on greed and power. It was everything about the male persona I felt threatened by, don't like, or trust. To me, he definitely magnified the masculine and feminine being out of balance. In my Magdalene workshops I would talk about how many of us are present-day Magdalenes and are currently part of the Magdalene Order of which we usually have no awareness. Magdalenes are masters of resurrection. I'd already shared the teachings in my workshops about how we live in crucifixion, resurrection, and ascension every day. I realized I was in full-on crucifixion mode with my extreme judgment about Donald Trump. How could I continue to teach that we live crucifixion, resurrection and ascension every day if I wasn't willing to apply it to myself? I knew I was so triggered by "The Donald" I had to do my inner work around him.

First, I quieted myself and went into my inner meditative state. In this state I asked him to show me where in my body he lived. Surprised when he showed me it was my cervix, it was like he was Captain Kirk on the bridge of the Starship Enterprise with a 360-degree view. He, the Donald aspect within me, said he chose that area because it was the threshold between the inner and outer world. It had to do with birthing creation, which he wanted absolute control over. I didn't like it. However, I acknowledged since he was an inner aspect of me, I'd love him and would be there for him. I asked him to show me how he got to be that way. In my inner vision a scene unfolded of a young boy, maybe 5 or 6 years old, who was being terrorized and locked in a dark closet. I felt I was seeing his "inner child." This child desired to never feel terrorized or victimized by anyone ever again. It seemed the terror of this was so great he figured out how to amass great wealth and power in order to crush anyone who would try to do such a thing against to him.

I asked his "inner child" what it wanted. The response came that all he wanted was to feel loved, to know people cared about him, and that he mattered. I then asked for the Divine Mother aspect of me to come in, open his heart and let him know love. She also reminded him that within his heart was a grand spark of light, which was divine and a part of God. She let him know it was his job to protect and nurture it at all times.

Then an extraordinary thing happened, as often does when doing shadow work. Shown his great mass of external wealth as money, real estate holdings, companies, investments, and other endeavors, because of the spark of light he claimed in his heart, now it was ready to mirror this reality internally, so that a balance between the inner and outer could take place. This also represented the balance between the masculine and the feminine. The extent of his outer wealth became golden light anchored and filtered through the pure spark of light he had now claimed through his inner child's heart and was there to nurture and protect. The golden light pouring into the void of his inner self was so immense it was enough to seed abundance throughout the entire grid system of the New Earth that was being birthed. What a gift!

This ability of the masculine part of me to make money and create well in a 3-D world has always been a missing piece. Now I have to know it is no longer missing, but will be an ally for me, instead of an enemy now. Now when I think of Trump, I can choose to not get pulled into the criticism, fear, or insanity of the ego personality, but to just focus on his inner child's heart shown to me and the gift he is bringing there.

As to the actual person, Donald Trump, I have absolutely no idea what his story really is. Do any of us really know about anyone else? All we ever have is our own response or reaction to another person. This exercise wasn't at all about the "outer reality" of what's happening, but the work to shift the low frequency energy and judgment of my 'inner reality' bringing myself into greater peace and balance. Either we're inspired by someone, triggered by them, or we are neutral. At least through this deep inner work, I know I have a choice within me of different perspectives of how I want to react.

After doing this inner shadow work session, I could watch Trump from a neutral place and not get sucked into the drama. This didn't mean I agreed or disagreed with him. I didn't know if I would vote for him or not. Every time I saw Trump from that point on, I realized I had a choice to see through the lens of the inner gold aspect of him within me, or the villainous way he was being portrayed through the media. Instead of getting pulled into division and being asked to take sides, I now could be in the world, but not of it.

Willing to go within, squarely face whatever I found there without trying to make it different until receiving guidance of what to do, allowed an organic unfolding of this gift within. This is the way I approach anything which intensely triggers me. There is "gold" in that shadow piece along with wisdom when one will confront it, rather than trying to sweep it under the rug, push it away, do battle with it, or pretend it isn't there. After this, I finally fell back to sleep.

This helped me navigate the deeper realms of awakening. My judgment and mistrust of the male persona out-pictured as the persona of Trump was the poison. I continued to see clearly how the "poison" was a necessary ingredient for transformation. When doing my coaching certification with Debby Ford, trying to be all sweet, light and lovey-dovey on top of the unexamined shadow beliefs which really creates our "reality," she referred to this as putting ice cream on top of poop. I had to go within and examine what I judged and couldn't live with. It was not the person "out there" but an aspect of myself that I couldn't be with within me.

I believe the chaos and darkness out-pictured in our world is all of the parts of ourselves we can't be with. It is all of the individual and collective ugliness we've refused to face and take responsibility for, which is now undeniably up in our face. We can change it by changing the frequency within ourselves. By doing so, we can create a new collective out-picturing. This is what I believe the New Earth is all about. I finally felt more rested and integrated within myself and was ready to move on.

After Greece, I flew back to the Netherlands to travel up to Ter Apel in the northern part of the Netherlands to do another *Seeding the Light* event followed by taking the overnight ferry from Holland to northern England to do another event in Hexham, Northumberland. Eventually I made my way up to Findhorn in Scotland, where I stayed for about two weeks. I gave a talk at the Findhorn Eco Village and enrolled in their week-long "Experience Week" course, which introduces people to the essence of the Findhorn Foundation.

Findhorn became famous in the 70s with the book *Findhorn Garden,* all about the small band of people who planted a miraculous garden in the inhospitable windswept and barren sand dunes of Scotland. Through communication and cooperation with the Devas and nature spirits, they produced vegetables of enormous size. Since then, the vegetables no longer grow to such an enormous size, as the Devas said humans had gotten the point.

Findhorn developed into a spiritual learning community, which continues to this day. Dorothy MacLean, one of the original founders of Findhorn, who had been a guest on Universal Contact in Seattle when Barry and I worked as the camera crew there in the 80s, was still living at Findhorn. Now well into her 90s, she came to daily meditation with us almost every day.

Even though Findhorn reached its peak many years ago, I still found it to be a wonderful experience. While I was staying there, I received word that my Uncle Paul who had been very ill for the past six months had just passed away that morning. I took a few minutes to sit quietly and tune into my uncle. As I tuned in, he was acting like a five-year old kid on Christmas morning, jumping up and down in excitement and gratitude that he was now free of the albatross of his ailing body. He excitedly darted back and forth, investigating thing after thing which caught his attention. I had never seen him so animated and full of joy. Tuning into the spiritual realm when I was able to experience it with clarity never ceased to amaze me.

After all the traveling throughout Europe, I needed to return to the States to rest. Coming back to North Carolina, my living arrangement had changed, so I again had to find another roommate to live with. Upon returning to North Carolina, I also noticed the fibromyalgia type of pain I started experiencing before I left for Europe seemed to get much worse. I finally figured out, as beautiful as North Carolina was, it was very damp in the Smoky mountains and full of mold. I am super allergic to mold. Also, I'd forgotten all about the heat and extreme humidity in the summer, especially in the south.

What was I thinking moving there?

I knew I was being guided to move back to the high desert to dry out this mold sensitivity in my body. Right after I got back to North Carolina, returning from a trip to France after the 2016 election, I heard a crystal-clear, distinct message in my head that I was now free to leave North Carolina.

Free to leave North Carolina?

I have no conscious awareness of what that was about. I figured we are guided to move to certain areas for specific lengths of time, which serves a larger purpose. Maybe our frequency or energetic codes are needed at certain times in certain places, which often we may not even consciously understand.

Not wanting to go back to Las Vegas, the other large metropolitan area in the high desert was Phoenix, so I chose Phoenix. Going on Craig's List looking for room shares in Arizona, I found one in a gated community in Sun City West, which looked good. I contacted the person to set up an appointment to see the house before even leaving North Carolina. I flew to Phoenix and rented a motel room for a few nights so I could look at places, but none of them were right for me. Finally, I went to the Corte Bella listing in Sun City West and knew that one was it, especially after the other places I'd seen. I gave the owner a deposit right away to hold it for me, which was a good thing as she received about twenty-five phone calls about the room right after I gave her my deposit.

Returning to Asheville, I packed up and got rid of, once again, most of my things. I couldn't really afford to rent a truck to drive across the country. I could only take what would fit in my little Ford Focus on one trip. I packed and unpacked the car several times as I tried to get the bare essentials into the car. Finally, I had to get rid of all the boxes and bags I'd put things in order to get things to fit. I just had to stuff clothes, socks, and other possessions in every nook and cranny that could take anything. Even with a rooftop bag on the top of the car, the car was so full it looked like it was practically dragging on the ground.

There was no way to see out the rear-view mirror, so I had to rely only on my side view mirrors. I ended up having eleven huge trash bags full of things I really wanted to keep but couldn't fit in the car. I had to let them all go. My roommate said he'd donate them to the Goodwill for me. Finally, I left Asheville around 2 PM on Christmas Day, six hours later than I intended to leave. I drove to Austin, Texas, facilitated another workshop there, and then continued on to Sun City West in Arizona. I arrived the afternoon of New Year's Eve and promptly went to IKEA and bought myself a bed. Here I was, back in the high desert, in a new place ready to ring in the New Year of 2017, starting yet another new chapter in my life.

Within a few months of being in Arizona, someone told me about a manufactured house for sale in an over 55 retirement manufactured home park in Surprise. Much to my surprise, I qualified for the land lease, so I purchased the house. I finally owned my first-ever home at age sixty-five, which I never

Chapter 27: Integration

thought possible as it had always been as crazy and unrealistic to me as traveling all over the world with no money, yet I'd done both. Things had surely changed for me on this journey of awakening. There were a lot of tough times, but as I've said many times to myself, I just kept the faith that like the cat I would always land on my feet no matter what.

Conclusion

There are many other facets of this journey of awakening which I haven't gone into including what it now referred to "Ascension Symptoms" in the body. Previously people thought these kinds of symptoms pointed to some physical abnormality or problem in the body. Now often, despite having medical tests, many times physical problems just aren't found.

People talk about these ascension symptoms as being part of a rapid evolution on primarily a cellular and DNA level of changing from a carbon-based structure to a crystalline- based structure. I had waves of Kundalini rising occasionally for short time periods throughout the years. In 1998, I began waking up each morning with an intense vibration and buzzing feeling throughout my body. I felt like the cat in the cartoons with its tail plugged into the wall socket all the time. A mild blanket of chronic anxiety emerged as I dreaded I might have some kind of adrenal cancer or other kind of cancer which might cause these sensations.

Finally, after having it persist day after day, month after month into year after year, when it hadn't killed me yet, I decided it was probably okay. Decades later, I came to understand these were just changes taking place in my body in order to allow the *energy* to come through me as I did my work. At the end of my two-day workshops, when I facilitated the personal Magdalene Grid Activation individually for people, several people later remarked that when they stood in front of me being anointed, the force of energy moving through me was so strong it almost knocked them over.

Of course, I didn't feel any of this. I've also come to understand that the *energy* I was always trying to understand is the *energy* of the feminine, which creates flow and vibration and is part of the essence of the mother whose balance is so needed on the earth right now. As my journey of awakening kept unfolding, I also began to understand more about how Mafu and Ramtha had come to the point in their self-mastery journey of loving every part of themselves, both the good and the bad. Once they could do this, they didn't need to be in polarity anymore to receive the lessons. To gain an understanding of this polarity, however, one has to walk through, first-hand, experiences of polarity, and the pairs of opposites: light-dark, oppressor-victim, narcissist-empath, expectation-disappointment, striving-surrender, wealth-poverty or whatever we most need to learn.

I came into a deeper understanding and appreciation of my soul directing my journey through the "treasure map of my soul." These were all the varied, random, and seemingly unrelated computer jobs, teaching dance and water aerobics, researching and writing for Greg Hutchins, countless moves, relationships, and encounters where I felt I was biding my time and going nowhere. I was unaware they were providing me with the exact training, the skill-sets and toolbox of experiences needed for entering into my work with Claire Heartsong, Anna, and the Councils of Light.

In this awakening process and through my experience as a hypnotherapist, I came to understand that through all of our various lives and experiences, we've experienced it all. We've learned first-hand the lessons and the wisdom of what it is to be a victim and what it is to be the oppressor. Throughout multitudes of lifetimes, we've been every race and gender. Our soul has set it up so that we have personally experienced throughout all of our lifetimes, all actions, reactions, behaviors, attitudes, trauma, drama, recognition, achievements, and situations until we've experienced everything. Then we finally come home to ourselves, finding only love is there. A new adventure can begin, perhaps in an alternative universe in which we are yet to create its journeys and experiences. The awakening will always continue to unfold.

In writing about this journey of awakening, it may appear that I've had direct loud and clear communication from the other side. Except in rare instances, this was not the case. I learned to listen to the still, small, inner voice which was often less than a whisper, more like a subtle inkling. Often, I've felt like I was in a soundproof room, with the shades pulled down and the lights out, trying to perceive and receive this communication. Most of the time it was anything but loud and clear. Throughout it all I've tried to be present to what was in the space at the moment as much as possible. At times some of the information and experiences may seem to be far-fetched or something I imagined. I don't discount imagination, but none of it was something I just conjured up for the sake of making up a tale.

I feel that opening up to our multidimensional aspects requires us to move beyond our third-dimensional boundaries and assumptions. Opening up to the larger aspects of ourselves as cosmic beings requires that we become adventurers in consciousness. In doing so we can allow the possibility of things we have not experienced before without being afraid to redefine life as we have previously known it. But this doesn't mean we have achieved perfection.

My friend Karen, a participant on the Israel tour in 2017, had gotten to know me well as we lived in the same area and became friends. When people first meet me, especially those enamored with the books I've written or co-authored, it's not unusual that they've somewhat put me up on a pedestal until they really get to know me.

After getting to know me and seeing me in the middle of my life's challenges, Karen would say, when I am "on," it's amazing who I am and what comes through me, but when I am in my 'stuff (fears, insecurities, concerns about money, the future, etc.), I am a real mess. Yup! It's called being human. As best I can, I walk my talk, and walk the path using all of my tools to keep bringing myself back to center, to peace, and back into the deep inner connection to spirit. Sometimes doing this is a big challenge and I don't always succeed. In those moments of significant challenge, I stop and remind myself yet again, I am like the cat that has survived nine or more lives. If I've done it those nine times, there is no reason I can't do it again.

I just always have to remember I will always land on my feet, dust myself off, and walk into the next adventure. I've come to understand when I am in cohesion and coherence within myself, then I am in a unified field of unconditional love where there is no more war within me. There is no longer a need to project my internal struggles outward onto others, blaming them for my problems. I have awakened to all of it, at least in some moments. I have equally walked through the light and the dark. I would like to close with one of my channeled messages from the Hosts of Heaven of how they see us and our potential. We just need to see ourselves this way.

Hosts of Heaven Message

"We are here, beloved. It is wonderful that you will accommodate us in this manner. Today we would like to address your understanding of the cosmos, for you see it as an external thing, something "out there" when it is an internal state of affairs much like the orbs you have been seeing in your photographs. They are each in a way their own universe or omni-verse. and so, it is with you and with all humans.

The externalized is the 'maya' or the illusion, as you have been made aware. Now the trick is to turn inward and to experience the holographic universe that you are and that all consciousness and "life" are.

It is up to each individual to care for and construct their own personal model, if you will, of the cosmos, for each holographic reality, although containing the whole, becomes individualized according to the individual–their wisdom, their needs, their accumulated experience and their desired outcomes. No two are alike, nor should they be. It is a grand playing field which has the potential of being much more fun if you will but allow it. There is that word "allow" again.

The universe, or the omni-verse, is a magical place of immeasurable possibilities, far beyond what the average human deems possible. You have within your grasp the ability to transmute matter, to transmute your consciousness, to transfigure your body and to re-invent not only yourself, but all that has gone on before. The ever-present moment of the God/Goddess, all that is, is constantly at a point of new creation repeatedly. It's a never-ending cycle, rapidly blinking on and off, of conscious intent, taking form. Not always what you think it is, rather it's a pulse of conscious creation.

These pulses of conscious creation gain momentum, as similar pulses magnetize one another so that eventually a repeated intention or thought form coagulates into matter. For what the consciousness persists in focusing upon, that focus coagulates into form, or an event, or a synchronicity. Why do we go into all of this? It is because you have asked for greater understanding and greater wisdom.

My dear beloved lady, we are so thrilled to be in communication with you like this. Remember it is always through the heart, through that lens of sensitivity and deep connection that the greatest kernels of profound wisdom become the simplest, most innocent experience of the divine, for we are all divine creatures. All of life is divine. That intimate connection to the divine is the missing piece. And it is the divine deeply rooted that is the foundation and at the center of all that you are, all that you desire, all that you could be, and all that you have ever done or will ever do.

That divinity realized is the Christ/Christess walking, living, and breathing, being and manifesting as a Master unencumbered with thoughts of doubt, failure, limitation and resistance. Divinity realized is like a sacred river of thought and feeling that flows on into infinity. We will help you become that in your own life and to share that process in its deeper understanding with others. You are well on your way, for there has been much attunement and progress already made towards this end.

Much of this you already know. Your concern that you will not get beyond what is already in your awareness is unfounded. Have no fear, dear one, for we are not entertaining fear here, you, see? Deeply know and understand that all will come again with allowance and gratitude, gratitude for each morsel of thought, experience, or feeling that raises one's vibration. Be willing to raise up in consciousness, to live fully immersed in the present moment, not fearing, nor expecting the experience of the next moment or comparing it to the experience of the last moment or a previous moment.

BE UNTO YOURSELF A GIANT BEACON OF LIGHT, unerring, unconcerned of how all will come about. That is the job of the greater part of you, the divinity within. When a Christ/Christess resonates within their being, it is a vibrational match to the highest form of what it is they desire, the highest form of their creation. It takes place within, within the many mansions of the omni-verse of their being.

You have wonderfully outlined the steps of consciousness that produce what we call the "right thinking," portals of greater levels of profound experience and awareness that one can open up to. It is a matter of re-aligning and re-defining one's template, if you will. You can call forth the template of your Christ/Christess self. Ask that the codes and energy signature of this template become fully activated within your bodies, within your DNA and within your quantum particles. It is a tone–sound–light–vibrational tuning that takes place just like tuning a fine instrument. Again, allow. Give thanks, allow and give thanks.

You can invoke this attunement daily or several times a day. Then one can intend and ask to align their Christ/Christess template with the Christ/Christess template in all other individuals, all other life *forms, centered in the divine heart. In doing this, the higher form of communication or energy transmission and transference invokes the highest form of interaction and communication with all life animate and inanimate.*

When activated and engaged, all life will rush to be of service and support to you. Just as you remembered in your experience with the sidewalk rushing up to cushion your feet, to love you–its entire motivation for existence was to serve you in that moment.

And just as all life can't wait to rush to be of service and support for you, then you too will only want to serve all life around you in the same way into infinity. And so, it is when you live as a Master of Divinity you unlock the doors of heaven. Love begets love, which begets love, in the womb of infinity.

Namaste,

~Alariel and the Hosts of Heaven."

Often through this journey of awakening I have been envious of what others had, not so much only the material things, but companionship, families, spouses, children, grandchildren, vacations, or a straightforward path in life. Now I understand I have a wild heart. I probably wouldn't have been content this time around to live a safe or secure life centered on a husband and children. Also, I realized if I had this, I wouldn't have done the deep inner work to gain the wisdom, nor the ever-expanding realization and expansion of who I am as a multidimensional being.

It has become clear there was a higher plan all along that my soul was following. What often seemed like mundane jobs, moves, or experiences seemingly unrelated, in retrospect, came together like an exquisite tapestry to provide what was needed for me successfully to accomplish what my soul had planned. I believe this is true for all of us if we develop inner listening, communication with our soul, and get out of the way of ourselves.

As I write this conclusion, I had yet another few ah-ha moments. I realized I still unconsciously qualify my life's experiences through my fourteen-year-old's lens of not quite achieving what she desired in her physical life. Rather than viewing this as a point of failure, as society's conditioning would have me believe, I needed to dissolve that lens and look at my life now through the lens of raising my frequency, awakening to the more of life and the more of who I am. I realized that the thread of irritation and challenge in my life has only served in birthing the priceless pearl that I AM. I can now own my wisdom, my inner beauty, and my capacity to anchor, expand, and share my light.

Also, when I think back to my initial meeting with St. Germain posing as the bum in Boston my visceral reaction was so pronounced and bewildering it made me wonder if this bum could be my soulmate. Working with Anna channeled through Claire Heartsong I came to understand that Portia St. Germain's twin flame is the oversoul of Anna. In finding out that I was part of the soul stream of Anna, I realized that St. Germain is also a soulmate of that soul stream. Rather than this being just a crazy thought, I was given verification of it being a truth. It further showed to me I could trust my "inner knowing" even when externally, it rarely made sense.

I thrive on adventure and the need to create outside the box. Also, I came to the realization there was no one else I wanted to be, nor anywhere else I wanted to go other than that place of awakening to my infinite self, unfurled from the light, so I can help light the way for others. That is all I will ever need to be. And that is enough!

Afterword: Know Thyself

- By Claire Heartsong

(Author of Anna, Grandmother of Jesus and co-author of Anna, the Voice of the Magdalenes and Twin Flame Union, the Ascension of St. Germain and Portia with Catherine Ann Clemett, and St. Germain, Twin Souls & Soulmates with Azena Ramanda)

With gratitude to Catherine Ann for this opportunity, I wish to share a few words about what I have learned over the past 17 years regarding "twin flame" and empath/narcissist relationships. As you are now aware, this is one of the important topics addressed in her memoir.

To give an update, I have been in spiritual retreat since 2006, except for 2010, when Catherine Ann and I finished and published "Anna, the Voice of the Magdalenes". During this long hiatus I have chosen to give my full attention to an intense ongoing initiatory process of awakening and transmutation overseen by Anna, St. Germain and other guides. This "out of the blue" invitation to enter retreat with a soulmate came in the later stages of bringing forth the Magdalene messages. In her memoir, Catherine Ann reveals how my radical choice abruptly and radically shifted her life's course. You have read how she was ushered out of the safety net of obscurity onto the world stage! Years later, we both can see how her wider service could not have occurred without my "disappearance".

Not hearing from Claire Heartsong, some of you may have thought I was tired and simply wanted to retire from my Anna activities. There might be others of you who envisioned me and my beloved twin flame riding off into the sunset to make our ascension. Yes, in the first scenario I was experiencing health challenges which have continued into this, my 78th year. In the second scenario, you may be disappointed (or perhaps relieved!) to know my twin flame fantasies evaporated like a mirage over hot desert sands.

If you have read my books, you know I hold soulmate and twin flame relationships close to my heart. This Afterword provides me with an opportunity to offer a more current, expanded view on this often-misunderstood subject. For it is, indeed, vast and fascinating, requiring cautionary signposts. As such, I would like to offer some of the wisdom I have experientially gained over the past 16 years of being in retreat.

Foremost, I desire you to know I am motivated to share these understandings with you because I have come to realize how vitally important it is to have a clear awareness of the intensity likely be encountered. By being informed, your physical health and empowered emotional well-being can be better supported. More importantly, your spiritual awakening will be deeply compromised if you choose to remain fragmented and in denial of the shadow energies that will arise. If you sincerely intend to fully awaken from your dream of separation and raise your frequency equal to that of a fully embodied twin flame energy, you must be willing to take off your rose-colored glasses and Know Thyself!

For these reasons I strongly encourage you to educate yourself and become aware of your underlying psychological patterns and unconscious dynamics. I say this because I have come to know we often co-create soulmate/twin flame fantasies as a way to sooth our deep-seated perceptions of feeling separate and alienated. Many of these feelings arise as soul memories and karmic cellular imprints from previous lives. In our current life we may have experienced early trauma and abuse that continues to cloud our perceptions and beliefs about our self, others and life in general.

These traumatic imprints become deeply imprinted in our brain and nervous system. They become behavioral patterns held in our subconscious which Jungian psychologists call the shadow. They live on in our bodies, in our subconscious, and in the stories, we repeatedly tell ourselves. Unhealed trauma gives rise to strategies that are intended to protect us from feeling relentless emotional pain, emptiness and worthlessness. However, as much as we try, we continue to feel unlovable and bound up with guilt and shame. In my case, I deeply internalized a very twisted silent injunction from my father, "You deserve abuse!" It has not been until recently that I have been able to dissolve this internal voice. It had been buried in my subconscious, trapped in my nervous system, and it has flared up as inflammation in every tissue and bone. I now realize that this script has been playing out over many lifetimes – often by assuming the role of martyr.

It took Anna's invitation to enter a "twin flame" initiation with a dear soulmate to awaken this suppressed self-destructive message. With four years of very effective psychotherapy, this "hidden" energy-form emerged out of internal bondage and is slowly dissolving. Remnants of ancient cellular memory continue to rise up from time to time, mostly as physical pain. Even so, it is now much easier to bring the angry energy into the light of self-forgiveness a – spacious, nonjudgmental, melting, maternal Awareness.

We don't like to admit it, but we often find our perceived *self* as lacking. With intense longing, we look outwardly, hoping to find wholeness in relationships. But hidden behind the hope is the fear of never finding our heart's "missing half". These feelings of hope and fear fuel a desperate search – an endless quest for the Holy Grail – our Twin Flame. But the searching proves to be futile. Our intense grasping obscures and darkens the mirroring glass of recognition. Ultimately, we come to know that the one who is searching IS the One we've been seeking! Desperation wearies and closes our intuitive hearts. For it is not by intellectual prowess, but by opening our hearts that we Know and clearly see the Beloved who has been here all along.

Are there such beings as soulmates and twin flames? I will answer, "Yes!". However, to be in an authentic relationship in which the Beloved is clearly mirrored, both partners need to be equally courageous, patient, and generous in spirit. Embodied empathy, kindness, compassion and humility are required by **both**. To assist in clarifying what obscures these intrinsic soul qualities, a soulmate (or a series of soulmates) with whom one has past life connections, may come forth. The soulmate container is alchemical in nature and it provides both partners with the profound, though intense, opportunity of facing, embracing and clarifying the shadows that obscure the ability to clearly see the Beloved that is Here - Now. The One who is always present, but not recognized.

At some point when you no longer <u>need</u> a "Twin Flame" in order to feel whole, he or she will appear. This vast energy field will spontaneously arise in a form you will recognize because you KNOW THYSELF. You are both clear vessels of boundless compassion in service to all life - a spontaneous giving that is truly without ego agendas.

Meanwhile, no longer fervently trying to fix ourselves or our partners, we can relax and enjoy our very ordinary daily human lives. Instead of searching online, we are free to use our time and energy to develop wisdom and skills that maintain our sovereignty and commitment to bring no harm to ourselves or others. We come to intimately experience our consciousness and bodies as vibrational frequencies of light, sound and color. We fall in love with the natural world and simply being. We learn how to discern different energy forms by examining our felt experiences. Are we feeling contracted or spacious? If contracted, we carefully look into our intentions and actions from one moment to the next. We trust our inner guidance in order to change what needs to change within us and to accept what cannot. Relaxed and open, life flows and manifests evolving growth through us effortlessly.

We also look into our psychology and cultivate wisdom and skills that enable us to embrace and unify our conscious light side and our unconscious shadows. Our light side is motivated by an intrinsic impulse to awaken and realize we already ARE the ineffable Beloved. Our shadow side blindly and selfishly pursues what it wants and rejects what it doesn't want. It stays busy and is blindly self-absorbed.

Early in my retreat I discovered that highly sensitive souls and empaths, like myself, who are in "spiritual bypass", inevitably attract people with a high percentage of narcissistic traits. They appear as our narcissistic parents, siblings, friends, lovers, spiritual teachers and bosses. We come together because our souls have agreed to assist each other to wake up. We are each other's energetic opposite. Being opposites, our synergy is powerfully catalytic. You could say we are like "twin flame" magnets. We automatically ignite and shine a very bright, torch-like light into each other's shadowy corners. We come together to mirror, trigger, and call out our unconscious, projected energies. A partner who mirrors us is not required, but the process of transmutation is greatly sped up, especially when you are both committed to not bypass spiritually, run away or implode into depression. Eventually the persona disrobes allowing the remaining essential aspects to spontaneously arise and integrate into a perfect wholeness. Outer relationships come and go; but the true Self is always present. Veils dissolve and the Beloved appears!

Soulmate relationships provide each partner with an opportunity to do deep self-inquiry. Even though it feels scary, we are motivated to turn inward and do our own personal shadow work which is mirrored and catalyzed by our soulmate. Instead of blaming, we turn within and relax the chronic resistance held in our tight body and mind. Rather than playing the victim game, we choose gratitude and self-care, even if that choice requires us to end the relationship. When inevitable challenges arise, we look within, take responsibility and receive the jewel of wisdom shining in the mud. Remembering to pause in the midst of distractions and busyness, we find peaceful calm and rest in our heart-center's vast expanse – the space between. And so it is, here and now, that we discover we have never left Home. All imagined separation dissolves. Laughing at the cosmic joke we are able to recognize our ineffable Beloved's face as our own!

RESOURCES for Knowing Thyself

(Books and You-Tube Videos)

Since I no longer offer private sessions or speak at public events, I would like to share with you the resources below should you be looking for assistance.

RECOGNIZING NARCISSISTS &DISOWNED EMPATH SHADOWS:

Joanna Kujath, *"Are You Tired of Being Exploited? Then Stop Doing This!"*
Christiane Northrup, MD, *"Dodging Energy Vampires"*

H. G. Tudor, (videos) With the precision of a surgeon, Mr. Tudor, (a diagnosed ultra-narcissist psychopath), removes the cat's rose-colored glasses while "taking it out of the bag"! Please use discernment and **do not** interact with him.

HEALING FROM TRAUMA AND NARCISSISTIC ABUSE:

Meredith M Miller, *"The Journey, A Roadmap for Self-Healing After Narcissist Abuse"*

Bessel Van Der Kolk, MD, *"The Body Keeps the Score: Brain, Mind, and Body in the Healing of Trauma"*

Peter A. Levine, PhD, *"Waking the Tiger"*, *"In an Unspoken Voice"* and *"Freedom from Pain"*

Martin Aylward, *"Awake Where You Are: The Art of Embodied Awareness"*

(Learn how to reset your Vagus Nerve when you are stuck in chronic fight, flight or freeze.)

Deb Dana, *"Polyvagal Exercises for Safety and Connection"*

RAISING YOUR FREQUENCY:

Catherine Ann Clemett, *"Soulweaving, Return to the Heart of the Mother"*

(Research alternative holistic psychosomatic modalities of **bodywork**, subtle **energy healing**, and traditions of **yoga** and **meditation**. **Evolutionary Astrology** can also provide insights.)

NON-DUAL AWARENESS:

Rupert Spira, Ramana Maharshi, Nisargadatta, Chan Buddhism, Kasmiri Shaivaism, Hafiz, Kabir, Rumi, http://www.nondualzen.com, **Tibetan**

Afterword

Buddhist Dzogchen, "Gnostic Gospels of Thomas, Mary Magdalene, and Phillip", and "A Course in Miracles"

Alex Shalier, *See his 2021 – 2022 You-Tube videos on awakening and non-dual awareness.*

Michael A Singer, "The Untethered Soul"

MY TIBETAN BUDDHIST MEDITATION TEACHERS:

Anam Thubten, "*The Magic of Awareness*"

Amita Lhamo (Connee Pike), "*Wisdom Moon: Presence in Dying*"

ST. GERMAIN'S ADVICE:

"*Wear your crown as a clown.*"

"*Laughter is the great aligner.*"

"*Easy glum, easy glow.*"

"*F-U-N: Freedom, Unity, and Nowness.*"

"*Enlightenment is Now, the only time there is.*"

"*When there's trauma in your drama, shift the tragic to magic!*"

"*Freedom is spelled R-E-L-A-X.*"

Images

My mother's house built in 1750 in Newport, Rhode Island.

Me at age 8, sitting on the fence in the front yard of our house in South Portland, Maine against the backdrop of the ship channel to Portland Harbor.

Age 14 when my awakening began.

Visiting the remodeled and expanded house I lived in as a child in Maine 53 years later. This is the opposite view from the image above.

Raising My Frequency

Age 14 in ballet class when my father relentlessly attacked me about my weight and my brothers made up stories at the dinner table.

Side view of the Harkness mansion in Watch Hill, Rhode Island where I attended the Harkness Ballet summer program when I was 16.

In my early twenties goofing around with my NY roommates.

Performing in a ballet at Connecticut College.

Images

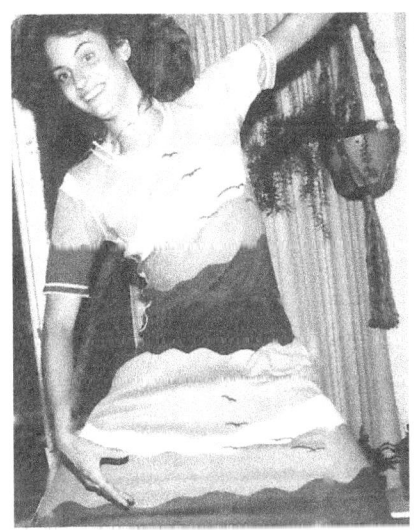

Practicing a pas de chat in the living room when I was in graduate school at the University of Hawaii.

Rehearsing with the other MFA candidate for our full evening concert.

Performing with Hawaii Dance Theater in 1978.

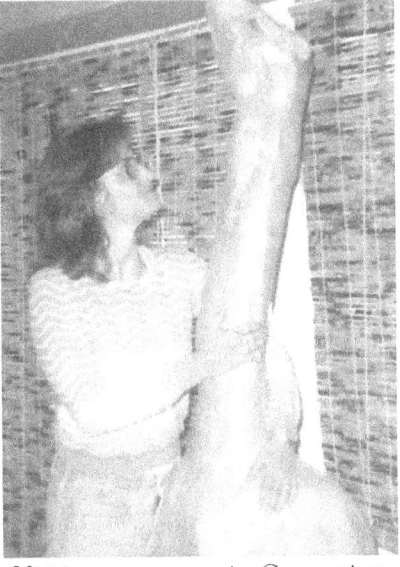

Visiting my parents in Connecticut for Easter break days before my car accident in 1978.

Raising My Frequency

Running the Paradise Inn post office at Mt. Rainier in 1984.

My Welsh boyfriend whom I met while working at Mt. Rainier.

Performing Argentine Tango for a friend's wedding when I worked at Portland Community College.

Images

Mt. Rainier Guide Service Building. Girl's dorm was on the top floor.

My father visiting me at Paradise Inn at the start of the season in May of 1984. Snow melted in a few weeks.

Hiking up at Mt. Rainier. It seems this was to become a theme in my life.

My old beater car, "Little Red Dent"

Raising My Frequency

Paradise Inn on Mt. Rainier where I ran the post office the summer I worked there.

Mt. Rainier

Images

Hiking the Inca Trail in 1988 in Peru wearing the camera which I also won.

Rest stop. The only flat stretch in 8 hours of hiking.

Indians sold us ice-cold Cocoa-Cola and Inca Kola on the trail.

Our daily bathing option on the trail.

Raising My Frequency

Hiking through Warmwanusqa pass (Dead Woman's Pass) at 13,780 ft.

Our nightly camp setup along the Inca Trail.

White Water rafting on the Urumbumba River.

Lunch along the Inca Trail.

Images

Performing a drumming ceremony in the cult probably around 1990.

Sign at area 51 warning us that we'd be arrested if we ventured beyond the sign.

Costume I devised on Halloween when in the cult.

Raising My Frequency

My friend Kay and me goofing around. Another yearly Halloween event. Definitely the 80s look.

Winning the Miata car at the Excalibur Hotel and Casino in Las Vegas in 1991.

Images

Took a flying leap in the park one day almost twenty years after my car accident which ended my dance career to see if I still had it in me. It was still there but I was very rusty.

Me and Claire in Springdale in 2006. Our 3rd collaborator wished to remain anonymous.

Claire looking out her living room window in Springdale.

Facilitating a session with Claire bringing through the characters for the sequel.

Theo, Claire's cat was always present and would 'hold space' during the sessions. We couldn't start a session without him.

Fire broke out on the Kolob plateau ridge (backside of Zion National Park) above Claire's roof line that threatened us. We were within 15 minutes of needing to evacuate. Fortunately, we didn't have to.

Images

Great White Throne, a twelfth dimensional portal in Zion National Park

You never knew what to expect. A flock of wild turkeys blocked the passage of the tram in Zion National Park.

Zion

Raising My Frequency

My second-floor apartment in Springdale, UT.

Climbing up to St. Baume while on the South of France tour with Finbarr in 2006.

At the top of the Tor looking out towards a rainbow.

Images

Me and my friend Alan, another participant on the tour, climbing up to the Tor. Glastonbury can be seen in the background down the hill behind us.

Climbing up to the Tor in Glastonbury.

Aigne, the snail village in France where Mother Mary's presence stood before me.

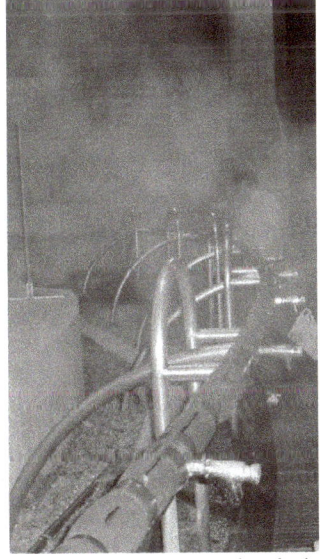

Mysterious mist at the holy water sinks at Lourdes. It only showed up in this one picture. It was not steam.

Raising My Frequency

Altar in St. Baume in France in chaptel built into a cave in the rock face.

Visiting the famous Ricoleta Cemetery in Argentina where Eva Peron (main character in the musical Evita) is buried.

My TEFL certification class in Buenos Aires in 2009. Most of my classmates were so much younger that me they thought of me as a grandma so I never really made any friends.

Dancing Argentine Tango at a Milonga in Buenos Aires.

Images

At Punta del Estes in Uruguay on a side trip I took from Buenos Aires.

In 2011 I started facilitating my own events. This is the Fortingall, Scotland *Magdalene Grid Activation* in 2012 in a field just down the road from the famous ancient Yew tree.

Participants found a peaceful spot during the *Fortingall Magdalene Grid Activation*.

317

Raising My Frequency

St. Brigid's Well on the highest hilltop on Isle of Iona in Scotland.

Visiting Rosslyn Chapel in Scotland.

My sound healer Gila and I leading a weekend workshop in Australia.

Images

Group process during one of the Australian weekend workshops.

The *Australian Magdalene Grid Activation* in 2013 took place in three different locations. This first location was on a rainy day in a park outside of Melbourne.

Raising My Frequency

Part 2 of the *Australian Magdalene Grid Activation* done by me and one other person took place on the Great Barrier Reef. We took a boat out to this island where people could snorkel on the Great Barrier Reef. We built an alter under the water on a piece of the coral for this part of the grid activation.

Well on Uluru where we did part 3 of the Magdalene Grid activation there.

Uluru in Australia previously known as Ayers Rock.

Images

Climbing up to the Gosford hieroglyphics north of Sydney.

Connecting with the well at Uluru during the Australian Magdalene Grid Activation.

The I AM Harmony Garden in Crestone, Colorado.

The actual ritual of the *Crestone Magdalene Grid Activation* in Colorado in August of 2013 had to be performed in the I AM Harmony Garden tepee since it was pouring rain that day.

Setting up the altar inside the tepee.

Images

Traveling down the Sinai Peninsula by van from the Taba border of Israel and Egypt to Sharm el Sheikh to catch a plane to Cairo prior to the start of the Egyptian *Valley of the Queens Magdalene Grid Activation*. This picture was taken next to the Gulf of Aqaba.

Holding the Ankh key which unlocks the Abu Simbal temple doors.

On the cold Giza plateau in December 2013 where it snowed the day before for the first time in over 100 years. Snow didn't stick though.

Raising My Frequency

The guide who oversees the Valley of the Queens led us to a private area out of site where we could do our *Valley of the Queens Magdalene Grid Activation* process. He even participated in some of it with us. He had twisted my scarf into a cobra hat for me.

Our wonderful Egyptian guide and his wife hosted a birthday party for me at their home in Luxor for my 62nd birthday.

Images

Lunch aboard our felucca boat on the Nile River.

Inside the Grand Bazaar Istanbul, Turkey

A Turkish waitress brought us piping hot bread to use to keep us warm under our jackets and shawls as we were headed out on a long walk in the cold wind.

Raising My Frequency

After waiting for decent weather for several days we were finally able to take a hot-air balloon ride over the fairyland of Cappadocia, Turkey.

A close-up view of the type of balloon basket our group rode in.

Images

Fairy house in Cappadocia. Natural rock formations are carved out to make dwellings.

Wishing Wall at Mother Mary's House Ephesus, Turkey.

The house of the Virgin Mary on Mt. Koressos close to Ephesus, Turkey.

Raising My Frequency

Our group in front of the ancient Ephesus library.

In the deep-water hot springs at Pamukkale swimming above ancient columns and ruins.

Images

Rumi Shrine, Konya, Turkey. I intended for us to go to the ancient archaeological site Gobelki Tepe but changed the itinerary 3 weeks before the tour due to fighting on the Syrian border 25 miles away for the safety of the group.

Women had to cover their heads in all the mosques.

Our group including our van driver performing part of the Ephesus Magdalene Grid Activation on a beach on the Aegean Sea about 8 km from the Virgin Mary's House.

Walking next to the travertine pools in Pamukkule, Turkey.

329

Raising My Frequency

Walking the labyrinth at the Sacred Garden in Maui.

Swimming in one of the 7 sacred pools on Maui.

Connecting with the elements during the Maui Magdalene Grid Activation.

Images

Whales greeting us in Maui.

Conducting a weekend workshop at Chalice Well in Glastonbury, Somerset, England.

Raising My Frequency

Red Spring at Chalice Well.

White Spring at Chalice Well.

Images

Remodel of an old mill into a healing center. My event was the first one to be held there in Enniscorthy, Ireland.

Speaking to almost 100 people in Bucharest, Romania.

Raising My Frequency

Channeling at a workshop in Cobh, Ireland.

Bologna, Italy workshop.

Erfurt, Germany workshop with my translator.

Athens, Greece event with my Greek translator.

Images

Lunch break during the weekend workshop at the Hague.

Resting in Greece.

Working in the Findhorn kitchen during my 2 week stay there.

Our Israel Tour group at Elija's Cave in Haifa.

Standing in the Sea of Galilee.

Images

On a wooden boat on the Sea of Galilee.

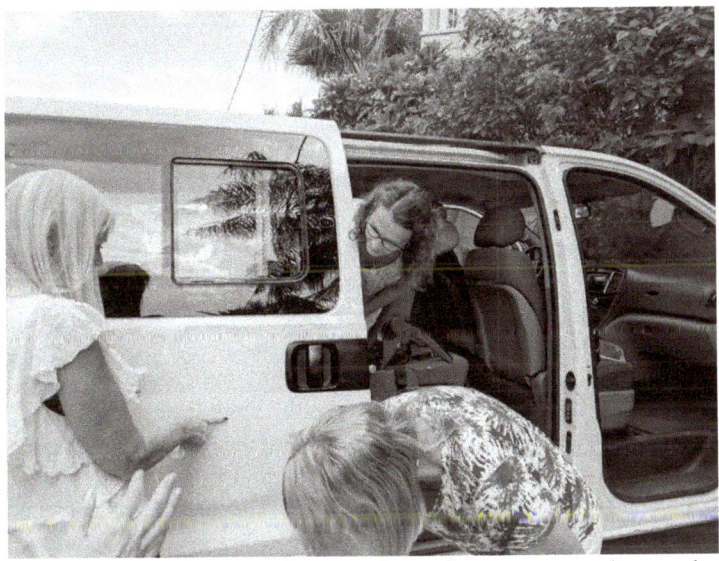

Our international group of women fixing the minor scratches on the rental van using a black magic marker and toothpaste.

Raising My Frequency

Site of the manger in Bethlehem. Not what I expected.

Giving a talk at Banyen Books, Vancouver, BC, Canada

Wading in the salt accumulation in the Dead Sea in Israel.

Book signing at the New Renaissance Bookstore in Portland, Oregon where I fist bought my *Anna, Grandmother of Jesus* book in 2004.

Images

The older manufactured house I bought in Surprise, AZ.

The Saint Germain picture I received for my 50th birthday.

Award-winning documentary movie in which I appear.

Events Calendar

Dates	Location	Event Type	Event Name
12/1/2010	Mountain View, CA	Speaker	East West Books
12/5/2010	Mountain View, CA	Workshop	Your Magdalene Voice
5/1/2011	San Jose, CA	Workshop	Magdalene Connection
7/14/2011	Santa Cruz, CA	Workshop	Secrets to Awakening
9/24-9/26/2011	Louisville, KY	Speaker/Workshop	Sound, Light, Ascension Expo
10/22/2011	Escondido, CA	Workshop	Unique Brilliance
10/25/2011	Los Angeles, CA	Speaker	Bodhi Tree Bookstore
10/27/2011	Santa Cruz, CA	Workshop	Unique Brilliance
11/5/2011	Mt. Bugarach, France	Workshop	Unique Brilliance
11/8-11/11/2011	Gazost, France	Tour	Lourdes Grid Activation
11/12-1/15/2011	St. Marie la Mer, Franc	Tour	France Grid Activation
11/24/2011	Mourex Grilly, France	Workshop	Embrace the Heart
12/3/2011	Borgerhout, Belgium	Workshop	Magdalene Order
4/8/2012	Pahrump, NV	Speaker	The Bunkhouse
4/20-4/21/2012	Pahrump, NV	Workshop	Embrace the Heart
5/12/2012	Pahrump, NV	Workshop	Magdalene Heart
6/10/2012	San Jose, CA	Workshop	Magdalene Heart
7/15/2012	Lake Arrowhead, CA	Workshop	Magdalene Heart
8/12/2012	Capistrano Beach, CA	Workshop	Embrace the Heart
8/15/2012	Mountain View, CA	Workshop	Embrace the Heart
8/18/2012	Seattle, WA	Workshop	Embrace the Heart
8/19/2012	Ladner, BC, Canada	Workshop	Embrace the Heart
8/25/2012	Post Falls, ID	Workshop	Magdalene Heart
9/9/2012	Phoenix, AZ	Workshop	Magdalene Heart
9/15/2012	Washington, DC	Workshop	Magdalene Heart
9/22/2012	South Portland, ME	Workshop	Embrace the Heart
9/26-10/5/2012	Fortingall, Scotland, UK	Tour	Fortingall Grid Activation

Dates	Location	Event Type	Event Name
10/10-0/20/2012	Isle of Man UK	Tour	Isle of Man Grid Activation
1/5/2013	Sedona, AZ	Speaker	Unity Church
1/17/2013	Pahrump, NV	Speaker	Bunkhouse
3/20/2013	Woy Woy Central Coast Australia	Speaker	Gnostic Forest
3/23-3/24/2013	Palm Beach, NSW, Australia	Workshop	Magdalene-Christed Being
3/30-3/31/2013	Central Coast, Australia	Workshop	Magdalene-Christed Being
4/6-4/7/2013	Melbourne, Australia	Workshop	Magdalene-Christed Being
4/13/-4/14/2013	Perth, Western Australia	Workshop	Magdalene-Christed Being
4/20-4/21/2013	Mullimbimby, Australia	Workshop	Magdalene-Christed Being
5/4-5/5/2013	Wellington, NZ	Workshop	Magdalene-Christed Being
5/12-5/13/2013	Auckland, NZ	Workshop	Magdalene-Christed Being
5/14-5/26/2013	Australia	Tour	Australia Grid Activation
6/8-6/9/2013	Ellerslie (Auckland), NZ	Workshop	Magdalene-Christed Being
8/5/-8/11/2013	Crestone, CO	Tour	Crestone Grid Activation
8/6/2017	Campbell, CA	Workshop	Seeding the Light
8/21/2013	Orange County, CA	Talk	Magdalene Order Talk
8/24-8/25/2013	Los Altos, CA	Workshop	The Magdalene Gateway
9/12-9/15/2013	Sedona, AZ	Speaker/Workshop	Walk-Ins Welcome Conf.
12/3-12/14/2013	Egypt	Tour	Egypt Grid Activation
6/16/2014	Studio City, CA	Speaker	Jean Trebek's House
6/17/2014	Orange County, CA	Talk	Magdalene Order
10/5/2014	St. George, UT	Speaker	The World Peace Garden
10/10-10/12/2014	Mt. Shasta, CA	Speaker/Workshop	Visionaries in Light Conf.
10/18-10/19/2014	La Verkin, UT	Workshop	The Magdalene Gateway
10/29-11/11/2014	Ephesus, Turkey	Tour	Turkey Grid Activation Tour
2/14-2/23/2015	Maui, HI	Tour	Maui Hawaii Grid Activation
9/9/2015	Austin, TX	Talk	Magdalene Order
9/16/2015	San Antonio, TX,	Talk	Magdalene Order
9/19-9/20/2015	Austin, TX	Workshop	Magdalene Mysteries
11/14-11/15/2015	New York, NY	Workshop	Magdalene Mysteries

Calendar

Dates	Location	Event Type	Event Name
1/31/2016	Asheville, NC	Workshop	Seeding the Light
2/3/2016	Studio City, CA	Workshop	Seeding the Light
2/8/2016	Orange, County, CA	Workshop	Seeding the Light
2/16/2016	Sedona, AZ	Workshop	Seeding the Light
2/17/2016	Asheville, NC	Workshop	Seeding the Light
3/11-3/20/2016	England	Tour	Little England Tour
3/12-3/13/2016	Chalice Well, Glastonbury, UK	Workshop	Magdalene Mysteries
3/22/2016	Cobh, Ireland	Workshop	Seeding the Light
3/23/2016	Enniscorthy, Ireland	Workshop	Seeding the Light
3/24/2016	Dublin, Ireland	Workshop	Seeding the Light
3/28/2016	Newry, Northern Ireland	Workshop	Seeding the Light
4/4/2016	Bologna, Italy	Workshop	Seeding the Light
4/8/2016	Bucharest, Romania	Workshop	Seeding the Light
4/11/2016	Erfurt, Germany	Workshop	Seeding the Light
4/16-4/17/2016	The Hague, Netherlands	Workshop	Magdalene Mysteries
4/27/2016	Athens, Greece	Workshop	Seeding the Light
5/4/2016	Athens, Greece	Workshop	Seeding the Light
5/9/2016	Ter Apel, Netherlands	Workshop	Seeding the Light
5/12/2016	Hexham, Northumberland, UK	Workshop	Seeding the Light
5/22/2016	Findhorn, Scotland	Speaker	Findhorn Eco Village
10/27/2016	New York, NY	Workshop	Seeding the Light
11/4-11/14/2016	Reims, France	Sessions	Partnering with Divinity
11/29/2016	West Hartford, CT	Workshop	Seeding the Light
12/1/2016	Rye, NY	Workshop	Seeding the Light
12/2/2016	Montvale, NJ	Workshop	Seeding the Light
12/4/2016	Trenton, NJ	Workshop	Seeding the Light
12/7/2016	Burke, VA	Workshop	Seeding the Light
3/1/2017	Surprise, AZ	Talk	Magdalene Order
5/6/2017	Sedona, AZ	Workshop	St. Germain Experience
8/2/2017	Burlingame, CA	Workshop	Seeding the Light
8/6/2017	Campbell, CA	Workshop	Seeding the Light

Frequency Raising

Dates	Location	Event Type	Event Name
8/9/2017	Brookings, OR	Workshop	Seeding the Light
8/22/2017	Portland, OR	Speaker	New Renaissance Bookstore
8/25/2017	Vancouver, BC, Canada	Speaker	Banyen Books
8/26/2017	Vancouver, BC, Canada	Workshop	Seeding the Light
8/28/2017	Edmonds, WA	Workshop	Seeding the Light
8/29/2017	Olympia, WA	Workshop	Seeding the Light
8/30/2017	Rhododendron, OR	Workshop	Seeding the Light
8/31/2017	Ashland, OR	Workshop	Seeding the Light
9/3/2017	Grants Pass, OR	Workshop	Seeding the Light
9/7/2017	Tustin, CA	Workshop	Seeding the Light
9/9/2017	San Diego, CA	Workshop	Seeding the Light
9/10/2017	Laguna Nigel, CA	Workshop	Seeding the Light
9/16/2017	Diamond Springs, CA	Workshop	Seeding the Light
9/20/2017	Salt Lake City, UT	Workshop	Seeding the Light
10/26-11/6/2017	Israel	Tour	Ancient Holy Land Tour
1/12/2018	Scottsdale, AZ	Workshop	Access Your Cosmic Being
1/28/2018	Scottsdale, AZ	Workshop	Access Your Cosmic Being
2/6/2018	Sedona, AZ	Free Talk	Literate Lizard Bookstore
2/13/2018	Sedona, AZ	Workshop	Seeding the Light
2/17/2018	Sedona, AZ	Workshop	Access Your Cosmic Being
2/28/2018	Scottsdale, AZ	Workshop	Seeding the Light
3/4/2018	Orange County, CA	Workshop	Access Your Cosmic Being
3/10/2018	Surprise, AZ	Workshop	Access Your Cosmic Being
3/24/2018	Santa Monica, CA	Workshop	Access Your Cosmic Being
3/29/2018	Surprise, AZ	Workshop	Seeding the Light
4/28-4/29/2018	Sedona, AZ	Speaker	Michael Gillardy's Event
11/4/2018	Diamond Springs, CA	Workshop	The Magdalene Path
11/7/2018	Sebastopol, CA	Talk	The Magdalene Path
11/10/2018	Burlingame, CA	Workshop	Seeding the Light
11/28/2018	Sebastopol, CA	Workshop	Divine Feminine Power
4/28/2019	Surprise, AZ	Workshop	Unique Brilliance

Dates	Location	Event Type	Event Name
8/18/2019	Denver, CO	Workshop	The Magdalene Path
8/29/2019	Denver, CO	Workshop	Heart Opening Tools
8/31/2019	Westminster	Workshop	Unique Brilliance
11/04-11/07/2021	Las Vegas	Speaker	Cosmic Consciousness in Disclosure
5/4/2022	Sun City, AZ	Speaker	AZ Enlightenment Group

Books and Products

(All books and products are available on Amazon)

Anna, Grandmother of Jesus

By Claire Heartsong

Although I did not write this book, it is the basis for much of my work that has come forth. Anna, Grandmother of Jesus became a publishing sensation when the self-published version sold 50,000 copies through word of mouth alone, amassing a worldwide following in the process. Anna is the mother of the Virgin Mary and the grandmother of Jesus. Her teachings and service birthed a spiritual lineage that changed the world. In this book, you'll discover missing pieces of history concerning Anna, Mary, and Jesus, as channeled by Claire Heartsong, who has been receiving telepathic messages from Anna for 30 years. Told through the gentle and heartwarming voice of Anna herself, this book offers insights into unknown places the holy family visited, people they knew, and intimate details of their daily struggle to complete the Resurrection challenges. You will learn about the Essenes of Mount Carmel and their secret teachings and initiations, and gain a new understanding of Jesus' mission. Containing encoded activations to bring Anna's wisdom and energy into your own spiritual life, this book is an invitation to complete a journey of initiation begun long ago.

Anna, the Voice of the Magdalenes

By Claire Heartsong and Catherine Ann Clemett

In this channeled sequel to the international bestseller *Anna, Grandmother of Jesus*, we journey with Anna, the Holy Family, and 18 other Magdalene-Essenes as they travel to France and Britain after Jesus's crucifixion and resurrection. Through Claire Heartsong and Catherine Ann Clemett's joint collaboration with the Councils of Light, this book divulges hidden aspects of Jesus' life, including marriages, offspring, and his continued presence on the earth plane for another 40 years. This book also addresses deeper sacred mysteries of how the 'bloodline' acts as a living catalyst for awakening the Christ-Magdalene potential in all people today. Not only does this book give a new view of the Christ drama 2,000 years ago, but of greater importance is its potential to lift the suppressed Divine Feminine voice in our time.

Twin Flame Union, the Ascension of St. Germain and Portia

By Claire Heartsong and Catherine Ann Clemett

This book presents an expanded view and understanding of Twin Souls, Twin Flames, and the nature of soul mate relationships. The ultimate goal of twin flame union is the journey back into remembered wholeness--the cosmic union of Twin Flames. St. Germain and Portia illustrate this journey through accounts of their joint Twin-Flame ascension. This book also includes a guided Twin Flame Union meditation CD, which offers the opportunity to integrate multiple levels of consciousness and energies through advanced practices.

Are You a Magdalene? Discovering your Divine Feminine Heritage and Purpose

By Catherine Ann Clemett

Are you drawn to Mary Magdalene? Are you curious about what made her such a unique, powerful, female disciple and counterpart to Jesus? If you are drawn to her energy and wisdom, it may be a signal asking you to remember you may be part of a larger picture in which Magdalene is not just an individual but an "Order of Consciousness" which you may be connected to. Find out more how you may be a present-day Magdalene.

Soulweaving, Return to the Heart of the Mother

By Catherine Ann Clemett

A gateway to accessing your true self through intimately sharing her personal journey, Catherine Ann has developed 12 powerful tools to access one's true divine nature. Harmonizing what's out of balance in your life by taking steps to heal the inner wounds and dysfunctional patterns built up over lifetimes reveals clues to accessing the living treasure map of your soul. By following the treasure map of your soul; claiming and living your life from your own inner authority and upgrading your consciousness and frequency, you can then live your soul's purpose and be of greater planetary service, which is ultimately every soul's journey back to wholeness. "This book is a powerful catalyst and 'must read' for anyone on a conscious path of Spiritual Awakening. I consider this book to be one of the most significant publications I've ever read, right up there with The Course in Miracles." ~ Jean Trebek, Studio City, CA (Science of Mind Practitioner and wife of Jeopardy Host, Alex Trebek).

Books and Products

Finding the One True Love: Why Breaking the Rules Will Change Your Life

By Angelina Heart and Catherine Ann Clemett

Has your search for the one eluded you? Do you feel someone is out there just waiting for you—if you could figure out how to connect? This Writer's Digest award-winning book will facilitate a quantum leap of understanding to help you find your true identity and authentic voice. Fourteen assumptions commonly held, are revealed which may prevent you from authentically being yourself and attracting your vibratory match. Learn the truth about natural laws you can easily apply to heal the broken and attract the genuine, unconditional love you really want.

Partnering with Divinity: Daily Inspirations & Contemplations for the Calendar Year

By Catherine Ann Clemett

Partnering with Divinity is a compilation of quotes from eleven books which Catherine Ann Clemett has either authored, co-authored, published through her company LightRiver Media, or been associated with. Just as in the books from which they originate, these quotes impart transmissions of light, codes which activate the reader into opening up to greater wisdom and the ability to receive and anchor light from the higher realms. Each quote is meant to either inspire, introduce subjects for deeper contemplation, or to serve as a catalyst for an individual's further awakening. These 366 quotes, one for each day of the year and the 29th of February during a leap year, can be read again and again over the years. Reading a quote each morning upon awakening helps start your day on a higher frequency. Quotes in this book are only assigned to a specific month and day, not a specific year so the quotes can be referred to during any calendar year.

The Awakening Series

Is This All There Is? The Call to Awaken

Book 1: The Awakening Series

By Catherine Ann Clemett

This guide helps you understand and navigate the confusion, uncertainty, questioning and, sometimes, the melt-down of reality as you've known it when your soul is prompting you to awaken. For some, this is a bewildering process, as so many beliefs come up for review. This book will help you understand what is occurring. It will help you understand you are being uniquely guided by your own soul to understand there is a larger picture at play and that you have a part to play in this. Reading this book will help you identify the signposts leading you to become your own inner authority, living your most authentic self.

Finding Your Inner Jewel: How to Access Your Authentic Self
Book 2: The Awakening Series

By Catherine Ann Clemett

You are like a diamond in the rough before being cut and polished. Within you, there is a valuable and precious jewel of creation. This book assists you in finding your authentic self. Most of us have become disconnected from our core in our awareness. This book shares how to move through any blocks, resistance or shadow frequencies which cover or hide the brilliance of your inner jewel and your light. You are here now because the world needs your gifts, talents and light.

Me Too – Time's Up: Bringing the Feminine & Masculine into Balance
Book 3: The Awakening Series

By Catherine Ann Clemett

Going beyond the 'Me-Too' movement, this book is about restoring the balance and equality of the masculine and feminine within our beings, society, our thinking, awareness, language, and constructs of reality. When you understand and embrace your own masculine and feminine, you can begin to awaken to the path of Twin Flame Union within accelerating your awakening process and the paradigm shift we are currently undergoing. Check back on Amazon for availability.

Unlocking the Magic of Money and Abundance
Book 4: The Awakening Series

By Catherine Ann Clemett

This book addresses the role of money and manifestation in your life, uncovering your beliefs about money and how the role of money impacts your life. Shift from striving to survive to thriving in all areas of your life so abundance can and will show up. Find out how your experience and perceptions about money sometimes can block or slow down your awakening. Discover how to become the master of money, rather than money having mastery and control over you. Check back on Amazon for availability.

Shine Your Light: Be All You Can Be

Book 5: The Awakening Series

By Catherine Ann Clemett

The final book in the series discusses who you are as a great cosmic being of light, what it means to be the light and live your light. It addresses the ascension process and how to navigate the waves of vibrational shifts which are now escalating. It also offers information to help you refine your inner jewel and your unique brilliance so you can enjoy the journey and the fruits of your labor and be a shining light to others. Check back on Amazon for availability.

Other Books and Products from Light River Media

What Every Human Must Know to Survive & Thrive on Planet Earth

By Virginia Essene

Virginia shares important practical guidance from the heavenly realms to help you move past your problems, fears, and concerns so you can more fully share your divine gifts and get on with the work you came here to do. It covers major concepts essential for all of us to understand in order to make the smoothest and safest transition through the present "ascension-of-sorts" that the planet and all of humanity are undergoing right now. (Published by LightRiver Media)

Blessings from the Heart of the Rose Oracle Card Deck

By Sheila Murphy (Published and manufactured by LightRiver Media)

This set of 44 cards and a guidebook are divination tools to help you enter the sacred space within yourself. These cards help you connect with the mystical marriage of Divine Feminine/Divine Masculine union; the path of Oneness. Each card is an exquisite work of art accompanied by relevant guidance for you at the moment.

Meditations

Meditation MP3 Downloads are Available at:
https://catherineannclemett.com/lightriver-media-2/

Yeshua (Jesus) "Breath of Oneness – Transmuting Through the Sacred Heart Meditation"

From *Anna, the Voice of the Magdalenes* by Claire Heartsong and Catherine Ann Clemett, this offers you a powerful inner meeting with Yeshua (Jesus) assisting you to move beyond any pain or suffering you hold in your body, mind, or spirit. Transmuting it through the crucible of his sacred heart, helping you can access your own Christ within where great peace, light and infinite love resides in your heart

Dancing Wind's Meditation Weaving Your Body Anew as a Receptacle of Light

Also from *Anna, the Voice of the Magdalenes* by Claire Heartsong and Catherine Ann Clemett, listening to this meditation invites you to become one with the energy of Mother Earth and Father Spirit as they amplify the magic of ascending and descending spiraling energies through your human form helping you remember you are a keeper of the sacred grail, the holy blood, and the keys and codes of the worlds whence we come.

Cosmic Twin Flame Union Meditation

From *Twin Flame Union, the Ascension of St. Germain and Portia* by Claire Heartsong and Catherine Ann Clemett, is the answer to your collective prayers for experiencing the unifying power of Love and Wisdom through the embrace of Twin-Flame union beyond the realms of duality. Your fervent prayers have been heard reverberating throughout all dimensions, levels, and timelines. Refining and empowering your consciousness through this meditation brings about ultimate joy and freedom for your own happiness as well as the happiness of all sentient beings. This same meditation is on the CD included with the print version of the book.

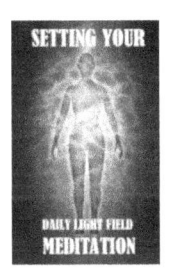

Setting Your Daily Light Field Meditation

Setting Your Daily Light Field Meditation assisting you to clear and release any lower frequency or intruding energy lurking in your body or energy fields, so that you can expand and intensify your own light throughout your helping you in keeping a higher vibration throughout the day.

Programs and Sessions

Frequency Healing Sessions

For a more personal journey, Catherine Ann assists clients through in-depth one-on-one private 60- or 90-minute sessions. These Divine Feminine Frequency Healing/Channeling sessions will help you to uncover and move beyond limiting beliefs and fields of consciousness keeping you 'stuck' in fear, pain or lower frequencies that have unconsciously programmed your life. Find the underlying reason and the gift of this pattern so you can finally release it and let go of the need in the trauma. With the assistance also of the Hosts of Heaven, the Councils of Light, you'll feel an expansion of your energy, allowing greater light to descend and expand through your body to a greater understanding and rise in frequency.

Past Life Regressions Sessions

Catherine Ann also facilitates Past Life Regression sessions in person with clients. Information regarding speaking engagements, workshops, tours, healing sessions can be found at: www.catherineannclemett.com

About the Author

Catherine Ann Clemett

Award winning Hay House author Catherine Ann Clemett's work focuses on returning the balance of the Divine Feminine to planet earth to assist the awakening of humanity. She has authored her own books and co-authored books with Claire Heartsong and Angelina Heart.

She has also published books under her own publishing company, LightRiver Media. Catherine Ann also brings her experience and training in various healing modalities: DNA Healing, Matrix Energetics, Transpersonal Hypnotherapy, Past-Life Regression, and Integrative Coaching with author Debbie Ford to the unfolding of her Divine Feminine and planetary awakening work.

She has conducted Magdalene Grid Activations and Sacred Site tours, awakening dormant feminine planetary lines all over the world. She appears in the award-winning documentary film *New Human, New Earth, New Humanity* available on Vimeo. She has also facilitated workshops and tours internationally throughout the United States, Europe, Australia, New Zealand and the Middle East.

Her passion is to seek, understand, download, and anchor who she is as a multidimensional spiritual being of light and to assist others in doing so as well.

For more information about the Magdalenes, the Anna books, and Catherine Ann's other books, products, courses, and events you can go to these websites:

www.catherineannclemett.com
www.frequencyraising.com
www.raising-my-frequency.com

If you liked this book, Catherine Ann would appreciate it if you left a review of it on Amazon to help others learn about this subject. Thank you.

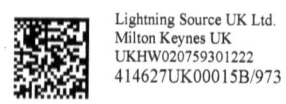